KV-354-853

Aldus® Persuasion™
PC/Windows

SELF-TEACHING GUIDE

Karen Brown
Diane Stielstra

John Wiley & Sons, Inc.
New York ▲ Chichester ▲ Brisbane ▲ Toronto ▲ Singapore

Adobe Type Manager and PostScript are trademarks of Adobe Systems, Inc.
Apple is a registered trademark, and LaserWriter is a trademark, of Apple Computer, Inc.
Hewlett-Packard and LaserJet are registered trademarks, and IntelliFont-for-Windows is
    a trademark, of Hewlett-Packard Company.
Microsoft is a registered trademark, and Windows is a trademark, of Microsoft Corporation.
NEC Colormate PS is a trademark of Nippon Electric Corporation Information Systems.

SUTTON LEISURE
LIBRARIES
0154284 20
JUL 1993
686.2252

Recognizing the importance of preserving what has been written, it is a policy of John
Wiley & Sons, Inc., to have books of enduring value published in the United States printed
on acid-free paper, and we exert our best efforts to that end.

This publication is designed to provide accurate and authoritative information in regard
to the subject matter covered. It is sold with the understanding that the publisher is not
engaged in rendering legal, accounting, or other professional service. If legal advice or
other expert assistance is required, the services of a competent professional person
should be sought. FROM A DECLARATION OF PRINCIPLES JOINTLY ADOPTED BY
A COMMITTEE OF THE AMERICAN BAR ASSOCIATION AND A COMMITTEE OF
PUBLISHERS.

Copyright © 1991 by John Wiley & Sons, Inc.

All rights reserved. Published simultaneously in Canada

Reproduction or translation of any part of this work beyond that permitted by section 107
or 108 of the 1976 United States Copyright Act without the written permission of the
copyright owner is unlawful. Requests for permission or further information should be
addressed to the Permissions Department, John Wiley & Sons, Inc.

Library of Congress Cataloging-in-Publication Data

Brown, Karen, 1952-
    Aldus Persuasion PC/Windows : self teaching guide / Karen Brown,
Diane Stielstra.
        p. cm. -- (Wiley self teaching guides)
    Includes index.
    ISBN 0-471-51411-x
    1. Aldus Persuasion (Computer program)   2. Business presentations-
-Graphic methods--Computer programs.   I. Stielstra, Diane, 1944-.
II. Title.   III. Series.
HF5718.22.876   1991
808.5'1'02855369--dc20   91-30354

Printed in the United States of America

10 9 8 7 6 5 4 3 2 1

Ba

30119 015428420

LONDON BOROUGH OF SUTTON

Aldus® Persuasion™
PC/Windows

SELF-TEACHING GUIDE

Wiley SELF-TEACHING GUIDES (STGs) are designed for first-time users of computer applications and programming languages. They feature concept-reinforcing drills, exercises, and illustrations that enable you to measure your progress and learn at your own pace.

Other Wiley Self-Teaching Guides

INTRODUCTION TO PERSONAL COMPUTERS, Peter Stephenson

QUATTRO PRO 3.0. Jennifer Meyer

PARADOX 3.5, Gloria Wheeler

Q&A 4.0, Corey Sandler and Tom Badget

FOXPRO 2.0, Ellen Sander

PERFORM, Peter Stephenson

QUARK Xpress, Paul Kaitz and Luther Sperberg

MICROSOFT WORD 5.5 FOR THE PC, Ruth Ashley and Judi N. Fernandez

WORDPERFECT 5.0/5.1, Neil Salkind

WORDPERFECT FOR WINDOWS, Neil Salkind

MICROSOFT WINDOWS 3.0, Keith Weiskamp and Saul Aguiar

PC DOS 4, Ruth Ashley and Judi N. Fernandez

PC DOS—3rd Edition, Ruth Ashley and Judi N. Fernandez

MASTERING MICROSOFT WORKS, David Sachs, Babette Kronstadt, Judith Van Wormer, and Barbara Farrell

QUICKPASCAL, Keith Weiskamp and Saul Aguiar

GW BASIC, Ruth Ashley and Judi N. Fernandez

TURBO PASCAL, Keith Weiskamp

To order our STGs, you can call Wiley directly at (201)469-4400, or check your local bookstores.

Mastering computers was never this easy, rewarding, and fun!

Contents Overview

Contents

Part II: Creating a Presentation from Outline View

4   Planning and Starting Your Presentation, 57

5   Using AutoTemplates, 73

6 Entering, Editing, and Rearranging Your Outline, 91

7 Tutorial: A Presentation Created from Outline View, 133

Part III: Working on a Presentation from Slide View

8 Enhancing the Text in Your Presentation, 165

9 Creating and Importing Graphics, 183

10 Creating Charts and Tables, 219

11 Tutorial: An Enhanced Presentation with Graphics, 251

Part IV: Creating Masters, Using Color, and Producing Your Presentation

14   Producing Your Presentation, 317

Appendixes

A   A Guide to Persuasion's AutoTemplates, 333

B   Transferring Slides Among Presentations, 347

Glossary, 349

Index, 353

Preface

Aldus® Persuasion™ is a sophisticated, fully integrated, and automated desktop presentation program. Persuasion lets you design every aspect of a presentation—text, graphics, charts—and then produce it as overhead transparencies, 35 mm slides, or on-screen presentations, complete with accompanying handouts and speaker notes.

Whether you're preparing for a weekly staff meeting or making a presentation to the board, Persuasion lets you create professional visuals quickly. To create a presentation in Persuasion, you select (or create) the slide masters you want, type your ideas into the outline processor, and then print out a finished presentation. That's it! And if you want, you can use Persuasion's advanced drawing and charting tools to embellish your presentation with special effects and color.

If you are creating overhead transparencies, you are not dependent on anyone else to produce your presentation. You can quickly prepare it yourself and print it out in time for the meeting. For 35 mm slides you can shoot the frames with a film recorder, and your presentation is ready as soon as you can get the film developed, perhaps in just one hour. Or you can send your created presentation on disk to a slide service bureau.

Why a Book about Persuasion?

Persuasion is a complex piece of software, combining several applications into one. It contains an outline processor, a drawing package, and a chart-making program. You could use any of these capabilities alone, but you'll probably want to use them together to release the full power of Persuasion for creating presentations.

In fact, Persuasion's uniqueness lies in the interactivity of its parts. Typing headings in the outline processor creates a slide; editing that text on the slide automatically registers those changes in the outline. Charts are generated from the data sheet and can be automatically reformatted.

Because Persuasion is so rich in possibilities, this book was written to show you a quick and easy path to creating presentations, as well as to demonstrate how to get the most from Persuasion. It begins with the Microsoft Windows environment and takes you through the creation process step by step. Short question-and-answer checkpoints sprinkled through chapters, exercises at the ends of chapters, and two major tutorials introduce you in a hands-on fashion to Persuasion's features.

Who Should Use This Book?

This book is designed for people who need to give presentations regularly and want to be able to create and produce them quickly. Such people might include a middle manager in a corporation, a public relations person, a teacher or trainer, a small business owner, or a graphic designer.

Rather than handing your ideas over to another person or department, you can retain complete control of the content and production of your presentation with Persuasion. This book will show you how to do that by giving you the basics and then allowing you to branch out from there, using the checkpoints and exercises as well as the tutorials.

What Is in This Book?

This book is organized to help you learn Persuasion as you go through it chapter by chapter. Within the chapters, you will find several helpful features:

▲ A list of the main topics is included at the beginning of each chapter.

▲ At the end of each chapter, the **Quick Command Summary** reviews the specific commands and procedures treated in the chapter (with the exception of Chapters 1 and 2, which do not deal with specific procedures).

▲ As you go through Chapters 3 through 14, you'll have opportunities to try out **procedures** as you read about them.

▲ **Check Yourself** sections enable you to practice information learned before moving on to a new section. These are followed by instructions so you can make sure that you've understood the topics covered.

▲ **Practice What You've Learned** sections are found at the end of chapters; these are another method for you to make sure you can do what's been discussed in the chapter. There are instructions with these practice sessions as well, in case you're having trouble.

▲ You'll see helpful **Tips** throughout the book where we call your attention to special points and shortcuts.

Chapter 7 and Chapter 11, the tutorials, serve as extended exercises at the ends of Parts II and III, respectively. As you build from the self-checks to the exercises to the tutorials, your understanding of Persuasion grows from procedural know-how into fluency with the entire process of creating presentations.

This book has four parts. After an orientation to Persuasion's eight easy steps, desktop presentations, and the Windows environment in Part I, you'll learn how to plan and create a simple presentation in Part II, and then how to create and produce presentations involving advanced features and special effects in Parts III and IV. If you are an experienced Windows user and have Persuasion already installed, you may want to skip Part I and go directly to Part II. If you are familiar with Persuasion, you can look through Parts II, III, and IV for tips on using Persuasion creatively and efficiently and refer to Appendixes A and B for quick reference information.

Part I: Introducing Desktop Presentations and Persuasion

Chapter 1, "Desktop Presentations and Persuasion: An Overview," introduces you to desktop presentation software, explains how Persuasion will change the way you create presentations, and establishes eight easy steps to creating a presentation using Persuasion. Chapter 2, "Setting Up Your Computer," discusses a reasonable system configuration for running Persuasion and gives you valuable information on some of the areas where hardware and software meet, such as fonts, printers, and type managers. Chapter 3, "Using Persuasion in the Windows Environment," familiarizes you with working in Windows and in Persuasion's environment.

Part II: Creating a Presentation from Outline View

Chapter 4, "Planning and Starting Your Presentation," teaches you how to plan, start, and set up a presentation; and Chapter 5, "Using

AutoTemplates," introduces you to the concept of slide masters and AutoTemplates, gives advice on choosing the appropriate AutoTemplate, and shows you how to assign masters to your slides. Chapter 6, "Entering, Editing, and Rearranging Your Outline," explains how to work in Outline view: entering, importing, changing, and rearranging your outline, as well as creating different types of charts. Chapter 7, "Tutorial: A Presentation Created from Outline View," guides you through the creation of a basic presentation.

Part III: Working on a Presentation from Slide View

Chapter 8, "Enhancing the Text in Your Presentation," describes how you can add text directly to your slides and change its attributes—font, color, alignment, size, style, and bullet marks. Chapter 9, "Creating and Importing Graphics," teaches you how to use Persuasion's drawing tools to add graphics to your presentation. Chapter 10, "Creating Charts and Tables," shows you how to turn data from a spreadsheet into a chart or table on your slide. Chapter 11, "Tutorial: An Enhanced Presentation with Graphics," suggests ways to add text blocks, graphics, charts, and tables to a presentation.

Part IV: Creating Masters, Using Color, and Producing Your Presentation

Chapter 12, "On Your Own: Creating Masters," gives you the key to total control of your presentation by explaining how to create masters for slides, speaker notes, and handouts; it also explains how to alter application and presentation default settings. Chapter 13, "Using Color in Your Presentation," explains how to add color to your presentation, how to define a color scheme, and how to set up Persuasion's color palette. Chapter 14, "Producing Your Presentation," provides you with a preprinting checklist of tasks: formatting your outline for print, using the spell checker, and previewing your slides. The heart of the chapter explains how to print overhead transparencies, notes, and handouts; how to do on-screen presentations; how to create color slides; and how to prepare a disk for a service bureau.

Appendixes

Appendix A, "A Guide to Persuasion's AutoTemplates," is an illustrated table describing the design specifications of Persuasion's 55 AutoTemplates. Appendix B, "Transferring Slides among Presentations," explains how to transfer slides among Persuasion presentations in the Windows environment.

We have also provided a Glossary containing terms helpful in using Persuasion in a Windows environment.

Acknowledgments

Our efforts in writing this book depended on the support of friends, family, and colleagues. Our appreciation to:

Pam Trebon, head of Persuasion Technical Support at Aldus Corporation, for her enthusiasm and efforts beyond any conventional definition of duty.

Lorretta Matson, Paul Lewis, Kerri McConnell, Mark Sherman, and Lynn Perry of Aldus Corporation for freely sharing their experiences with Persuasion.

Katherine Schowalter and Marcia Samuels of John Wiley & Sons, our editors, for guidance and patience.

Rob Mauhar and Lenity Himburg for guidance on design and production.

Aldus® Persuasion™
PC/Windows

SELF-TEACHING GUIDE

PART I

Introducing Desktop Presentations and Persuasion

1

Desktop Presentations and Persuasion: An Overview

Since they began drawing in the sand with sticks, people have attempted to give their ideas visual impact. In fact, time has proven that the best way to inform, convince, or move an audience is by combining the spoken word with a graphic image.

The value of images in communication is acknowledged in everyday language—"A picture is worth a thousand words," or "Do you get the picture?" Communication is a fragile thing; meaning easily slips through the cracks between words. Pictures help to seal these cracks and even enhance the meaning presented in the words.

Today, when you want to get your ideas across, you still rely on a graphic way of presenting them. Instead of drawing in sand, though, you probably project your words and images on a screen with slides or overhead transparencies. But the basic ingredients for a powerful presentation are still the same: a compelling idea expressed in clear words supported by a striking image. With modern desktop presentation software, you can get that idea across much more easily—and leave behind a great impression!

In this chapter, you'll learn the following:

▲ **How Persuasion has changed the process for creating presentations**

▲ **What makes Persuasion distinct from other presentation programs**

▲ **What the eight steps for creating a presentation in Persuasion are**

The Evolution of Presentation Technology

If you've been making presentations for years, you remember the "bad old days," when producing them was tedious and time-consuming—and, mainly, out of your hands. After scribbling your ideas down and planning the overall presentation on paper, you'd hand it over to a series of professionals to be turned into slides or overhead transparencies.

Because each task in the process was specialized, the process was necessarily fragmented. Different people performed different tasks:

▲ Planning and writing the overall presentation

▲ Designing the look of the presentation and drawing the slide background and illustrations

▲ Selecting or shooting the pictures needed for the presentation

▲ Typesetting the words on paper

▲ Pasting up each of the elements produced to create camera-ready copy

▲ Photographing the camera-ready copy to produce film for a 35 mm slide or an overhead transparency

This was expensive, and it took a lot of time. Other than writing down your ideas and sketching out the flow of the presentation, you had little control over the presentation's production quality or its completion time. You could approve the outcome—or spend more money and send it back for another try. Money, time, loss of creative control—these considerations would frequently stop you before you began. Who wouldn't try to think of an alternative for making a formal presentation?

Using a Combination of Software Programs

Now that draw programs, chart packages, and desktop publishing software are commonplace, you are probably tempted to use them instead of simply scribbling on paper and handing your ideas off to professionals. In fact, with the right desktop publishing program, you can fashion your own overhead transparencies, but it's a lengthy and painstaking process.

For each transparency, you have to import graphic elements from a draw program and text from a word processor or outliner into a desktop publishing program, where you manipulate them to create the look you want. And if you want to go to the trouble of adding a chart, you have to use a chart program or a spreadsheet application to create the type of chart you want and then import that into the desktop publishing program as well.

As you can see, this process involves a lot of copying and repetition. Making changes can be difficult under this setup, especially if you have to make them to a number of frames or slides. Because you are using so many software applications, you have to worry about having all those applications available, as well as learning how to use them. Furthermore, all you can produce from this convoluted process is overheads. Creating 35 mm slides is still out of reach without turning to professionals.

Using Desktop Presentation Software

A number of software companies have come to the aid of presenters by combining some of these software programs into a single program dedicated to creating presentations. Instead of struggling to use an outliner, a word processor, drawing tools, and a chart package in conjunction with desktop publishing, you can now use one piece of software: a desktop presentation program.

Not all presentation programs, however, give you a full range of capabilities. Some Windows presentation programs give you charting abilities; others have an outliner. Most have drawing tools, but they vary widely in sophistication.

However, a dedicated presentation program should have not only charting, drawing, and outlining capabilities, but also templates or slide masters, speaker notes and handouts creation, on-screen slide shows, and a slide sorter. These functions are missing when you need to move from program to program to build a presentation. Editing, positioning, and previewing, for example, are all more expediently performed with a dedicated presentation program.

Using Persuasion

Persuasion for Windows includes all the features you'd expect from a presentation program, and they are integrated. Not only are the outliner, drawing program, and spreadsheet/chart package under one software roof, but they are also linked in ways that make them truly a single product.

The outliner, drawing program, and chart package in Persuasion are combined in such a way that a change made using one tool is reflected elsewhere throughout the presentation. For example, if you change the title of a slide in the outline, that change is automatically made in the title on the slide itself. A change in the text for an organization chart is made simultaneously in the chart on the slide.

The advantage of an integrated presentation program is clear from the minute you start working. Instead of organizing your thoughts on paper, the first thing you do is type them into Persuasion's outliner. This step essentially creates every slide in your presentation. Because Persuasion is integrated, the text you enter into the outline is entered on your slides simultaneously; each main heading in the outline serves as a slide title and each subordinate heading serves as a piece of text on that slide. Therefore, creating a simple presentation can be as easy as typing your outline.

But Persuasion's link between outline and slides goes beyond sharing text. By using slide masters, you can predetermine the look and placement of text and graphics on any slide. In fact, a slide master provides a model format for your slides. Instead of handing over the various pieces of your presentation to a professional to put together, Persuasion's slide masters make it easy to integrate the text and graphics yourself. Figure 1.1 illustrates how the slide masters communicate information from the outline to the slides.

With Persuasion you now have the power to get your ideas across with maximum impact, whether you need them for a staff meeting, a planning session with your manager, or a sales conference with a client. Gone are the days when you avoided creating presentations because they were too time-consuming, expensive, or frustrating to produce. Persuasion will completely change the way you think about presentations. Instead of using them only for special occasions to impress a client, you can now use them for your day-to-day communications. In fact, Persuasion can become one of the most effective tools of communication you have.

Eight Steps to Creating a Presentation with Persuasion

Unlocking the power of Persuasion is easy if you follow this series of steps for creating a presentation from inception to production. As you become familiar with the process, you can adapt it to suit your purposes. Above all, the basic sequence of thought and action established in this step-by-step model will help you develop a habit of mind that makes creating effective presentations second nature.

▼ *Figure 1.1. How Persuasion uses slide masters to format the outline into slides*

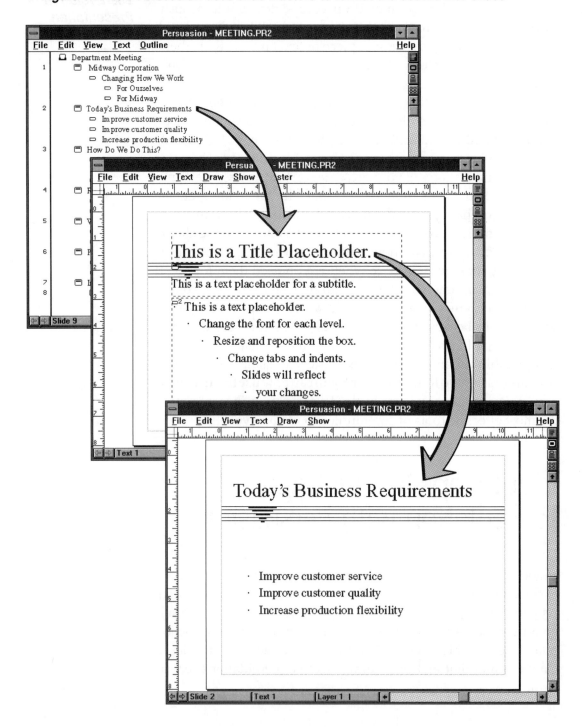

Writing your outline is the backbone of creating any presentation. But before you begin, you must do some planning, and after your outline is finished, you'll want to create effective graphics for your slides. To understand the flow of this process, review the eight steps illustrated in Figure 1.2.

Eight Steps to Creating a Presentation with Persuasion

1. *Determine your presentation medium.* The first thing you must do is think about the end product and decide what the medium of your presentation will be. Envision the setting in which you'll be giving this presentation. How large is your audience? How large is the room in which you will be making your presentation? For example, a color slide presentation of a corporate annual report to a large audience in an auditorium requires a very different look and setup from an overhead presentation of a college course syllabus to a classroom of 25 students. To plan your presentation medium and get started in Persuasion, see Chapter 4.

▼ *Figure 1.2. Eight steps to creating a presentation*

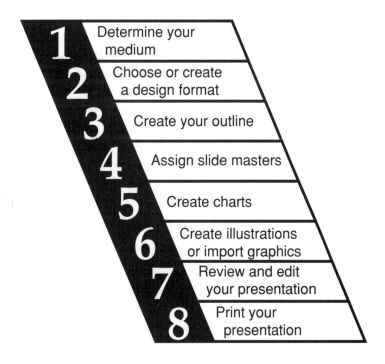

2. *Choose or create a design format.* Once you open Persuasion, you determine the look of your presentation by selecting a design format or creating one of your own. You can start with another presentation that you want to modify, or you can use one of Persuasion's AutoTemplates to provide an instant format. (An AutoTemplate is a collection of slide masters that you can use repeatedly as the basis for new presentations.) If you want to start from scratch, you can create your own slide masters. To start with an AutoTemplate or other presentation, see Chapter 5 or the tutorial in Chapter 7. To create your own masters, see Chapter 12.

3. *Create an outline of your presentation.* This is the main step in creating any presentation; here you establish its content, structure, and flow. In fact, if you want only text in your presentation and no graphics, it would be finished after this step. To find out more about creating an outline, see Chapter 6.

4. *Assign slide masters.* The text you type in the outline flows to each slide according to the format of the default slide master that Persuasion automatically assigns. To give a slide another format, you need to assign a different slide master to it. To learn how to assign slide masters and preview their effects, see Chapter 5.

5. *Create charts.* Charts can be created from Outline view by entering or importing the relevant data into the data sheet and plotting it. You are free to choose from a wide variety of chart types and special effects for enhancing charts or tables. To explore this step further, see Chapter 10.

6. *Create illustrations on the slides or import any graphics you need.* Once you type your outline and enter data for charts, you have automatically created your slides. You can use Persuasion's drawing tools to draw directly on each slide, creating the diagram or illustration you want to support your words.

   To use an existing graphic, such as your company logo, you simply import it. To learn more about drawing and importing graphics, see Chapter 9.

7. *Review and edit your presentation.* You can review your presentation by two different means: the slide sorter or the slide show.

The slide sorter lets you look at miniatures of your slides laid out in order so that you can easily rearrange them if you need to. The slide show simply gives you an on-screen preview of what each slide in your presentation looks like. For tips on how to use these features to edit your presentation, see Chapter 14.

Eight Steps to Creating a Presentation with Persuasion

8. *Print your presentation.* You can print your overhead transparencies, notes, and handouts on the printer you connect with in Windows and select in the "Slide setup" dialog box. Alternatively, you can produce 35 mm slides either by attaching a film recorder to your computer or by sending your presentation to a slide service bureau. To learn more about producing your presentation, see Chapter 14.

As you review these steps, you can see that some are more essential than others. For example, if you are creating a simple, text-only presentation, you can omit steps 5 and 6. However, if you are creating an elaborate color slide presentation, you may spend the majority of your time on these steps. The process outlined here is flexible and can be easily modified according to your needs.

As you become familiar with using Persuasion in this way, you will soon adapt this process to your personal work habits. Persuasion gives you the freedom to concentrate on developing your ideas to the fullest without getting distracted by production details. At last, you have the control that has eluded the presenter for so long.

2

Setting Up Your Computer

Thinking about computer hardware gives most people an instant headache. The options are staggering. How, then, can a person know what computer configuration will do the job? In this case, using Persuasion requires a computer that can run Microsoft® Windows 3.0™ or higher. If you can run Windows 3.0 on your computer with some ease and also print to your printer, chances are good that you can also use Persuasion effectively to produce presentations.

This chapter will help you to make some important decisions:

▲ **What issues to consider in purchasing hardware components**

▲ **What the best hardware configuration is for you, based on the type of presentations you'll give most frequently**

▲ **What output device will serve you best**

IBM-Compatible Computers and Windows 3.0

The hardware configuration that Aldus recommends is a 386-based computer with 2 MB of random-access memory, at least a 20 MB hard disk, and a mouse. You should also have a floppy disk drive capable of reading either 1.2 MB 5¼ inch disks or 720 K 3½ inch disks, and a monitor that uses a VGA graphics adapter. We agree with this recommendation. If you have a 286-based computer, Persuasion will run much more slowly, especially if the machine runs at 16 MHz or less. Additional memory is always useful, whatever type of computer you have. More memory gives you more system resources so that you can run slide shows with layering and transition effects at a desirable speed. In determining the amount of hard disk space you need, consider the fact that if you install all of the Persuasion files (all the AutoTemplates, clip art, and so forth) and you have Windows installed, you have already used up about 10 to 12 MB of your hard disk. You always need to keep about 2 MB of hard disk space free to operate—before you have started creating presentations, which can be 1 MB or more in size.

What if your system doesn't exactly fit into this recommended profile? Since there are so many possible hardware configurations available, the best way to answer that question is to say that if you can run Windows 3.0 or higher and if your hardware, including your printer, is compatible with Windows, you can probably use Persuasion successfully.

Fonts and Type Managers

The look of a presentation depends a great deal on the attractiveness of the typeface you use to create it. Good-looking type is important for on-screen slide shows, for 35 mm film imaging, and for printed slides or overheads. The fonts you work with are of two basic types: printer fonts and screen fonts.

Printer fonts are used to print your presentations; screen fonts are used to show on-screen how text will look when it is printed and to create smooth, pleasant-looking type for on-screen slide shows. Sometimes inconsistencies may exist between printer fonts and screen fonts. For example, you may choose a printer font for your presentation that has no matching screen font in the same point size. In that case, Persuasion substitutes a generic screen font, and as a result your presentation may look different on your monitor than it does when it is printed (although the text line lengths will be the same). You should always print proof copies of your presentation to make sure that you have achieved the look you want, but doing so is especially important if your printer fonts and screen fonts are mismatched.

You can prevent mismatching printer and screen fonts by installing a type manager, which scales the correct type size you need for the screen from its own outline fonts. For example, Adobe Type Manager™ (ATM) can display PostScript® fonts on non-PostScript devices, such as your computer screen or a PCL printer. FaceLift™ and IntelliFont for Windows, two other type managers, provide screen representations of Bitstream® and Hewlett-Packard® printer fonts, respectively.

We strongly recommend that you install a type manager. Persuasion has created its AutoTemplates using two ATM fonts, Gill Sans and Times New Roman PS. The version of ATM that shipped initially with Persuasion contains these fonts. Because Persuasion's AutoTemplates use these fonts, you should install this version of ATM if possible. If you do not install ATM, you will need to change the fonts used on the slide masters in the Persuasion AutoTemplates. In any case, we recommend that you install some type manager on your PC to minimize the problems of inconsistency that can crop up between screen and printer fonts and to give the text on your monitor a smoother look.

Fonts and Type Managers

Printers

No matter what type of presentation you're creating, you'll need to have access to a printer. You'll use a printer as a proofing device for

35 mm slide presentations or on-screen slide shows, as well as for printing notes and audience handouts. For overhead transparency presentations, a printer will be your primary production device.

The black-and-white laser printers available to you fall into two groups:

▲ PCL printers, which use Hewlett-Packard's Printer Command Language (PCL), such as the Hewlett-Packard LaserJet™ family of printers

▲ PostScript devices, which use the Adobe PostScript page description language, such as the family of Apple LaserWriters®

In addition to black-and-white laser printers, the world of color is becoming more accessible as the prices of color printers come down. Because color printers are becoming more common, some of the AutoTemplates that come with Persuasion are set up to be printed on color printers.

PCL Printers

Hewlett-Packard designed its Printer Control Language in the early 1980s to support its full line of printers, from dot matrix to laser to color ink jet. As Hewlett-Packard developed printers during the 1980s, PCL continued to support the advances in printer technology through the LaserJet Series II and IID. PCL printers during this time relied on bit-mapped fonts. In other words, when you use a PCL printer made before the LaserJet III, you are dealing with fonts for which you need to store an image of each character in every size, either in cartridges or as downloadable fonts on disk.

With the advent of PCL 5, the latest version of the printer control language, and the introduction of the HP LaserJet III, scalable fonts came to PCL printers, as did a number of advances in printing graphics, such as vector graphic support and compressed bit-mapped graphics. The new features in PCL 5 and the LaserJet III are quite helpful in eliminating the main differences between PCL and PostScript printers, though the two are still unique and cannot share fonts.

PCL printers can use built-in fonts, cartridge fonts, or downloadable fonts. If you have installed a type manager, you can download character bitmaps. ATM, for instance, uses font metric and image files (.PFM and .PFB, respectively) to generate bitmaps for both the screen and the PCL printer.

PostScript Printers

In 1986 Apple introduced the LaserWriter family of printers. The LaserWriter IINT and IINTX and Personal LaserWriter NT use the PostScript page description language. PostScript printers are recommended for printing presentations not only because they can handle text well, but because they also perform well with illustrations, scanned images, and other graphics.

PostScript printers use outline fonts rather than bit-mapped fonts as the HP LaserJet Series II printers do. PostScript printers can use both resident fonts or downloadable fonts, but they do not use cartridges. If you install a type manager such as ATM, you can install additional fonts that the PostScript driver can download.

Color Printers

Color is a subject of considerable technical complexity. The way color is displayed on the screen is very different from the way color overhead transparencies or slides are produced. (For an in-depth discussion of color, see Chapter 13.)

Of the color printers available on the market today, none can match the quality or quantity of colors in an on-screen slide show, on slides produced with a film recorder, or on slides created by a slide service bureau. Even though the price of color printers is coming down, you'll find that printers that produce high-quality color overhead transparencies are generally more expensive than using either a film recorder or a slide service bureau. However, if you need to produce color overhead transparencies frequently and are willing to do a little research, you can find a color printer that produces acceptable quality.

Current printer technology uses a number of techniques to print in color—color laser, dye sublimation, dot matrix, inkjet, and thermal transfer—but the most relevant in terms of quality and affordability are the last two. Dot matrix printers lack the resolution and color capabilities necessary for most overhead transparencies, and color laser printers and dye-sublimation printers are relatively new technologies that are exciting but still far more expensive than inkjet or thermal transfer.

Color laser printers have been developed from the technology for color photocopiers, using a micro-fine color toner to reproduce colors. Canon and Adobe are both working on color laser printers that currently run just under $60,000. Dye-sublimation printers transfer dyes from ink ribbons onto custom paper in a very precise manner that renders high-resolution images with color gradations that are exceptionally smooth. Dye-sublimation printers are at this time more affordable than color laser printers, ranging from $14,000 to $48,000.

Inkjet Printers

Inkjet color printers can produce low-resolution color (about 160 to 216 dots per inch, or dpi) on transparencies. They produce color from four ink reservoirs—(cyan, yellow, magenta, and black)—by spraying a mix of these colors onto the paper as controlled by the computer. This liquid ink is absorbed into the paper to a larger extent than the wax film used in thermal transfer technology, producing colors that are less intense. Many inkjet printers, however, can overprint lines on transparencies to produce fairly rich colors. You must keep in mind that overprinting will, of course, extend your printing time.

In evaluating inkjet printers, you should also know that they lack built-in PostScript. There are software interpreters for many inkjet printers, such as Custom Applications' Freedom of Press® or QMS's UltraScript, but print processing takes much longer. Inkjet printers usually have a limited font selection and can benefit from a type manager such as ATM. However they are the most affordable color printers, currently ranging from $1,400 to $3,000.

Thermal Transfer Printers

Thermal transfer color printers, which use color ribbons with a waxlike coating of color and a heat process to transfer the color to the printed page, produce quality color overhead transparencies quickly. Resolution is good—from 200 to 300 dpi, which, at the upper end, matches that of the black-and-white transparencies produced by using a member of the LaserWriter printer family. You'll also find that thermal transfer printers are handy as proofing devices for color slides, since slide film is developed off-site.

Printers

Some thermal transfer color printers, such as the QMS ColorScript™ 100, NEC Colormate PS, or Océ Color, are PostScript printers and thus offer all the advantages of this software. In addition, some, including the QMS ColorScript 100, offer PANTONE MATCHING SYSTEM® certification by simulating the PANTONE colors with process color.

TIP

The printable area of the QMS ColorScript 100 is significantly smaller than that of other printers. Check the online text file PRNTDVRS.TXT on your Persuasion disks for information on how to deal with the smaller printable area of ColorScript. (To find any online text file, look at the top level of the "PR2US" directory, double-click the .TXT file you want to read to open it in Notepad, and then read it on-screen or print it.)

Although the inkjet printers cost about half of what a thermal transfer printer does, they also generally have lower resolution, a more limited color range, and no PostScript support. If the volume of color transparencies or slide proofs you must produce is high enough to justify the expense, your best bet is a thermal transfer printer, which ranges in price from about $5,000 to $10,000.

Printer Drivers

When you install Persuasion, it is a good idea to install printer drivers for both PCL (LaserJet Series II) and PostScript printers. A Persuasion AutoTemplate must be targeted either to a PCL printer or to a PostScript printer. Although you are probably not connected to both of these printers, it is nonetheless advisable to install the drivers to avoid multiple messages requesting a missing driver.

When you begin to create your presentation, you should target your printer in the "Slide setup" dialog box, so that when it comes time to print, you print with the fonts you actually have. You should also target your printer in the "Notes setup" dialog box. If the printer you target at print time is not the one you targeted in "Slide setup" and "Notes setup" at the beginning, you may be in for some surprises in font substitution.

You may have already installed the PCL and PostScript drivers in Windows; however, drivers are updated frequently. Check to see if newer versions of the PCL and PostScript drivers are on your Persuasion disks (that is, the files HPPCL.DRV and PSCRIPT.DRV).

Printer drivers are installed using the Printers icon in the Windows Control Panel. You can follow the procedure outlined in the Windows documentation, or you can do the exercise at the end of this chapter to update your printer drivers. If you have an HP LaserJet III printer, you can install its driver (HPPCL5A.DRV) as "unlisted." The specific steps for installing an unlisted printer are spelled out in the online file that comes with Persuasion, called PRNTDRVS.TXT.

Film Recorders and Slide Service Bureaus

When it comes to producing professional-quality color presentations, 35 mm slides provide the truest colors and the sharpest image. Only slides offer you the entire spectrum of colors available, and only slide resolution—as high as 10 to 20 times that of the computer screen—can be sharp enough for presentations given to large audiences in an auditorium.

You have two choices for producing quality slide presentations: You can attach a film recorder to your computer to expose 35 mm film that you then have developed into slides, or you can take your Persuasion files to a slide service bureau, which will create the slides for you.

TIP

When you are creating a 35 mm slide presentation, always choose "35mm" in the "Slide setup" dialog box to establish the correct 3:2 aspect ratio for 35 mm film. Even if the actual size of your film varies from the 10.14 x 6.75 inches given in the "Slide setup" dialog box, your printer driver will report the actual size of the device targeted and correct this setting. You do not need to establish a custom size.

For other tips on creating slides and information on using specific film recorders and slide service bureaus, read the online Persuasion file in the PR2US directory called 35MMDRVS.TXT.

Film Recorders

At one time, people had to take their ideas for slides, along with any illustrations, to a professional at a slide service bureau, who would then create the slides for them. The process was expensive and time-consuming—from overnight to several days, depending on the complexity of the slides. The introduction of desktop film recorders that can be attached directly to your computer has changed that process, shortening it to a few hours and letting you have creative control over your slides.

Most film recorders are easy for you to set up and use: Plug it into the back of your computer, install the driver using the Windows Control Panel, and you're ready to go. A film recorder contains a standard 35 mm camera. You specify the film recorder as the target device in Persuasion's "Print" dialog box, and then print. Once the film is exposed, take it to any film developer—even a one-hour developer.

As you can see, the process is relatively simple. But film recorders are a fairly new technology. If you are considering purchasing a film recorder, you should think about the following issues:

▲ A film recorder can save you money. Service bureaus charge anywhere from $10 to $15 for each slide in your presentation. If you want extremely complex graphics or a rush order, the price can go as high as $100 per slide. Alternatively, the cost of each slide that you produce with a film recorder can go as low as 50 cents per slide, and the time it takes to expose and develop the film is a few hours instead of overnight. Even with the expense of the film recorder ($4,500 and up) and the labor-hours it takes to create the slides, you can save money on every presentation.

▲ Using a film recorder is more convenient and faster than using a slide service bureau. You can create slide presentations in shorter time frames and update your slides more easily. In addition, confidential information that might appear on the slides never has to leave your company.

▲ Some film recorders come with an extra camera—a Polaroid Instamatic—for previewing slides. This can be helpful because you don't have to wait to get the slides back from the developer to see what they will look like. However, changing cameras poses problems: You can get dust inside the film recorder, which can settle on the monitor screen or the camera lens, spotting your images. To solve this problem, you can clean the monitor screen and camera lens with lens-cleaning solution.

▲ The number of fonts supported also varies from one film recorder to the next. Check that the fonts you plan to use for your presentations are supported by the film recorder you want to purchase.

▲ The quality of colors produced varies from one film recorder to the next. These variations can be caused by calibration drift, different film types, or any number of other factors.

▲ There is also a trade-off between resolution and the reproduction of hairlines and small text. When you create a slide at 2 K resolution, hairlines and small text will reproduce accurately; at 4 K resolution on some film recorders, hairlines and small text are lost.

▲ Because film recorders are a new technology, ongoing technical support is an issue. Be sure that the manufacturer you choose has a support staff dedicated to answering your questions and helping you with any production problems that can arise.

In general, if you are producing color slides on a regular basis, a film recorder is well worth the original investment of time and money. In fact, it can pay for itself in the first few slide presentations that you produce. But, given the current state of the technology, you should insist that you be allowed to create a representative set of slides on the film recorder you are considering before you purchase it. This is the only way to ensure that you are purchasing one that will meet your needs.

Slide Service Bureaus

Even though film recorders are more convenient, there will be times when you want to use a slide service bureau. For that extra-special presentation, a service bureau's graphic artists can provide design expertise. They also have equipment that lets them create unusual special effects on slides. For presentations given to very large audiences in an auditorium, the resolution of the slides produced on their equipment is superior (8 K) and won't blur when projected at large sizes.

To use a slide service bureau, you have to install the service bureau's driver on your computer. Persuasion's "Print…" command will then create a disk file that you send over a modem or mail to the service bureau. Most service bureaus sell a starter kit that includes the driver and instructions for its installation; the price of the starter kit is typically deducted from the charge for the first set of slides you send to them.

Although the cost of creating slides using a slide service bureau is relatively high, it should fall as film recorders become more commonplace and service bureaus have to compete. For now, they offer an excellent alternative if you create slides infrequently and don't want to take on the expense and learning time involved with purchasing and using a film recorder or if you want to add special effects to your slides. Service bureaus also offer other technologies, such as high-resolution color transparencies or prints, that can be a cost-effective alternative to purchasing a color printer for the occasional presentation that requires color transparencies and handouts.

Alternative Large-Screen Projection Techniques

If your presentation site has a computer, you have several alternatives for giving presentations. More and more companies are now offering projection panels that can be used with an overhead projector, as well as large-screen (up to 432-inch) projectors or projection systems in both monochrome and color. Using either of these technologies requires that you have a computer available and that you use Persuasion's "Slide show" command to give the presentation.

You can attach a projection panel to the computer and place the pad on an overhead projector so that an image drawn on the pad is then displayed by the overhead projector onto a screen. The image can be in black and white or in color, depending on the capabilities of both your monitor and your projection panel. If either is monochrome, then your image will be also. Some of the newer projection panels can display thousands of colors, and they are lightweight (some weigh as little as 5 pounds) and easy to set up and operate. They range in price from about $700 for a monochrome model to $1,200 or more for simulated color to $5,000 and up for true color.

On the other hand, you can connect a large-screen projector to a computer to run your presentation. Most projectors have three lenses—one for each of the primary colors. This means that the projectors require a delicate adjustment called *convergence*, in which the three colors are overlaid and focused to achieve a white image. Projectors come in three flavors: LCD, CRT, and light-valve projectors. LCD projectors are priced at the lower end of the scale, from $3,000 to $5,000, and are easy to transport, set up, and operate. However, they are not capable of displaying fine detail and rarely possess the full color range that CRT projectors do. CRT projectors, sometimes called three-gun projectors, have higher picture quality than the LCD models, but are heavier and require regular convergence adjustments. CRT projectors generally cost from $5,000 to $20,000. The highest-priced projectors are the light-valve projectors, which run from $45,000 to $300,000 and more. Because the price of light-valve projectors is far outside most budgets and because they are complex enough to require a trained technician to operate, these projectors are not really a viable option for most users. Thinking about purchasing a projector or a projection panel really requires you to assess your presentation situation. How frequently would the projection device be used? Will it mainly be used in one location, or does it need to be transported? How large is the audience and how much detail do they need to be able to see? In other words, classrooms have different requirements and budgets from those of corporate boardrooms. A projection panel may be ideal for one, while the other can justify a high-end CRT projection system.

Alternative
Large-Screen
Projection
Techniques

Putting It All Together

So what's the bottom line when purchasing hardware for presentations? Buy the configuration that best suits your needs based on the presentations you'll create and produce most frequently.

If you will be using Persuasion primarily as a tool for informal meetings and work group sessions, you can purchase a system that matches the minimum requirements:

▲ A computer with an Intel 80286 processor with at least 2 MB of memory that runs Windows 3.0

▲ A 20 MB hard disk

▲ An EGA graphics adapter

▲ A mouse

▲ A PCL printer

If you will be using Persuasion to produce quality black-and-white overhead transparencies, but rarely to produce color slides, a flexible and upgradable configuration that will not unduly stretch your budget is comprised of the following:

▲ A computer with an Intel 80386 processor with 4 MB of memory that runs Windows 3.0

▲ A 40 MB hard disk

▲ A VGA graphics adapter and a color monitor

▲ A mouse

▲ A laser printer—either a PCL printer, such as Hewlett-Packard LaserJet Series II or LaserJet III, or a PostScript printer, such as an Apple Personal LaserWriter II NT

However, for producing high-quality color presentations—either slides or transparencies—you should consider retaining the items in the configuration just described, but upgrading it in these ways:

▲ Upgrade to a Super VGA graphics adapter.

▲ Add a desktop film recorder, a slide service bureau starter kit, or a thermal transfer color printer.

▲ Install additional memory, if possible.

Your hardware requirements, then, are actually rather simple. All you need to run Persuasion is a computer that can run Windows 3.0 in standard or 386-enhanced mode, at least 2 MB of memory, a hard disk, a mouse, and a disk drive that can read either 1.2 MB 5¼ inch disks or 720 K 3½ inch disks. With this equipment, you can create any presentation you want using Persuasion. Producing it is another issue.

Once you've set up your computer, the more difficult hardware question is, "What shall I use for an output device?" To some extent you can avoid an answer to that question by sending your presentations to a slide service bureau. However, you cannot deny the usefulness of a printer in creating notes, handouts, and proofs. Before you send anything off to a service bureau, you'll probably want to see how it looks in print, so a printer is next on the shopping list after a computer. With those ingredients you can cook up and serve any presentation, but you'd be particularly well prepared for creating overhead transparencies or on-screen slide shows.

Color presents the next challenge. Even though you can create color presentations on a black-and-white monitor by assigning colors as shades of gray using the color table and color IDs in the color palette, you'd prefer to see what you're doing on a color monitor. For output you could use a film recorder or, in some cases, a color printer. These two areas of technology are changing the most rapidly in feature development and price fluctuation. In order to sort out these issues before you purchase, your best course would be to consult magazines covering the world of computers and desktop publishing and presentations, such as *Publish!*, *PC World*, or *PC Magazine*.

Your hardware decisions should be straightforward if you know what kind of presentations you'll be turning out. Keep in mind your budget and the types of presentations you'll be making; those two realities should narrow down the field to the hardware configuration you'll need.

Putting It All Together

PRACTICE WHAT YOU'VE LEARNED

In this exercise, you'll install a printer driver.

1. Install the PCL driver using the Windows Control Panel.

2. Configure the new printer driver.

ANSWERS

1. In the Main group window of Program Manager, double-click the Control Panel icon, and then double-click the Printers icon. In the "Printers" dialog box, click "Add Printer." Select your printer from the "List of Printers" (or, if you do not have a PCL printer, select any PCL/HP LaserJet printer listed). Click "Install…." If you already have a PCL driver on your computer, you will get a message indicating that you already have a driver for this printer and asking whether you want to install a new driver. Click "New" in the confirmation message, and then you'll get the "Control Panel—Printers" dialog box. If you do not have a PCL driver currently installed, you'll get the "Control Panel—Printers" dialog box immediately. Insert the disk containing the new driver into drive A, and then click "OK" in the dialog box. After the driver is installed,

click "OK" in the "Printers" dialog box. (Close the control panel by double-clicking the control box in the upper-left corner of the window, and then reopen it. This is necessary in order to update the WIN.INI correctly.)

2. In the "Printers" dialog box, select the new driver entry in "Installed printers," and then click "Configure...." In the "Printers—Configure" dialog box, select a port (such as LPT1), and then click "Setup." Select the printer from the drop-down list box, choose any other configuration options you want, and then click "OK" in all three dialog boxes. Close the control panel, and then restart Windows.

Using Persuasion in the Windows Environment

You've set up Windows 3.0 (or higher) and Persuasion on your PC and, if you're new to Windows, you're saying to yourself, "Where's the command line? Where do I type the name of the program I want to run?"

If disorientation is setting in, relax. Windows looks different because it *is* different. Instead of issuing commands by typing in arcane codes, you pull down menus and click a command name, or point to icons and double-click. Aldus has carried the philosophy of Windows graphical environment through in the design of Persuasion so that, in general, the way you operate in Windows—for instance, when you issue a command—is the way you work in Persuasion.

In this chapter we'll take a close look at the Windows graphical environment, and then we'll use that knowledge as the basis for learning Persuasion's working environment. If you've used Windows before, you may skip the first half of the chapter. However, the information provided there will be used as the basis for the explanations about Persuasion's environment, so you may want to browse and refresh your memory.

In this chapter, you'll learn several steps requisite to working with Windows and Persuasion:

▲ **How the Windows environment works**

▲ **How to use the mouse and menus in Windows**

▲ **How to respond to dialog boxes**

▲ **How to move among Persuasion's views**

▲ **What the range of Persuasion's commands and menus is**

Working in Windows

If you've never used Windows before, you're in for a treat—and some minor adjustments. If you have used a Macintosh before, the transition to Windows should be fairly easy. Both Windows and the Macintosh are designed on the premise that the computer should provide an environment that is analogous to the workaday world. For example, both use the metaphor of the desktop for the computer screen. This graphical environment is designed to be intuitive, as well as easy to learn and use.

The Desktop and Its Windows

Microsoft Windows comes by its name honestly: it works by displaying your work within windows on the screen. When you first type *win* at the C> prompt to open Windows, you see the desktop and the window of the Program Manager application. The small pictures of objects that sit on the desktop are called icons. For example, to open Persuasion, you use the mouse to point to the Persuasion icon in the Aldus window, as shown in Figure 3.1, and double-click it.

You run applications, then, inside windows. In fact, you can have several application windows open at once. This is useful for copying something from one application to another—say, from a spreadsheet to a word processor. And it can be useful for comparing two files. In addition to application windows, you can open windows—document windows—within an application. An application may let you open several document windows within it or, like Persuasion, it may not. In Persuasion you can have only one presentation open at a time.

A window is simply the framework for viewing something. You can make windows as large as the screen or as small as you want to. Or you can minimize them—that is, make them back into icons even as they continue to run. Manipulating a window—moving it, overlapping it with another window, or resizing it—does not affect the content of the window, just your view into it. You

▼ *Figure 3.1. Components of a window*

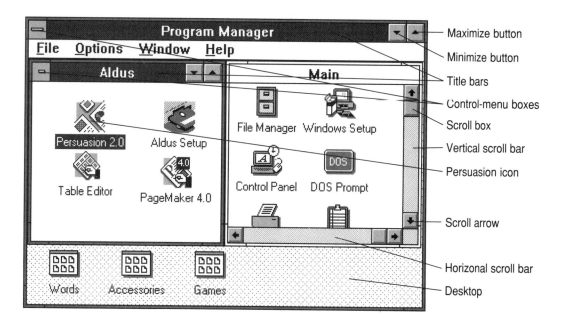

can arrange objects in the window the way you want them and move objects from one window to another. See *Microsoft Windows User's Guide*, Chapter 2, "Basic Skills," for detailed instructions on working with Windows.

All Windows applications have common elements, as shown in Figure 3.1. Whether you are in the Program Manager window or in the Persuasion window, you can use the components to manipulate windows in the same way.

The bar running across the top of a window contains the name of the application and the name of the file open in it. Below the title bar is the menu bar, which contains the names of commands that you use to work in the application. Commands are available in Program Manager, for example, to create new application icons, to group icons in new windows, to define the look of the desktop, and so on.

The scroll bar on the right and sometimes at the bottom of the window also gives you a way to move around the contents of your window. You can scroll by clicking the scroll bar, by dragging the scroll box, or by clicking one of the scroll arrows.

In order to understand the Windows environment—and therefore Persuasion's environment—you need to become familiar with more than the window itself. You also need to understand these elements of the desktop interface: the mouse, menus, dialog boxes, and the keyboard.

The Mouse

Although you can operate in Windows without a mouse, Persuasion requires one. With the mouse, you can point to objects, select objects with a click of the mouse button, drag selected objects about, and choose actions to apply to selected objects.

Simply moving the mouse moves the pointer on the screen. You use the left mouse button for these actions: clicking, double-clicking, pressing, and dragging. (Under certain circumstances in Persuasion, the right button provides a shortcut.)

To *click*, press down the mouse button and quickly release it without moving the mouse. Use clicking to select an object, to move an insertion point, or to turn on a dialog box control.

To *double-click*, click the mouse button twice rapidly without moving the mouse. Double-clicking is typically a shortcut for performing some type of action. For example, you can double-click a Persuasion AutoTemplate filename in File Manager to start Persuasion as well as to open a copy of the AutoTemplate file.

To *press*, hold the mouse button down for a time without moving the mouse. Pressing on a scroll bar's arrows, for example, scrolls the document in the window until you release the mouse button.

To *drag*, point to an object, push down the mouse button, move the mouse to a new location, and then release the mouse button. You primarily use dragging to move an object to a new location, but you can also drag diagonally to define a box around objects—blocks of text or a range of objects—to select them. In addition, you can drag an object's handles or the corner of a window to resize it.

On the screen, the pointer that indicates mouse movement can assume different shapes depending on what you are doing:

▲ Arrow—a general-purpose pointer for selecting and choosing

▲ I-beam—used to place an insertion point in text

▲ Hourglass—indicates that the computer is busy and you can't do anything until the pointer changes back to one of the other shapes

Persuasion has additional pointer shapes that correspond to tools that you use to draw graphics and do precision work. For more information about these pointers, see Chapter 9.

One of the ways you most frequently use the mouse is to select an object for the next action you will take. Typically, you select an object by clicking on it. Some sort of visual feedback lets you know that you have selected an object, such as highlighted text or handles (boxes) around an object (see Figure 3.2). In most cases, you can undo any selection by making another selection or by clicking elsewhere on the screen. For more about how to select headings, text, and objects, see Chapters 6, 8, and 9.

▼ *Figure 3.2. Selected text and a selected object*

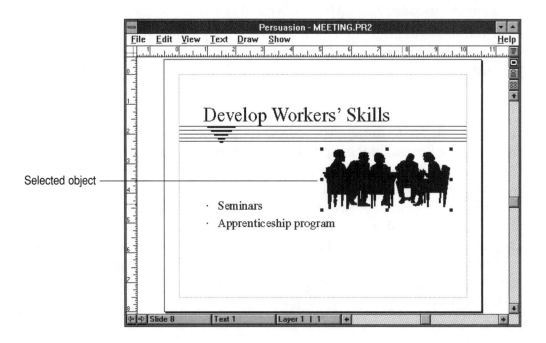

Selected text

Selected object

Menus

Menus are used to browse and to choose from the full range of actions available. To browse, simply click the menu name to pull down that menu. To choose an item on a menu, click the menu to open it, and then click the command you want. (Instead of clicking twice, you can also drag the pointer down the menu until you highlight the command you want and then release the mouse button.) The menu item will blink briefly, the menu will disappear, and the operation will be executed.

Three of the menus in the menu bar—the Control menu, the File menu, and the Edit menu—are standard menus that appear as the first three menus in almost every application, including Persuasion. The Control menu is not named, but is represented by the small box in the upper-left corner of each window. The Control menu is used primarily for closing an application or document, which is accomplished by double-clicking the Control-menu box. In addition to the three standard menus, each application has its own unique menus that appear to the right of the standard menus. Figure 3.3 shows the File menu from Persuasion's Outline view.

▼ *Figure 3.3. The File menu; a pull-down menu*

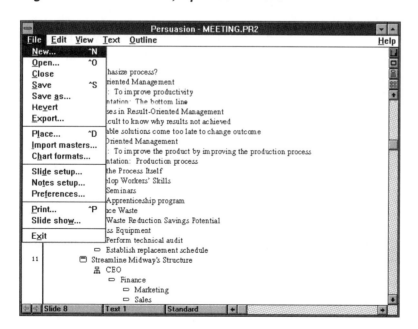

Two types of menus exist in the desktop interface: pull-down and pop-up. Pull-down menus are the most common, appearing from the menu bar at the top of the screen. Pop-up menus aren't in the menu bar but appear elsewhere—in the case of Persuasion, at the bottom of the window. When you press on the title of a pop-up menu, it "pops up" from that location. Pop-up menus are not "sticky" like pull-down menus—that is, they will not stay open unless you hold down the mouse button. The only way you can choose from a pop-up menu is to point to it and drag the pointer with the mouse to highlight the selection you want.

Dialog Boxes and Messages

Dialog boxes and messages present you with alternative actions. The computer is asking you for responses, typically several at one time. For example, in Persuasion's "Print" dialog box, you specify the number of copies to be printed, the range of slides to be printed, whether or not to print notes, and so on. If the command you choose has an ellipsis (…) after its name, a dialog box will be displayed. If your action causes a response that is unexpected or that you should be warned of, a message box will be displayed.

Dialog Boxes

Dialog boxes require additional information from you in order to carry out a command. Ellipses (…) following a command indicate that choosing that command opens a dialog box. Figure 3.4 illustrates a dialog box from Persuasion with various types of options.

A dialog box presents you with as many as five types of options:

1. *Command buttons.* Typically, the command buttons in a dialog box are "OK" or "Cancel." Alternatively, a command button may open yet another dialog box—for example, an "Options…" button. Clicking "OK" carries out the command; clicking "Cancel" closes the dialog box without carrying out the command. The default command button, indicated by a dark outline, identifies the most frequent action taken. If you want, you can activate the default button simply by pressing Enter on the keyboard.

▼ *Figure 3.4. The Slide Show dialog box.*

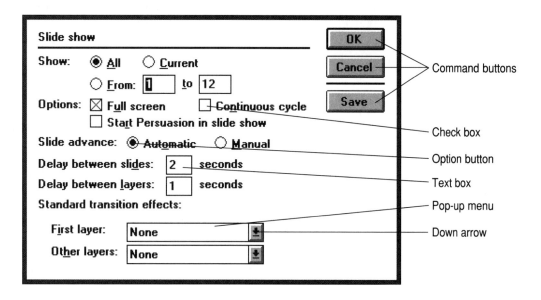

2. *Text boxes.* You type information into text boxes. If the blinking vertical bar, the insertion point, is not already at the far left side of the box, you can click an insertion point in the text box with the mouse. If the box already contains text, you can drag to highlight it and replace it by typing new text.

3. *List boxes.* List boxes are of two types: regular and drop-down. You click to select the item you want from a regular list box. You may have to scroll to see all the items in the list. In some cases, you can select more than one option by holding down Ctrl and clicking the items you want. Drop-down list boxes are not fully displayed in the dialog box. To display a drop-down list box, click the down arrow next to it to unfurl the list, and then click to select your choice from it.

4. *Check boxes.* You can click to check as many items in a group of check box options as you want. The check box operates like a toggle switch—you click to uncheck it, just as you clicked to check it.

5. *Option buttons.* You can click to select only one option button at a time; they are mutually exclusive. A selected option contains a black dot. An option is dimmed if it is not available.

Message Boxes

Message boxes notify you that something unusual has happened. They warn you of dangerous situations, recommend corrective actions, or provide information that might change your plans. Figure 3.5 shows a typical Persuasion message box.

CHECK YOURSELF

1. Start the Persuasion application found in the Aldus group window.

2. Resize the Persuasion application window, maximize it to fill the screen, and then return it to its previous size.

3. Open a copy of the default AutoTemplate by choosing "New..." from the File menu.

4. Open each of the menus along the top and bottom menu bars.

5. Minimize the presentation into an icon on the desktop.

ANSWERS

1. Locate the Aldus window. If it is still in icon form, double-click it. Then double-click the Persuasion icon within the Aldus window.

2. Position the mouse pointer at the lower-right corner of the window until it turns into a double-headed arrow, and then press the mouse button while you drag the corner to resize the window. Click the Maximize button in the upper-right corner of the window to make it fill the screen, and then click it again to return the window to its previous size.

3. Click the File menu and then click "New...."

4. Click on the menu name to open the menu. The menus on the top bar are sticky and will stay open until you make another click. The menus on the lower menu bar close as soon as you release the mouse button.

5. Click the Minimize button in the upper-right corner next to the Maximize button.

▼ *Figure 3.5. A Persuasion message box*

The Keyboard

There are three basic types of keys on the keyboard: character keys, modifier keys, and function keys. When you press a character key, that character appears on the screen—for example, a letter of the alphabet. If you hold down a modifier key while pressing a character key, the modifier key alters the meaning of what you typed. Function keys (F1 through F12) are often shortcuts for commands, sometimes in combination with modifier keys. The assignment of commands to function keys varies from application to application; function key assignments are usually indicated beside the relevant commands on the menus. You should become familiar with the uses of important character, modifier, and function keys, so that when you use them in Persuasion, you'll fully understand the actions that you are taking.

Character Keys

There are five character keys that you will use quite often when you are working with Persuasion:

▲ *Enter* tells the application that you are finished entering information in a particular area of a document, such as a dialog box. Pressing Enter while typing creates a carriage return in text.

▲ *Tab* in text in Persuasion moves the outline unit one level to the right. In a dialog box, Tab moves the cursor to the next option.

▲ *Backspace* deletes text. If you have an insertion point in text (the I-beam cursor), pressing Backspace erases one character at a time.

▲ *Delete* is a shortcut for the "Clear" command in the Edit menu; that is, it removes the selection from your document without putting it in the Clipboard.

▲ *Esc* lets you "get out of there." For example, you can press Esc instead of clicking Cancel in a dialog box.

Modifier Keys

You should be familiar with the following three modifier keys and their uses in Persuasion:

▲ *Shift*, when used together with another character key, produces the uppercase letter on alphabetic keys, or the upper character on two-character keys (the same as on a typewriter). The Shift key is sometimes used in combination with a character key to provide a shortcut, such as using Shift + Delete for the "Cut" command or Shift + Insert for the "Paste" command. The Shift key is also used in conjunction with the mouse for extending selections or for constraining movement in graphics applications—for example, holding down the Shift key while using the rectangle tool in Persuasion limits the tool to drawing squares.

▲ *Alt*, when used together with other keys, produces a set of international characters and special symbols. For example, Alt + 0150 produces an em dash (—). For a full description of the keystrokes required in combination with Alt to create special characters, see the presentation on the Persuasion disks called XCHARSET.PR2.

   The Alt key can also be used in conjunction with the mouse to modify the effect of a click or drag. For example, holding down Alt while dragging in the Persuasion window turns the pointer into the grabber hand, which moves a slide in the window so you can see different parts of it.

▲ *Ctrl*, when used together with other keys, tells the application to interpret the key as a command—known as a keyboard equivalent. For example, in Persuasion, pressing Ctrl + S is the same as choosing "Save" from the File menu. The meaning of these key combinations can vary from application to application.

For more information about how Persuasion uses modifier keys in conjunction with mouse actions, see Chapter 9.

Function Keys

The following is a brief summary of the function keys and their uses in Persuasion:

▲ *FI* opens online Help.

▲ *F3* is the shortcut for the "Find…" command.

▲ *F4* is the shortcut for the "Change…" command.

▲ *F5–F8* are the shortcuts for various character formatting commands, such as bold or italic.

▲ *F9* displays the toolbox.

▲ *F10, F11, and F12* display these palettes, respectively: Lines, Fills, and Colors.

Persuasion's Environment

Any Windows application such as Persuasion uses the basic elements of the Windows environment—windows, menus, icons, and so on—to create its own work space. Therefore, what you see when you start Persuasion is what you are already familiar with— a desktop that has a menu bar at the top, icons that represent objects you can point to and use, and a window that gives you a view into Persuasion's environment.

Because you need to work with the elements of a presentation—the outline, slides, charts and tables, notes, handouts, and so forth—Persuasion provides windows into each of the working environments that you need to create and maintain those elements. Those windows (or views), the transitions between them, and their associated menus are the key to understanding and working with Persuasion.

Views

Take a look at Figure 3.6 and you'll notice that the first menu unique to Persuasion—just below the Control menu box, File, and Edit menus—is the View menu. If you're in Persuasion right now, pull down that menu and take a look: What you see is a list of commands, each of which will take you to one of Persuasion's views.

Persuasion's views are organized around the elements of a presentation—the outline, slides, masters, and notes—and are carefully designed to give you the commands and tools you need to work with each element.

It's not necessary to work with all of Persuasion's views for each presentation that you create; in fact, you may work with only a few of them on a regular basis. (If you use Persuasion's AutoTemplates, you may not need to use any of the views, except Outline and Slide.) However, each view gives you complete control over some aspect of your presentation, and having a working knowledge of Persuasion's views gives you the power and flexibility you need to create any type of presentation you want.

▼ *Figure 3.6. Persuasion's View menu*

Use to go to a specific view

Use to go to a specific slide or master

Use to assign a slide master

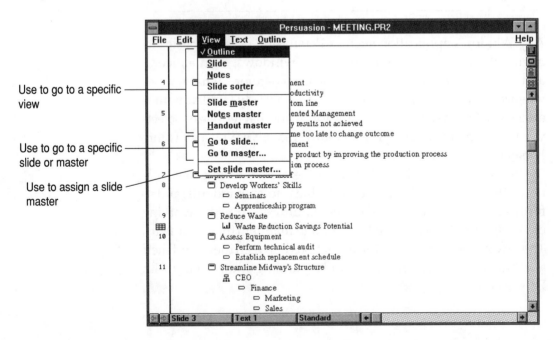

Outline View

Outline view (Figure 3.7) is one of the most powerful views in Persuasion because from it you can enter almost everything, excluding graphics, that you want in your presentation—text, charts, and organization charts. Outline view is typically the view you see when you open an AutoTemplate or a presentation.

In Outline view you can enter or import text to be used on your slides, enter data for charts and plot them, reorganize slides and slide text, and assign slide masters and transition effects. As long as you are using an AutoTemplate or have at least one slide master defined, whatever you enter into your outline automatically flows to your slides.

Pull-down and pop-up menus contain commands for entering text, assigning masters, and manipulating items of your outline. Figure 3.7 shows the icons from the upper-right edge of the window that appear in every view and represent Persuasion's views. (The icon for the view you are currently in is highlighted.) Use these view icons as shortcuts for going to other views.

Persuasion's Environment

▼ *Figure 3.7. Outline view*

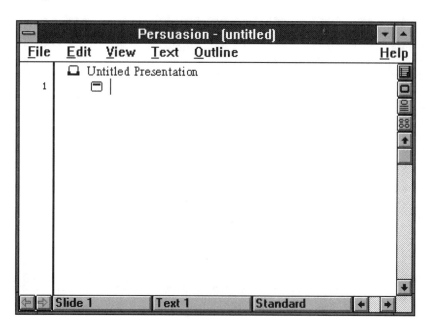

In addition to choosing the "Outline" command from the View menu, you can go from any view in Persuasion to Outline view by clicking the Outline view icon at the upper right edge of the window. For more information about working in Outline view, see Chapter 6.

Slide View

Slide view (Figure 3.8) lets you work directly on the slide to draw or import graphics, create charts and tables, and enter or edit text. Rulers are supplied at the left and the top of the slide for precision alignment, and you can track the movement of the pointer in both rulers. Icons representing Persuasion graphics tools are available in the toolbox. You can remove the rulers and the toolbox from the window by choosing each from the Show menu. Choose "Rulers" or "Toolbox" again to display it. Pull-down and pop-up menus contain commands that can be used to format text, plot charts, draw graphic objects, set special effects, define drawing layers, and assign masters.

▼ *Figure 3.8. Slide view*

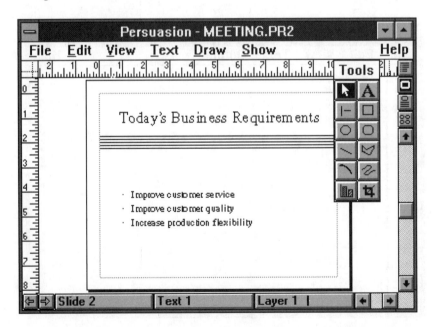

By choosing a tool (that is, by clicking on one of the tool icons shown in Figure 3.9), you set the shape of the pointer and define the type of work you can do, from typing text to drawing various shapes. The spaces below the tools in the left side of the window are used by Persuasion to indicate the default settings for tools.

Persuasion's Environment

You can go to Slide view in any of these ways:

▲ Click the Slide view icon.

▲ In Outline view, click the slide number in the left margin of the slide you want to see.

▲ Choose the slide you want to see from the Slide pop-up menu at the left in the lower menu bar.

▲ In Slide sorter view, click the slide you want to see with the right mouse button.

For more information about using Persuasion's tools, see Chapter 9.

▼ Figure 3.9. Persuasion's toolbox

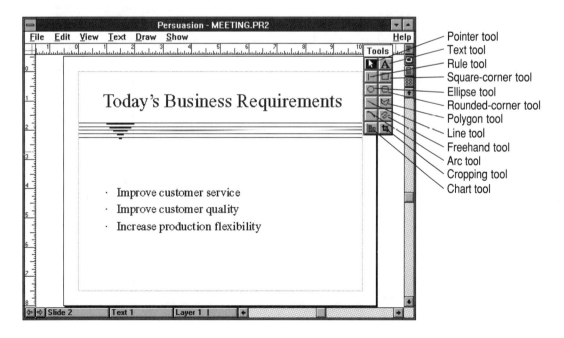

Notes View

You can enter or import text directly onto the speaker notes page in Notes view, as shown in Figure 3.10. You can also resize or change the position of the slide miniature, or use Persuasion's toolbox to draw graphics. One notes page exists for each slide.

To go to Notes view, click the Notes view icon. For more information about creating speaker notes and the notes master, see Chapter 12.

Slide Sorter View

Once you have created your slides, it's convenient to use the Slide sorter view (Figure 3.11) to rearrange slides or to assign masters and transition effects to groups of slides. Changes made in Slide sorter view are reflected in Outline view. To go to Slide sorter view, click the Slide sorter view icon. For more information about using Slide sorter view, see Chapters 5 and 6.

▼ *Figure 3.10. Notes view*

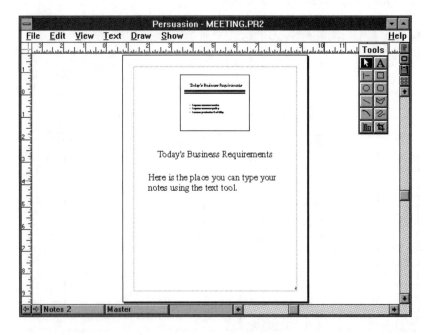

▼ *Figure 3.11. Slide sorter view*

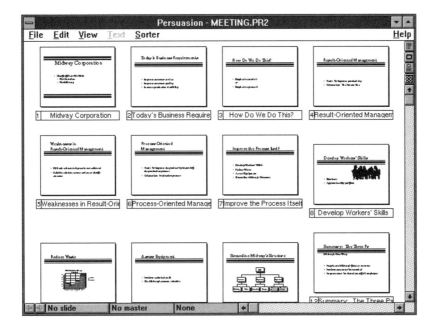

Slide Master, Handout Master, and Notes Master Views

Persuasion provides three master views—Slide, Handout, and Notes—so that you have the tools to define or modify the design of your presentation materials (Figure 3.12). If you are starting your presentation from an AutoTemplate, most design issues are handled for you and you may not need to use these views. However, if you decide to create your own design, you'll need to use the master views for positioning and formatting placeholders, defining backgrounds, and so on.

To go to any of the master views, choose them from the View menu. To take a shortcut to Slide master view (or Notes master view), click the right mouse button on the Slide view icon (or Notes view icon), or hold down the Ctrl key while you click the Slide view icon (or Notes view icon). For more information about designing your own masters, see Chapter 12.

▼ *Figure 3.12. Slide master view, Notes master view, Handout master view*

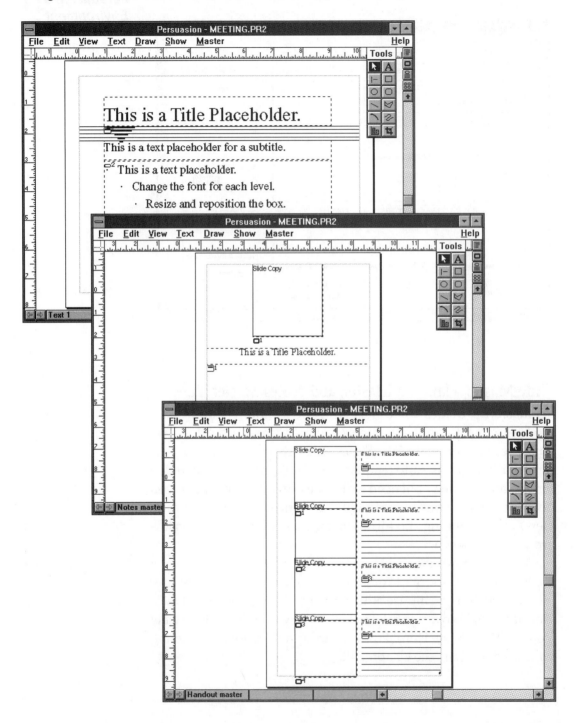

CHECK YOURSELF

1. Expand the presentation currently running as an icon (minimized).

2. Use a menu command to go to Slide view.

3. Use an icon to return to Outline view.

4. Use a mouse shortcut to go to Master view.

ANSWERS

1. Double-click the Persuasion icon at the bottom of your screen.

2. Choose "Slide" from the View menu.

3. Click the Outline view icon in the upper-right corner of the window.

4. Point to the Slide view icon in the upper-right corner of the window and click the right mouse button (or hold down Ctrl and click).

Persuasion's Menus

Persuasion uses both pull-down and pop-up menus. Eleven pull-down menus are available from the menu bar at the top of the window. Although the three standard menus—Control, File, and Edit—appear in each view, the others appear only in those views that are appropriate for the commands they contain.

To choose a command from a pull-down menu, click the name of the menu in the menu bar and then click the command you want. You can also point to the menu and drag the pointer down to the command you want, releasing the mouse button when it is highlighted.

Table 3.1 provides an explanation of each of Persuasion's pull-down menus. For a quick reference to all of Persuasion's commands, see the index entry for "Commands." For more information about the commands on a particular menu, see the chapters referenced in the table.

▼ *Table 3.1. Persuasion's pull-down menus*

Pull-down menu	*Description*
Control menu	Contains the commands that allow you to change the window size and location, make the window an icon, enlarge the window to full screen, close the window, and move from one open application to another.
File menu	Contains commands that operate on the entire file, such as "Open…," "Close," "Save," "Slide setup…," "Notes setup…," "Print…," and so on. In addition, it contains commands for importing text, graphics, slide masters, and chart formats and exporting your outline, as well as commands for customizing the Persuasion environment by setting preferences or running a slide show (Chapters 4 and 14).
Edit menu	Contains commands for revising and editing your presentation, such as "Cut," "Copy," "Paste," "Spelling…," and so on (Chapters 6, 8, and 14).
View menu	Contains commands for going to other views. (Chapter 3).
Text menu	Contains commands for formatting text, such as "Character…" and "Paragraph…" (Chapter 8).
Outline menu	Contains commands for entering, editing, and rearranging your outline. The Outline menu is available only in Outline view (Chapter 6).
Draw menu	Contains commands for editing and enhancing graphics or charts. The Draw menu is available in all views, except Outline and Slide sorter views (Chapter 9).
Show menu	Contains commands for opening special effects palettes, such as Colors, Fills, and Lines. In addition, you can change the display size of the slide up to 400% and in other ways customize the working environment. The Show menu is available in all views, except Outline and Slide sorter views (Chapters 9 and 13).
Sorter menu	Contains commands for determining the size of the slide miniatures shown on your screen in Slide sorter view. In addition, you can choose to view your slides in black and white, which will speed up rearranging slides or reassigning masters, and to expand or collapse subordinate slides. The Sorter menu is available only in Slide sorter view (Chapter 6).
Master menu	Contains commands for creating and formatting your own slide masters, as well as formatting notes and handout masters. The Master menu is available only in Slide master, Notes master, and Handout master views (Chapter 12).
Help menu	Contains the "Index…" command for opening the Help window and the "About Persuasion…" command for displaying the startup screen with the version number and serial number of the program.

In each view, the bottom bar of the window has an area set aside for pop-up menus. These menus provide shortcuts for the actions that are most frequently taken in each view. For example, it is common to assign masters and transition effects in Outline view, so Persuasion provides pop-up menus for that purpose. Table 3.2

▼ *Table 3.2. Persuasion's pop-up menus*

Pop-up menu	Description
Slide menu	Contains a list of slide numbers. Choosing one displays that slide. Choosing "New" creates a new slide with the default slide master assigned. The Slide pop-up menu is available in Outline, Slide, and Slide sorter views.
Master menu	Contains a list of slide master names. Choosing a slide master in Outline, Slide, or Slide sorter views assigns that master to the selected slide. Choose "Reapply master" to return a slide to the format of the assigned master. ("Reapply master" is the only command on this menu in Notes view.) The Master pop-up menu for assigning masters is available in Outline, Slide, Slide sorter, and Notes view (Chapter 5). In Slide master view, the location and function of this menu changes; it moves to the left on the lower menu bar. Choose a master name from the menu to display that master. Choose "New..." to create a new slide master. The Master pop-up menu for displaying masters is available in Slide master view only (Chapter 12).
Transition menu	Contains a list of transition effects that you can assign to the selected slide. In addition, you can choose "Layers..." to assign transition effects by slide build layers. The Transition pop-up menu is available in Outline and Slide sorter view (Chapter 9).
Layer menu	Contains a list of drawing layers to which you can assign selected objects. You can specify the current drawing layer, as well as which layers are active or inactive. The Layer pop-up menu is available in Slide view only (Chapter 9).
Notes menu	Contains a list of notes pages. Choose one to go to that notes page in Notes view. The Notes pop-up menu is available in Notes view only (Chapter 12).

briefly reviews Persuasion's pop-up menus. For more information about the actions you can take with pop-up menus, see the chapters referred to in the table.

Customizing Persuasion's Environment

Much of Persuasion's desktop can be customized to suit your work habits. Using the "Preferences" command, you can tell Persuasion to always open to the view of your preference, change the rulers to the measurement system you prefer, change the default slide master, or display break labels. You can also set options on menus (such as to display the rulers) and in dialog boxes (for example, font and size in the "Character specifications" dialog box) using the pointer tool with nothing selected. For more information about how to customize your working environment by setting presentation defaults, see Chapter 12.

QUICK COMMAND SUMMARY

In this chapter you have learned to do these procedures using these commands:

Commands/Icons	Procedures
Persuasion application icon	Start Persuasion
Minimize/Maximize buttons	Change the window size and iconize Persuasion
Control menu box	Close a window

View menu commands
    Outline
    Slide
    Notes
    Slide sorter
    Slide master
    Notes master
    Handout master
	Go to a specific view

View icons
    Outline
    Slide
    Notes
    Slide Sorter
	Go to a specific view

Rulers and Toolbox Show menu	Display the rulers or the toolbox
Drawing tool from the toolbox	Change the pointer to a particular tool

PRACTICE WHAT YOU'VE LEARNED

In this exercise, you'll move around the Persuasion window in different views to get familiar with the working environment.

1. Start Windows and open Persuasion.

2. Start a new presentation.

3. Make the window fill the screen (maximize it).

4. Go to Slide view.

5. Look at the Show menu. What function key controls the display of the toolbox? Remove the toolbox from the window.

6. Using the Show menu, turn off the rulers.

7. Go to Slide master view.

8. Use the Master pop-up menu to go to the "Graphic 1" master.

9. Return to Outline view.

10. Open the "Print" dialog box and find an example of each of these: command button, text box, drop-down list box, check box, and an option button.

11. Close the "Print" dialog box without printing and close Persuasion without saving the presentation.

ANSWERS

1. Type *win* at the C> prompt. Double-click the Persuasion icon in the Aldus window. Click "OK" in the "Slide setup" dialog box.

2. Choose "New…" from the File menu.

3. Click the upward-pointing triangle in the upper-right corner of the window.

4. Click the Slide view icon along the upper-right edge of the window, choose "Slide" from the View menu, or click the number "1" in the left margin.

5. Press F9.

6. Choose "Rulers" from the Show menu.

7. Click the Slide view icon using the right mouse button.

8. Point to the pop-up menu at the left end of the lower menu bar (it probably says "Text 1," the current slide master), hold down the mouse button, and drag up to select "Graphic 1."

9. Click the Outline view icon along the upper-left edge of the window.

10. Choose "Print…" from the File menu to open the dialog box. The command buttons are "OK," "Cancel," and "Setup…." An example of a text box is "Copies." A drop-down list box is "Slide printer" or "Notes printer." A check box is any of the options in the middle of the dialog box for "Print," "Graphics options," or "Outline options." An option button is "Pages."

11. Click "Cancel" in the "Print" dialog box, and then double-click the Control menu box in the upper-left corner of the Persuasion window. Click "No" if you see a message box asking whether you want to save changes. You have now closed both the presentation window and the application window.

PART II

Creating a Presentation from Outline View

Planning and Starting Your Presentation

What kind of presentation do you want to create? A great one, of course! But what makes for a great presentation? In part, a great presentation results from a skillful matching of the medium with the message.

So what type of medium should you choose—slides, overhead transparencies, or an on-screen slide show? Usually it all depends on your purpose, your audience, your presentation environment, and the equipment available. Some of those elements may already be determined; the rest you need to choose.

Then how do you formulate your message? By concentrating on how to get your point across to the targeted audience. Writing a great presentation takes into account both audience and purpose.

In this chapter you'll learn the following:

▲ **How to determine whether to create 35 mm slides, overheads, or an on-screen presentation**

▲ **How to plan the content of your presentation**

▲ **How to start a presentation**

▲ **How to save and name a presentation**

Planning Your Presentation

Most of the planning and writing you do for your presentation can be done using Persuasion. However, before you do anything, it's best to decide what kind of presentation you want to make so you can choose an AutoTemplate appropriate to the medium (or so you can indicate the chosen medium for the presentation setup if you start from scratch).

▲ Will you use overhead transparencies?

▲ Will you show slides?

▲ Will you display your presentation on-screen—either directly on the monitor or by projecting it onto a large screen from a personal computer?

Determining the Presentation Medium

The shape of a slide, a transparency, and a computer screen are all slightly different from one other, as you can see from Figure 4.1. Before you start putting anything on a "canvas," you need to know what size it is. AutoTemplates are already set up for a particular shape; thus, in choosing your AutoTemplate, you choose your medium. If you want to start from scratch, you need to define your own setup, a process described later in this chapter. For informa-

▼ *Figure 4.1. Shapes of screen, 35 mm side, and overhead*

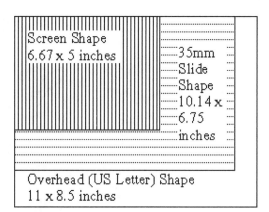

tion on choosing an AutoTemplate, see Chapter 5, and for information on creating an AutoTemplate, see Chapter 12.

Starting with the right shape is important. Changing your mind later may mean having to go from slide to slide or moving and resizing text and graphics so they fit within the new margins. Changing the setup of a finished presentation from "35 mm" slide to "Screen" can result in strange dislocations of elements on your new slide, as shown in Figure 4.2. It's best to design your message to fit the medium from the start; resort to converting a presentation from one medium to another only when there's no other way to avoid recreating it all.

How can you figure out what your presentation medium should be? Often the available preparation time or production equipment determines what kind of presentation you can produce and deliver. But let's assume you have the luxury of using any of the options listed earlier. Which should you choose?

In order to decide, consider these topics and ask yourself these questions:

▲ *Audience.* How large is my audience?

The size of the audience usually determines the size of the room and, thus, the audience's proximity to the screen. A smaller audience—for example, an audience small enough to fit around a conference table or in an office—could see a presentation run right on the screen of your computer. A

▼ *Figure 4.2. A slide set up for "35 mm" and changed to "screen"*

35 mm setting

Screen slide size with
elements from 35 mm
presentation

medium-sized audience, however, might be situated in a classroom and require the larger screen of an overhead or slide projector. A large audience seated in an auditorium needs the crisp resolution that slides provide.

▲ *Situation.* Will the room be dark or light? Will projection equipment be available?

The lighting of a room affects the audience in a number of ways: They cannot take notes in a room darkened for slides, nor can they see the presenter or each other for purposes of discussion. (Keep in mind, however, that you can always use Persuasion to prepare handouts to compensate for the audience's inability to take notes in the dark.) Because the audience cannot usually see the presenter or each other, the slides bear the full weight of the audience's attention and need to be particularly well-designed. Slide presentations tend to be more formal in subject and purpose than overhead transparency presentations: Darkness focuses attention on the slides and discussion is inhibited.

If you want to encourage audience participation, overhead transparencies or large-screen projection from a computer are better choices. However, the audience's attention will not be as focused as with slides. In a lighted room, people attend not only to what you say and show them, but to how others in the audience react. This environment tends to be more informal and invites discussion more easily than slides.

Finally, you need to know whether projection equipment is available at the presentation site. Any presentation other than a small, informal one on your computer requires special projection equipment, such as an overhead projector or a slide projector and screen.

▲ *Preparation time and equipment.* How much time do I have to produce the presentation? What means of production do I have available?

These considerations should be secondary to audience and situation, but the availability of production time and equipment may prevail in determining your medium. Obviously, producing transparencies is faster and easier than producing slides. All you need to create overhead transparencies is a printer and the time it takes to print your presentation, hand-outs, or speaker notes. Slides, however, require a film recorder—either your own or that of a service bureau—and the time it takes to develop and mount that film into slides.

▲ *Purpose.* What do I want the presentation to accomplish?

Answering this question shapes the content and structure of your presentation far more than its medium, but you should not ignore it in considering whether you want to use slides or transparencies. To the extent that the medium is the message, you want to link the content of your presentation to the way it's presented.

For example, consider the message you may be sending by using an inappropriate medium. If you simply need to prepare a status report for your manager, slides are clearly overkill and may cause your manager to question your judgment. However, if the purpose of your presentation is to impress shareholders, well-designed color slides should do the job. The distinctions here may be subtle, but you should be sensitive to them.

Formulating Your Message

Once you've chosen your presentation medium, you can begin by using Persuasion to organize your thoughts. Persuasion is not just a means of producing a presentation; it's a useful means of *creating* a presentation. Do not expect to scribble on paper first and only at the end type your final outline in Persuasion. Instead, use Persuasion's outliner from the beginning as you would a word processor—to generate, try out, and edit your ideas.

Take the sense of audience and purpose you defined in determining your medium and expand on them to write your presentation. Start by asking yourself these questions:

▲ How knowledgeable is my audience? How homogeneous or diverse are the members of the audience?

If your audience is unfamiliar with your subject matter, you'll need to provide a context for what you have to say. Remember to explain your terms, use plain language, and invent simple analogies to bridge the gap between what the audience knows and what it doesn't know. However, a more sophisticated audience will require less background information and explanation of terms; in fact, you need to take care that you don't talk down to them.

In dealing with a diverse audience, you need to establish a common ground of understanding. You need to be explicit about your assumptions—for example, state whom you assume your audience to be. A well-drawn image of its commonality can unite a diverse audience, so that for the length of your presentation the various people sitting in front of you become the audience you've described. Carefully examine your assumptions about both your audience and the subject of your presentation before you begin writing. Make sure that your starting point is clear so that people will know how to interpret what follows.

▲ What am I trying to accomplish with this presentation? Is my goal to convince my audience, to inform them, to impress them, to change their behavior, or to accomplish something else?

Make the goal of your presentation operational. An operational goal is concrete: It describes exactly what you want your audience to know, do, or feel after experiencing your presentation. After establishing that goal in your own mind, use it to assess each slide of your presentation as you go. Such a strategy will help you keep on track and finally reach your goal.

Once you have established what you want to accomplish, think about how you can do that within the presentation. Try to connect your own purpose with some need or interest of the audience. You end goals will be met if you can make the audience see how your information benefits them. If your audience does not understand why they should care about what you have to say, your chances for success in persuading them of anything are limited. Your personal goal for the presentation must be translated into information they can understand, care about, and act on.

In addition to these general guidelines for thinking about your presentation, keep in mind the following rules for putting information on a slide. The single most common mistake presenters make is to put too much information on a slide. Keep each slide as simple as possible so that all the information on it can be absorbed before moving on to the next one. Do not be afraid to use several slides to convey a multifaceted point; putting all that information on one slide for the sake of unity would be a mistake. The same advice goes for graphics: Be restrained. Color, patterns, and images can all be effectively used, but don't fall into the trap of using them for their own sake. The graphic elements should support your point; don't let them distract from it.

Finally, a word about organization. The old standby rule of "tell 'em what you're gonna tell 'em, tell 'em, and tell 'em what you just told 'em" works. Don't keep the point of your presentation a secret because you want to surprise them by divulging it at the end. They won't be there at the end to hear it, long ago having tuned out. You need to grab them at the beginning—with something as simple as the reason for your presentation and why they'll benefit from it!

Starting Your Presentation in Persuasion

Whether you create your presentation by using an AutoTemplate, modifying an existing presentation, or starting from scratch, the steps you take to begin are clear and simple:

▲ Start Persuasion.

▲ Open an existing Persuasion document or use the "New..." command to start from scratch.

▲ Name and save your presentation.

Starting Persuasion

Once you have installed Windows and the Persuasion application, you can start Persuasion by double-clicking the Persuasion icon in the Aldus group window (see Figure 4.3). Persuasion briefly displays its startup screen, opening to the Persuasion desktop.

▼ *Figure 4.3. Persuasion icon in the Aldus Group window*

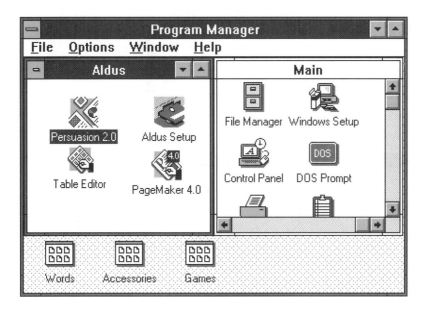

Opening an Existing Presentation

Most of the time you'll build one presentation on the foundation of another, working from a presentation that you previously created or from some other model. For example, Persuasion comes with 55 different AutoTemplates, which are shell presentations with background design and type conventions already established. All you need to do is add your words and your graphics, as you can see in Figure 4.4. Why duplicate a lot of work when you can build on the past so easily?

To open an existing presentation or copy of an AutoTemplate:

1. Choose "Open…" from the File menu. (The "Open" dialog box appears, as in Figure 4.5.)

2. Open the directory containing the presentation or AutoTemplate you want.

   ▲ For presentations, the PR2US\PRES directory is already open by default.

▼ *Figure 4.4. Text automatically formatted by the AutoTemplate*

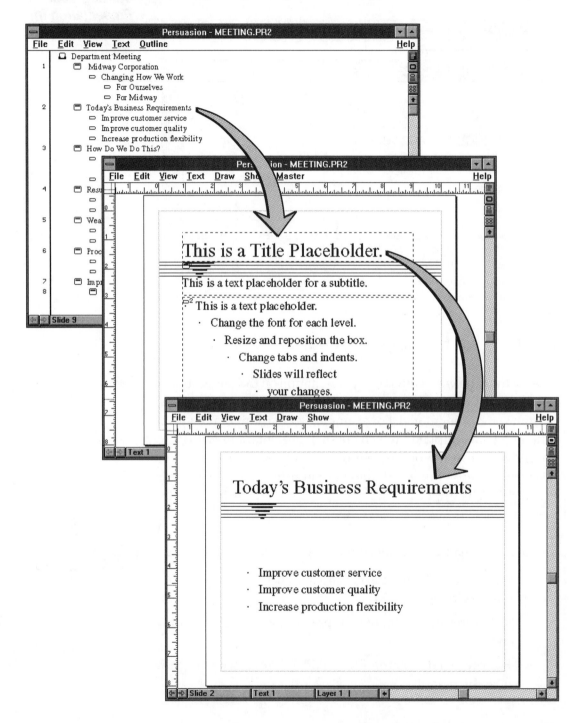

▼ *Figure 4.5. "Open" dialog box*

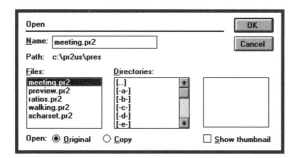

Starting Your Presentation in Persuasion

▲ For AutoTemplates, double-click [..] to go to the PR2US directory, and then double-click [autotemp] to go to the PR2US\AUTOTEMP directory.

3. Click to highlight the name of the AutoTemplate or presentation you want.

4. Click "OK." The "Slide setup" dialog box appears so that you can confirm the printer you'll use and the slide size you want. It is important to choose the output device that you will use to produce your presentation now.

5. Click "OK" in the "Slide setup" dialog box.

TIP

You can combine starting Persuasion and opening an existing presentation (the original) or AutoTemplate (a copy) by simply double-clicking on the name of the AutoTemplate or presentation in File Manager.

When you open an existing presentation (or AutoTemplate), it is already set up to be either a slide, overhead transparency, or on-screen presentation. AutoTemplates with the prefix OB are set up to be black-and-white overhead transparencies; AutoTemplates with the prefix OC are set up to be color overhead transparencies; and AutoTemplates with the prefix S are set up to be 35 mm slides. You can always check to see what the slide setup is by looking at the "Slide setup" dialog box settings.

CHECK YOURSELF

1. Open a copy of an AutoTemplate that is set up for 35 mm slides.

2. Open a copy of an AutoTemplate that is set up for black-and-white overheads.

ANSWERS

1. Choose "Open…" from the File menu. In the "Open" dialog box, double-click [..] to move up to the PR2US directory and then double-click [autotemp] to open the contents of PR2US\ AUTOTEMP. Now double-click one of the AutoTemplate filenames beginning with S, for example, S07.AT2. The "Slide setup" dialog box automatically appears. Check to be sure that "35mm" is selected for "Slide," and then click "OK."

2. Choose "Open…" from the File menu. The open presentation will automatically close, asking if you want to save changes. Click "No." Now click one of the AutoTemplate filenames beginning with OB, for example, OB15.AT2. The "Slide setup" dialog box automatically appears. Check to be sure that "US Letter" is selected for "Slide" and that you have selected your printer for "Target device." Click "OK."

Starting from Scratch

For those occasions when you feel you need a new and different look, you can build a presentation from the ground up by using the "New…" and "Slide setup…" commands. When you choose "New…," Persuasion opens the default AutoTemplate you designated during installation, which is the one stored in NEW.AT2 in the PR2US directory. If you made no selection at the time of installation, the default AutoTemplate is OB37, a plain AutoTemplate with no background design.

To start from scratch:

1. Choose "New…" from the File menu. An untitled copy of an AutoTemplate opens, and the "Slide setup" dialog box appears, as shown in Figure 4.6.

▼ *Figure 4.6. "Slide setup" dialog box in untitled presentation*

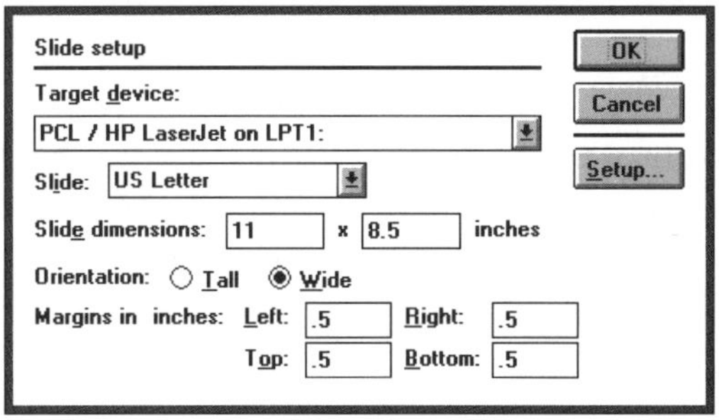

Starting Your Presentation in Persuasion

2. In the "Slide setup" dialog box, select the appropriate target device and slide size, and then click "OK."

   ▲ "Target device": You can choose any target device for which you have a driver installed. Even though you may not have a printer currently hooked up, you should target the device on which you eventually intend to produce your presentation. If you plan to print or produce your presentation yourself, you should target the printer or film recorder you currently have installed.

   ▲ "Slide": Select "US Letter" for overheads (black-and-white or color), "35mm" for 35 mm slides, or "Screen" for a slide show on a computer monitor.

Persuasion opens an untitled copy of NEW.AT2, which is actually either OB37.AT2 or the AutoTemplate you chose to be the default during installation. Basically, the default AutoTemplate is any AutoTemplate you save as NEW.AT2 to the PR2US directory. For more information about defining your own default AutoTemplate, see Chapter 12.

Naming and Saving Your Presentation

To create a new presentation from an existing one, you need to open an untitled copy of the old presentation or AutoTemplate and give it a new name. Once you give it a new name and save it, both the old and the new presentations exist, each with different names. Alternatively, if you have started from scratch, your presentation is not titled yet and exists only as a temporary file. You must name and save it to create a permanent file on the disk.

To name a presentation:

1. Choose "Save as…" from the File menu. The "Save as" dialog box appears, as in Figure 4.7. By default, the directory open in the list box is PR2US\PRES. You may want to change to another directory, but probably you'll want to save your presentations in the PRES directory.

2. Type the name of the new presentation.

3. Leave "Presentation" selected. Your presentation is given the filename extension of .PR2 to indicate that it is a presentation. If you save it as an AutoTemplate by selecting "AutoTemplate," the filename extension is .AT2.

    The only difference between a Persuasion document saved as a presentation and one saved as an AutoTemplate is how they open. Double-clicking an AutoTemplate automatically opens a copy of it; double-clicking a presentation opens the presentation itself. If you are creating a presentation that you intend to use as an AutoTemplate in the future, save it as an AutoTemplate.

4. Click "OK."

▼ *Figure 4.7. "Save as" dialog box*

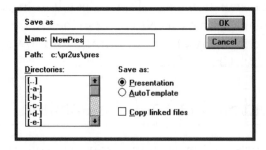

QUICK COMMAND SUMMARY

In this chapter you have learned to do these procedures using these commands:

Commands	Procedures
"Open..." (File menu)	Opening a presentation or AutoTemplate
"New..." (File)	Starting a presentation using the default AutoTemplate
"Slide setup..." (File)	Setting up the target device and slide size of your presentation or AutoTemplate
"Save as..." (File)	Saving and naming your presentation or AutoTemplate

PRACTICE WHAT YOU'VE LEARNED

In this exercise, you'll start a presentation, set it up for one medium, and then change it to another. Finally, you'll name and save it.

1. Start a presentation from scratch.

2. What medium is it set up for?

3. Change the medium.

4. Name the presentation "FIRSTONE."

ANSWERS

1. Choose "New..." from the File menu. In the "Slide setup" dialog box, choose an appropriate target device (printer) for your computer setup.

2. Look at the options in "Slide" in the "Slide setup" dialog box. If you are using the default AutoTemplate that comes with Persuasion (OB37.AT2), the answer is "overheads." ("US Letter" indicates the paper size that your overheads are printed on.)

3. Select "35mm" or "Screen" instead. Then click "OK." You'll get a warning about the results of changing slide size; proceed by clicking "OK."

4. Choose "Save as..." from the File menu. Type "FIRSTONE" and click "OK."

5

Using AutoTemplates

AutoTemplates are the key to Persuasion's ease of use: They provide a mold into which you pour the text and numbers you want to use in your presentation. That mold shapes your information into bulleted lists, pie charts, or whatever format you establish for the information on your slides. For example, once the background design or the color of your slide title is set in an AutoTemplate, it is automatically repeated on every slide connected to it. Persuasion comes with AutoTemplates in a variety of designs and for a variety of media: 35 mm slides, overheads, or on-screen display.

Once you have an AutoTemplate, you can use it repeatedly or modify it for new uses. In fact, one of the main reasons to use AutoTemplates, besides ease of use, is to give your slides a unique, but uniform, style that enhances the image of your organization. By setting its own design standards in its AutoTemplates, your organization makes it possible for any of its employees to easily create presentations that project a consistent image.

In this chapter you'll learn the following:

▲ **What an AutoTemplate is**

▲ **How masters and placeholders work**

▲ **How to import slide masters from other AutoTemplates**

▲ **How to change the default slide master**

▲ **How to assign slide masters**

What Are AutoTemplates?

The AutoTemplates that come with Persuasion are basically collections of slide masters—although, technically, an AutoTemplate can be any group of slides or slide masters created in Persuasion and saved as such. The only real difference between slides saved as a presentation and slides saved as an AutoTemplate is the way in which each file is opened by Persuasion:

▲ *AutoTemplate.* If you save a group of slides as an AutoTemplate, the next time you double-click its name in the "Open" dialog box, Persuasion automatically opens a copy of the AutoTemplate to prevent opening and altering the original by accident.

To open the original AutoTemplate, you need to click "Original" in the "Open" dialog box. Unless you specifically click "Original," you always get a copy.

▲ *Presentation.* If you save a group of slides as a presentation, Persuasion opens the original presentation when you double-click its name in the list box (see Figure 5.1).

Persuasion comes with 55 different AutoTemplates that employ 37 different designs. A single design may be used to create two different AutoTemplates, one set up for 35 mm slides and one set up for overheads. Persuasion's AutoTemplates consist of seven slide

▼ *Figure 5.1. Opening an AutoTemplate or a presentation*

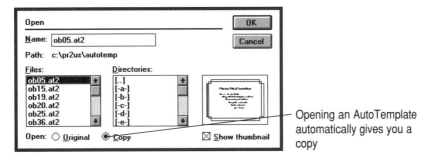

Opening an AutoTemplate automatically gives you a copy

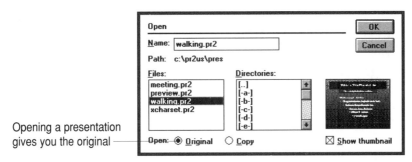

Opening a presentation gives you the original

masters. You can also create your own masters and then save them as an AutoTemplate. To create your own masters, see Chapter 12.

You should keep in mind, however, that you can also save a full presentation as an AutoTemplate—complete with outline, slides, charts, and slide masters. In fact, if you have a presentation you frequently use as the basis for other ones, you may want to save it as an AutoTemplate and start new presentations by modifying a copy of it. In that case, not only are your slide masters in place, but an outline and other elements are already partially finished.

Slide Masters and Background Masters

You can create your own slide masters or use the ones from a Persuasion AutoTemplate. Slide masters are different from slides in that they contain only formatting instructions, not actual information. Placeholders on the slide master give it this formatting capability. Placeholders exist for titles, text, charts, and organization charts. These placeholders define the look of the information that flows into them from the outline or data sheet. The only way for information entered in the outline or data sheet to flow to a slide is by associating the slide with a slide master. This connection is a powerful one, making Persuasion easy to use.

While you assign slide masters to slides, you assign a background to slide masters. The background "master" provides the background design and any graphic or textual elements you want repeated on the slide masters. The slide masters, in turn, transfer those design elements to the slides. The background master is composed of design elements only; it does not use placeholders. You can apply the background master to a slide master, but it is not always necessary. In some cases, you may want to create a unique background on a single master for a special purpose.

Placeholders

A placeholder marks the location on the slide master where you want certain text or objects to go. A placeholder defines the size, format, and look of information that flows through it from the outline or the data sheet to the slide.

Placeholders provide a dynamic connection between a slide and either the outline or the data sheet. Information can flow in both directions: If you edit title text on a slide, for instance, the change is automatically made in the outline, and if you make changes to a title in the outline, they are reflected on your slide. Changing a number in a table on your slide automatically changes that number in the data sheet, and vice versa.

Two types of placeholders (Title and Text) format different kinds of text and two others (Chart and Organization chart) format charts on a slide master. (Another placeholder for adding a miniature copy of the slide to a notes or handout master is also available.)

Placeholders are all form and no substance (well, almost). There's just enough substance in a placeholder (for example, "This is a Title Placeholder") to illustrate its formatting. From looking at the placeholder on the master, you have some idea of what your text or chart will look like on the slide (see Figure 5.2).

▼ *Figure 5.2. Slide master with placeholders*

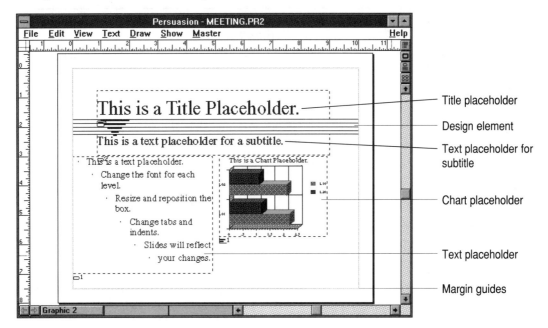

A text placeholder defines the font, size, style, and color of text. The color, size, and font of the bullets you use for bulleted lists are also defined in the placeholder—or the placeholder can eliminate them altogether.

A chart placeholder specifies the number of categories and series (rows and columns for a table) so that adequate space is saved on the slide for a chart or table. The number of categories or series in the placeholder, however, does not limit the number you can have on a chart. The organization chart placeholder similarly defines the default number of levels and boxes you want in an organization chart. Both placeholders can define the font and style of labels or text and exhibit fill patterns, shadows, or color in the rest of the chart or table.

Persuasion's AutoTemplates

Each AutoTemplate in the Persuasion package contains seven slide masters. Table 5.1 provides the names of the seven masters and the placeholders in each slide master.

▼ *Table 5.1. Slide masters and placeholders in Persuasion's AutoTemplates*

Slide master	Placeholders	Comments
Title	Title Text	As a rule, the layout of this slide master differs markedly from the others in the AutoTemplate, since it is usually assigned to the opening slide of a presentation.
Text 1	Title Text (#1—formatted for a moderate amount of text) Text (#2—as subtitle)	Since text on a slide should be pared to its essentials, you'll probably use this slide master most frequently. It functions as the default slide master (each slide is initially assigned to this master).
Text 2	Title Text (#1—on left) Text (#2—beside 1) Text (#3—as subtitle)	For two side-by-side text blocks on a slide, you can insert a break between each block of text in the outline (see Chapter 7).
Text 3	Title Text (#1—formatted for a larger amount of text) Text (#2—as subtitle)	To accommodate more words, the text placeholder reduces the point size of the text. Since this smaller text is harder to read, use this slide master only if your audience is going to be close enough to read small type.
Graphic 1	Title Text (as subtitle) Chart	Data plotted from the data sheet turns into the chart defined by the chart placeholder. The placeholder specifies the type of chart, its location on the slide, and the various fill patterns used to differentiate the data represented by bars or columns, for example. You do not have to put a chart on this slide; if you want, you can put some other graphic element on this slide, and the chart placeholder is ignored.
Graphic 2	Title Text (#1—block on left) Text (#2—as subtitle) Chart	This slide master is designed to accommodate text as well as a chart. Depending on the AutoTemplate, the chart type used in this placeholder may vary from the one used in Graphic 1.
Org Chart	Title Text (as subtitle) Organization chart	The boxes of the organization chart placeholder are frequently formatted to show depth.

Choosing an AutoTemplate

The guidelines for choosing an AutoTemplate are reminiscent of the design advice given in Chapter 4. The main considerations are the medium you choose and the proximity of your audience.

First, choose an AutoTemplate that is set up for the medium you intend to use. Your choice of medium strongly influences whether you'll use color or not: Overhead transparency presentations are usually in black and white and slide presentations in color. With the increasing availability of color printers and copiers, color overheads may be your medium of choice. Persuasion's AutoTemplates give you a number of options in each of these three categories.

Next, you must consider the relationship of the audience to the screen. A general rule of thumb to follow is this: The more distant the audience, the simpler the design must be. An audience in a large auditorium may not be able to readily sort out the information on an AutoTemplate dense with design elements. To be as clear as possible with a large audience, choose a design that is as simple (and elegant) as possible.

TIP

To choose a Persuasion AutoTemplate, preview the AutoTemplates on your screen. Choose the "Open..." command from the File menu. If you check "Show thumbnail," a small sketch of one of the masters from the AutoTemplate selected in the list box appears in the lower-right corner of the dialog box, as shown in Figure 5.3.

Importing an AutoTemplate

Within Persuasion you can mix slide masters from several Auto-Templates to create a new AutoTemplate or replace your current AutoTemplate with a different one. As you work on your presentation, you might realize that the slide masters you used for a previous presentation are more appropriate to your purpose than the one you are currently working with. It's not too late, since you can import those masters and assign them to the slides in this presentation.

▼ *Figure 5.3. "Open" dialog box showing thumbnails*

Sketch of master

Show thumbnail checked

Each of the seven slide masters in the Persuasion AutoTemplates has a unique name. Because these names are consistent across Persuasion's AutoTemplates, the "Text 2" master in one AutoTemplate can replace the "Text 2" in another.

TIP

Make sure when you import masters from another presentation or AutoTemplate that the slide setup size is the same for both. For example, if you are working on a 35 mm slide presentation and you want to change or add slide masters, they need to be from an AutoTemplate or presentation that is also set up for 35 mm slides. If you want to import an AutoTemplate with a different slide size, consider avoiding "Import masters..." altogether. Instead, select the entire presentation in Outline view and copy it, open the new AutoTemplate, select the empty unit where you want the copied outline to begin, and paste the outline into the new AutoTemplate (its charts and graphics come along, too). By doing this, you avoid all the slide-by-slide adjustments you would otherwise have to make in importing an AutoTemplate set up for a different size of slide.

To import masters:

1. Open the presentation whose masters you want to change.

2. Choose "Import masters..." from the File menu. The "Import masters" dialog box appears, as demonstrated in Figure 5.4.

▼ *Figure 5.4. "Import masters" dialog box*

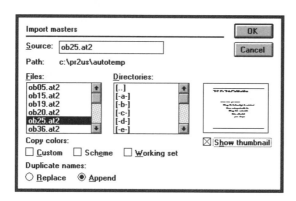

3. In the "Import masters" dialog box, choose the presentation (or AutoTemplate) whose masters you want to use. You may need to change directories or disk drives to locate the presentation you want. When you select a presentation, you can preview its AutoTemplate in the window in the lower-right corner of the dialog box by clicking "Show thumbnail," just as in the "Open" dialog box.

4. In "Copy colors," click to check the colors you want applied to the current presentation.

   ▲ *Custom.* Check to replace current custom colors with the custom colors from the "Source" presentation or AutoTemplate.

   ▲ *Scheme.* Check to replace current color scheme with the color scheme from the "Source" presentation or AutoTemplate.

   ▲ *Working set.* Check to replace current working set of colors with the working set from the "Source" presentation or AutoTemplate.

   (Refer to Chapter 13 for more information on how color works in Persuasion.)

5. Click "Replace" or "Append," then click "OK."

   ▲ *Replace.* Check to replace masters in the current presentation with masters of the same name in the "Source" presentation or AutoTemplate.

▲ *Append.* Check to add masters from the "Source" presentation to the masters in the current presentation. With "Append," names that are the same in the "Source" presentation are changed so that all masters are retained.

To decide whether to replace the masters in your current presentation or to append the new masters to them, review the results of each action in Table 5.2. In general, when you import a different set of AutoTemplates, whether you replace or append, the slide size of the original prevails.

▼ *Table 5.2. "Import masters" replace and append options*

Element	Replace	Append
Names	Imported masters will replace masters of the same name in the current presentation. Masters in the current presentation whose names are different from the imported masters remain as they are. Existing slides are redrawn to reflect the change in masters.	Imported slide masters are added to the masters in the current presentation. If one of the new masters has the same name as an existing master, the name of the new master will be modified.
Sizes	If the imported masters have a different slide size from those in the current presentation, a message appears warning you that the page size or orientation of the two presentations do not match. The size of the current masters remains in effect, so the design elements from the imported presentation could need significant adjustment in the new slide area. It is best if both presentations have the same slide setup and target output device to begin with.	Works the same as "Replace."
Backgrounds	The imported background master replaces the current background master, but retains the slide size of the current one. If they are the same, this presents no problem. If not, significant adjustment to each master could be required. Slide masters based on the old background master will now be based on the new one.	The fill of the imported background master becomes the fill of all the masters, but the design elements on the background master are retained from the current presentation. The imported background master is renamed and added as a slide master. It no longer functions as a background master.

▼ Table 5.2. "Import masters" replace and append options (continued)

Element	Replace	Append
Notes	The Notes master from the new presentation is not imported. The current one remains in effect.	Works the same as "Replace."
Colors	Custom colors and colors in the scheme and working set are replaced according to the selections you make in the "Copy colors" option. If no selections are made in "Copy colors," no colors are added to the current presentation. The current colors remain in effect.	Works the same as "Replace."
Chart formats	The custom chart formats in the current presentation remain, but the placeholder charts change with the replacement of "Graphic 1" and "Graphic 2." No existing charts are redrawn.	Masters with chart placeholders from the imported presentation are added to the masters in the current presentation, but no custom chart formats from the imported presentation are added.

CHECK YOURSELF

1. Find an AutoTemplate you want to work with using the "Show thumbnail" feature, and open it.

2. Look at each master in the AutoTemplate. What placeholders appear on every master?

3. Import a different set of masters from another AutoTemplate and add them to the masters you already have.

4. Look at the masters you just added. How do they differ from ones you already had?

ANSWERS

1. Choose "Open…" from the File menu, and click "Show thumbnail" in the "Open" dialog box. Go to the AutoTemplate directory and select an AutoTemplate (do not double-click or click "OK"). Notice the design of a master from the selected AutoTemplate on the right side of the dialog box. Look at

several AutoTemplates in this way, and when you find one you like, click "OK" to open a copy of it. (Click "OK" in the "Slide setup" dialog box.)

2. Hold down the Ctrl key and click the Slide view icon on the upper-right side of the window to go to Master view of the Text 1 slide master. Notice the placeholders: a Title place-holder and two Text placeholders (usually), one formatting a subtitle and one formatting the main slide text. Choose a different slide master from the Master pop-up menu at the left end of the lower menu bar. Go to every master, including Background. Examine the different kinds of placeholders and their placement on the slide. Use Table 5.1 as a guide. A Title placeholder and at least one Text placeholder appear on every master, except for Background, which has no placeholders.

3. Choose "Import masters..." from the File menu; in "Copy colors," click "Custom," "Scheme," and "Working set," and make sure that "Append" is selected. Then select an AutoTemplate that is set up for the same slide size to import; you can preview the designs of AutoTemplates in the "Show thumbnail" window as you click the AutoTemplate names in the list box. When you have found one you like, click "OK."

4. Use the Master pop-up menu to look at the masters that have been added to your presentation. The names of the new masters have been changed slightly so that they can be differ-entiated from the current ones. The background fill all masters use is from the imported presentation, but the design elements are from the current background master. The placeholders of the new and old AutoTemplates stay the same.

Assigning Masters

Assigning a master to a slide provides the connection between the information you've entered in the outline or data sheet and the formatting directions in the placeholders. At first, all your slides are automatically assigned to a master—specifically, the master designated as the default. In Persuasion's AutoTemplates, the default slide master is Text 1 because Persuasion assumes that it will be the most common slide layout people will need. If you create your own AutoTemplate, the first slide master you create serves as the default, but you can change the slide master that is the default in any AutoTemplate using the procedure described in the following section.

When you use an AutoTemplate, all your slides will appear similar at first, since they are formatted by the default slide master. Most likely, some of your slides will need a different format; different masters must be assigned to those slides. First, make sure the default master is the one you'll need for most of your slides. Next, assign masters to the slides requiring a different format from that of the default master.

Changing the Default Slide Master

Selecting the right slide master to be the default can save you some time later on. The default is automatically assigned to every slide in your presentation until you specifically assign a different master to a slide. Clearly, you will have to make fewer reassignments if your default slide master works for most of your slides.

What is the most common slide layout in your presentation? Frequently, it is some type of text slide. In that case, it makes sense to make your default master one containing an appropriately formatted text placeholder. If your presentation requires mainly slides containing text and a chart, you can make a text-and-chart master your default and avoid making a lot of repetitious individual master assignments.

To change the default slide master:

1. In Slide view, choose "Preferences…" from the File menu. The "Preferences" dialog box appears, as shown in Figure 5.5.

   Note: Go to Slide view to set the default slide master. Although using "Preferences…" to change the default slide master *should* work from Outline view, it currently does not do this procedure from Slide view.

▼ *Figure 5.5. "Preferences" dialog box*

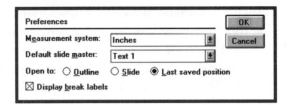

2. In the "Default slide master" drop-down list box, select the slide master you want for the default. If you have already assigned masters in your presentation, changing the default does not change those assignments. Any new slide you create will be assigned the new default.

3. Click "OK."

Assigning Masters in Outline View

Even though most of your slides have been appropriately formatted by the default master, you'll need to make some special slide master assignments to those slides whose format varies from the default.

To assign slide masters from Outline view:

1. Click in a slide title in the outline.

2. Choose the master you want to assign from the Master pop-up menu in the lower menu bar.

TIP

You can assign a slide master to several slide titles at once by holding down the Ctrl key while you click on their icons to select the slide titles you want and then choose the master from the Master pop-up menu in the lower menu bar.

If you do not need to see your slides or review your slide masters, you can do all your master assignments from Outline view as soon as you type your outline. If you are familiar with your AutoTemplate and the requirements of your presentation, you need never leave Outline view; in fact, this can be a very efficient way to create a presentation. If it helps to look at your slides to decide what master to assign to them, go to Slide view or Slide Sorter view.

Assigning Masters

Assigning Masters in Slide View

Assigning slide masters in Slide view is similar to assigning them from Outline view: You assign slide masters by selecting from the Master pop-up menu in the lower menu bar, though you can only assign them one at a time in Slide view.

To assign slide masters from Slide view:

1. Go to the slide whose master assignment you want to change.
2. Select the new assignment from the Master pop-up menu (see Figure 5.6).

▼ *Figure 5.6. Assigning slide masters in Slide view*

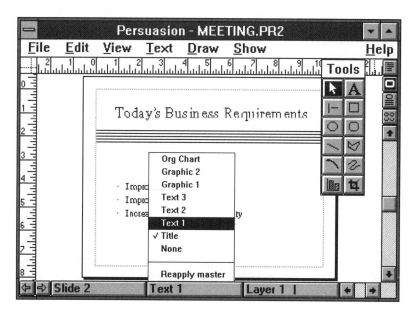

Assigning Masters in Slide Sorter View

In Slide Sorter view, you can change master assignments to several slides at once. You are not limited to assigning slide masters one at a time like you are in Slide view.

To assign slide masters in Slide Sorter view:

1. Go to Slide Sorter view by clicking the Slide Sorter view icon on the upper-left side of the window.

2. Select the slide or slides whose master assignments you want to change. Remember to hold down the Ctrl key while you point and click to select multiple slides, or drag a box around adjacent slides to select them.

3. Choose the slide master you want to assign from the Master pop-up menu in the lower menu bar, as shown in Figure 5.7.

▼ *Figure 5.7. Assigning slide masters in Slide sorter view*

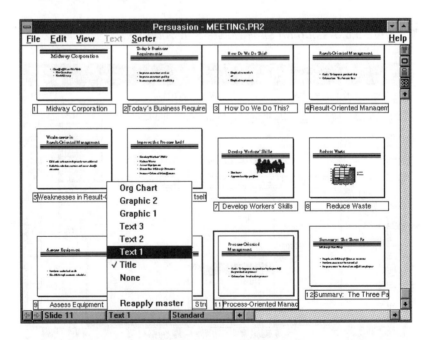

QUICK COMMAND SUMMARY

In this chapter you have learned to do these procedures using these commands:

Commands	Procedures
"Open" (File menu)	Previewing AutoTemplates
"Import masters..." (File menu)	Adding or replacing slide masters in a presentation
All commands (Master pop-up menu)	Assigning a slide master to a slide
"Preferences..." (File menu)	Changing default slide master

PRACTICE WHAT YOU'VE LEARNED

Here you'll begin a presentation, enter the text for a few slides, and see what those slides look like formatted by different slide masters. We will deal only with text and text and title placeholders in this exercise. You'll learn how to use chart and organization chart placeholders in the next chapter.

1. Open a copy of one of Persuasion's AutoTemplates.

2. Type the text for these two slides in Outline view:

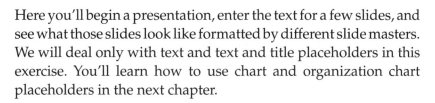

```
My Company <Enter><Tab>
    A Winner <Enter><Backspace>
Status Report <Enter><Tab>
    Delivered 500 widgets in April<Enter>
    Received 500 new orders in May <Enter>
    Increased production by 50% in May
```

3. In Slide view, assign the "Title" master to Slide 1. How is the slide different from when "Text 1" was assigned?

4. Go to Slide 2 and see how it looks as you assign a succession of different masters. (Compare your screen with what Table 5.1 would lead you to expect.) What happens if you assign "Graphic 1" or "Org Chart?"

ANSWERS

1. Choose "Open…" from the File menu, and double-click any of the AutoTemplates listed in the [autotemp] directory. Click "OK" in the "Slide setup" dialog box that automatically appears.

2. Type the text using the Enter, Tab, and Backspace keys to change indent levels.

3. Go to Slide 1 by clicking the number "1" in the left margin of the outline. The Master pop-up menu in the lower menu bar reads "Text 1," which is the default master that is originally assigned to all slides. Choose "Title" from the Master pop-up menu. Notice the difference in the look of your slide—the words stay the same, but the size and location of the text has changed.

4. Go to Slide 2 by choosing "2" from the Slide pop-up menu to the left of the Master pop-up menu in the lower menu bar. Notice what Slide 2 looks like with "Text 1" assigned. Choose "Title," "Text 2," "Text 3," "Graphic 1," "Graphic 2," and "Org Chart." "Graphic 1" and "Org Chart" do not have main text placeholders, so your text will not show up when either of those masters is assigned.

Entering, Editing, and Rearranging Your Outline

Persuasion's outliner is useful for brainstorming and developing your ideas, but its main purpose is to provide the text for your slides. In the end, your outline serves as the narrative flesh and bones—the textual content and structure—of your presentation.

From Outline view, you can do almost everything you need to create a presentation—short of drawing illustrations. Besides entering your outline, you can also assign slide masters and apply transition effects in Outline view. Organization charts can be generated automatically according to the levels of text you enter in the outline. Even charts can be plotted from Outline view—though you cannot see the results until you go to Slide view. However, Outline view is primarily a versatile tool for developing the text of your presentation.

This chapter explains the basics of working in Outline view:

▲ **Entering text in the outline**

▲ **Importing text to the outline**

▲ **Editing the outline**

▲ **Rearranging slides (Outline view or Slide Sorter view)**

▲ **Creating nested slides**

▲ **Creating charts and organization charts**

▲ **Inserting breaks in the outline**

▲ **Collapsing and expanding the outline**

Entering an Outline

You can create your outline by typing it or by importing it from another application. But why bother with an outline when you just want to get your slides done? Because Persuasion creates your slides automatically from your outline. The information you enter in the outline flows to the slides by way of slide masters that tell that text where to go and what to do.

If you prefer, you can avoid using Outline view altogether and work on your presentation slide by slide. By entering text and chart data within the placeholder boundaries on each slide, you can take advantage of the consistency that slide masters provide and still work in Slide view. However, Slide view is not quite as powerful as working in Outline view: You cannot create organization charts in Slide view or nest slides. The best way to work is to create the main part of your presentation from the view that is comfortable for you, and then go back and forth between Outline view and Slide view, working in one and then the other according to the advantages each affords.

Overview of Outline View

As a rule, you see Outline view when you first open an AutoTemplate. Outline view has a look all its own with its own icons and menu. This section explains the significance of what you see when you look at Outline view.

TIP

You'll see Outline view when you first open a copy of an AutoTemplate because that is the position in which the AutoTemplate was saved and the AutoTemplates always open to the last saved position. Once you have saved your copy of the AutoTemplate as a presentation, you may want to change the view it opens to. If you do not want your presentation to open to the last saved position, you can change that setting by choosing "Preferences" from the File menu and selecting "Outline" or "Slide" instead.

Outline Organization

The icon beside each outline entry indicates its purpose: divider, slide title, slide text, a chart, or an organization chart. The dynamic link between text in the outline and that same text on a slide is a placeholder. Placeholders exist for each kind of icon in the outline, except for the divider. Title, text, chart, and organization chart placeholders can be placed on slide masters. For more information about placeholders and slide masters, see Chapter 5.

Here's an example of how this dynamic linkage works for a slide title. Persuasion takes the title for, say, Slide 5 in your outline along with the formatting instructions from the title placeholder on the slide master assigned to Slide 5 and generates a slide with that title (see Figure 6.1). The title is positioned and formatted on the slide according to the title placeholder on the slide master.

Starting at the top level of your outline, the function of the text you enter in Outline view is determined by the icon beside it, as shown in Table 6.1. But you must also have a corresponding placeholder on the assigned slide master.

▼ *Figure 6.1. Slide title and text are formatted by slide master placeholders*

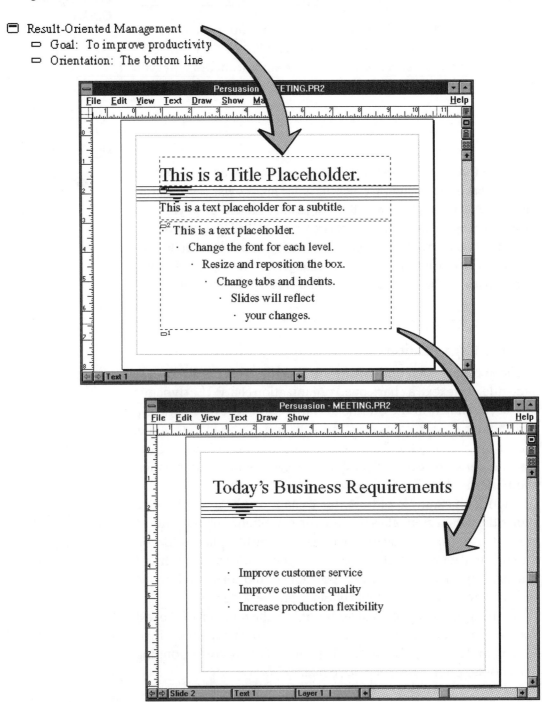

▼ *Table 6.1. Icons and cursors in Outline view*

Unit icons

The *divider icon* appears only in Outline view. You can indicate the name of your presentation or a section of your presentation in the divider unit, much as you might label a slide carousel. And, because it appears only in Outline view, you can enter comments here to yourself or others who might use the presentation. Keep in mind that this unit prints when you print your outline.

The *slide title icon* generates a new slide and the text in that unit functions as the slide's title. The number of the slide is opposite the slide title in the left column. The title placeholder on the assigned slide master formats this text for the slide.

The *text icon* indicates a unit containing text for your slide. You can have six hierarchical levels of slide text that are visible on your slide. Most commonly, the text placeholder on the assigned slide master formats this text for the slide as a hierarchical list. However, text units can also be the text in an organization chart when they are subordinate to an org chart unit.

The *chart icon* shows the presence of a chart; the icon changes to indicate the chart type you've specified in the "Chart info" dialog box. The text in the chart unit is the title of the chart.

The *org chart icon* marks the top level of an organization chart. All the text units subordinate to the org chart unit become the corresponding levels in the organization chart on the slide. The style of the organization chart is governed by the organization chart placeholder on the master slide.

Other icons

The *data sheet icon* is opposite the chart icon in the left margin. They work together— you click the data sheet icon to open the data sheet, a spreadsheet-like work area where you can enter the data you want to plot in the chart.

The *break character icon* (a downward-pointing triangle) indicates that the text units that follow are formatted by the next placeholder on the assigned slide master. The break label beside the break character specifies the slide number and the placeholder number of the text that follows.

The *left-pointing triangle* beside a unit indicates that the unit has subordinate units collapsed within it. Double-click it to see all of the subordinate units.

Cursors

The *pointer* lets you click icons to accomplish a variety of tasks, such as select an outline unit, drag an outline unit to a new location, open a data sheet, go to a different view, or go to a specific slide. The pointer also lets you click a horizontal insertion point between two outline units to indicate where a copied or cut unit will be pasted or where a new unit will be created.

The *I-beam* lets you select text and click a vertical insertion point. A vertical insertion point indicates where you can type, insert text, or begin selecting a text block.

Outline Menu

The Outline menu, shown in Table 6.2, is available in Outline view only and contains commands that govern the various actions you can take to organize and manage the outline.

Commands on some of the other menus are also used in Outline view, notably the various style commands and "Outline format..." from the Text menu.

▼ *Table 6.2. Outline menu*

Command	Function
Divider	Changes the selected unit in the outline to a divider unit
Title	Changes the selected unit in the outline to a slide title unit
Text	Changes the selected unit in the outline to a text unit
Chart	Changes the selected unit in the outline to a chart unit
Org chart	Changes the selected unit in the outline to an org chart unit
Chart info...	Opens the data sheet so you can enter or edit data for that chart and causes the "Chart info" dialog box to appear so you can define that chart's type and its other characteristics (available only when a chart unit is selected in the outline)
Insert break	Inserts a break character in the outline, indicating that the text units that follow are assigned to the placeholder with the next higher number
Expand	Displays all the units subordinate to the selected unit (Shortcut: Double-click the icon of the selected unit.)
Collapse	Hides all the units subordinate to the selected unit (Shortcut: Double-click the icon of the selected unit.)
Expand all	Displays all the units in the entire outline (Shortcut: Double-click the divider icon.)
Collapse all	Hides all the units in the entire outline in the divider unit (Shortcut: Double-click the divider icon.)
Show levels...	Displays all the levels in the outline up to the level you specify in the "Show levels..." dialog box

Typing the Outline

You see an empty outline when you open an AutoTemplate. The empty outline contains one divider that for now says "Untitled presentation" and one slide title icon next to an empty text unit with the number "1" in the left margin. The name of the file is at the center top of the window: Untitled 1.

You can edit the divider unit, if you wish, by dragging to highlight "Untitled presentation" and typing your own title or comments.

To begin your outline:

Click an insertion point to the right of the first slide icon and type.

When you press Enter, Persuasion starts another slide title with a "2" in the left margin. You can continue to add units or slide titles in this manner, or you can create several levels of indented units within each slide. Use the guidelines in Table 6.3 to type additional units in the outline. Whenever you want to create a new unit, be sure to have your cursor at the end of a unit.

▼ *Table 6.3. Typing in the outline*

To accomplish this	Do this
Begin a new unit at the same level	Press Enter
Start a new line within the same unit	Hold down Shift and press Enter
Begin a new unit one level to the right	Press Enter and then Tab
Move a unit to the right	Click in the unit and press Tab
Start a new unit one level to the left	Press Enter; then press Backspace
Move a unit to the left	Click in the unit; then hold down Shift and press Tab

CHECK YOURSELF

1. Open one of Persuasion's AutoTemplates.

2. Create a slide with several lines of text on it.

3. Create another slide with several lines of text.

4. Save this practice file as Practice.PR2.

ANSWERS

1. Choose "Open..." from the File menu. Double-click [..], then double-click [autotemp], and then double-click one of the AutoTemplate filenames listed.

2. When you open a copy of an AutoTemplate, the insertion point is at the beginning of Slide 1, so you can simply type the text you want for the slide title. Next, press Enter to create a new slide title unit, and then press Tab to move the unit to the right and make it a text unit. Type the text for the first bullet on the slide. Press Enter and type another line of text for the slide. Repeat until you have the text you want on Slide 1.

3. Press Enter after the last text unit on Slide 1. Then hold down Shift while you press Tab to move the unit back to the left one level. Now type the slide title for Slide 2 and proceed to create text for Slide 2 as you did for Slide 1.

4. Choose "Save as..." from the File menu. Type "Practice" for the "Name" in the "Save as" dialog box, and then click "OK."

Importing an Outline

If you have an outline that you created in some other software application and you want to use it in Persuasion, you can import it. Persuasion lets you "place" outlines created in a variety of programs, including Microsoft Word 5.0 and WordPerfect 5.0.

Persuasion recognizes tabbed indents from the left margin in word processing files as different unit levels. Persuasion also respects most text formats, such as fonts, type sizes, and type styles, specified in the word processing file. You can retain the text formatting in the original file by saving the file in a format other than text-only and by checking "Retain format" in Persuasion's "Place" dialog box.

Entering an Outline

If you do not want to retain the text styles, uncheck the "Retain format" option in the "Place" dialog box.

To place (import) an outline:

1. In Outline view, use the pointer to click a horizontal insertion point between outline units where you want the imported file to begin. Or, if you want to replace existing text with the imported outline, select the outline units you want to replace.

2. Choose "Place…" (Ctrl + D) from the File menu. The "Place" dialog box appears, as in demonstrated in Figure 6.2.

3. From "Files," select the name of the file you want to import. If necessary, change directories to locate the appropriate file.

    Note: If you cannot find the file you want to import, you may not have the appropriate import filter installed. Use Aldus Setup to make sure the correct filter is installed.

4. For "Place," verify that the option you want is selected:

    "Inserting text" adds the selected file at the insertion point.

    "Replacing selection" overwrites the selected text with the selected file.

▼ *Figure 6.2. "Place" dialog box*

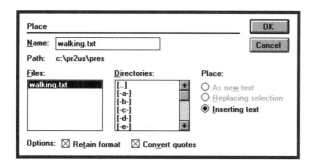

5. For "Options," make sure the option you want is checked:

   "Retain format" imports the file with its original text attributes.

   "Convert quotes" changes regular quotation marks (" ") to typeset quotation marks (" "); two hyphens (--) to an en dash (–); and three hyphens (---) to an em dash (—).

6. Click "OK." The formatted text flows into the specified place. If you are placing a text-only file, you'll get the "Smart ASCII import filter" dialog box. Leaving the default settings as they are, click "OK" to have the text imported.

Exporting an Outline

You can export your outline from Persuasion as a text-only file under a name you specify.

To export an outline:

1. Select the outline units you want to export. (You do not need to select anything if you want to export the entire outline.)

2. Choose "Export…" from the File menu. The "Export" dialog box appears, as shown in Figure 6.3.

3. Locate the drive and directory where you want the exported file to go.

▼ *Figure 6.3. "Export" dialog box*

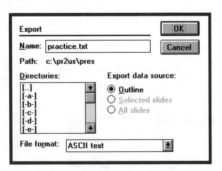

4. In the text box, type the name for your exported outline.

5. Click "OK." A file containing a copy of the selected text or the entire outline, with the name you just typed, now exists in the folder you chose. The outline levels are represented by tabbed indents. The text you selected to export also remains in its original position in the outline.

Editing an Outline

Outlines are made to be changed—from rewording a slide title to deleting several sections of your presentation. You can edit the outline by cutting, copying, or pasting text, or by adding, moving, or deleting units. Basically, editing in Persuasion's outline is consistent with standard Windows editing techniques. You can cut, copy, and paste text—or an entire unit—the way you would in most Windows applications.

Selecting Text and Selecting Units in the Outline

A Persuasion outline consists of text arranged in outline units. *Text* refers to a word or collection of words, and *unit* refers to the entire outline unit, including the icon. Understanding the distinction between text and units is crucial to learning how each is selected. Notice the difference between selected text and selected units in Figure 6.4.

You can select as many units in the outline as you want. Your selections can be contiguous or noncontiguous. Multiple selection saves you from repeating the same action for a variety of slides that need the same treatment. Figure 6.5 illustrates selecting a range of units. Tables 6.4 and 6.5 show you all the ways to select text and to select one or more outline units.

▼ *Figure 6.4. Selecting text and units*

Drag-selecting text highlights it.

Outline unit is selected when its icon and text are both highlighted.

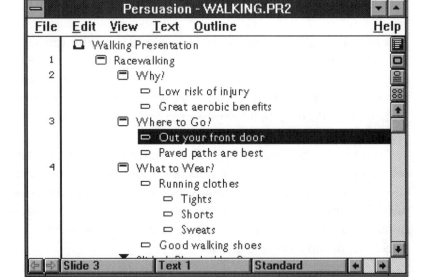

▼ *Figure 6.5. Range selection*

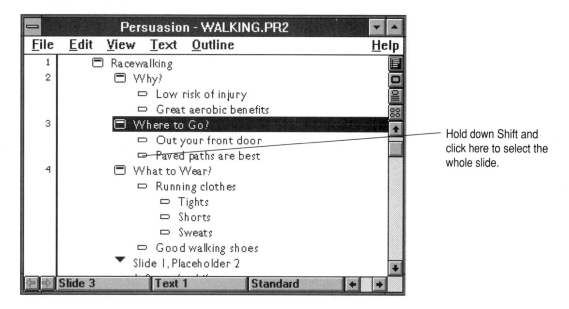

Hold down Shift and click here to select the whole slide.

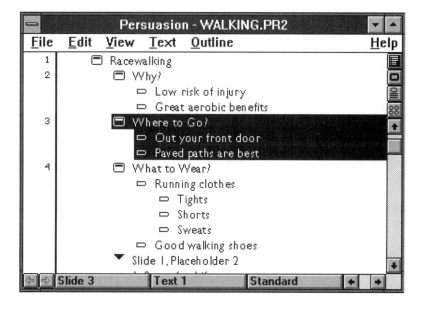

Now the whole slide is selected.

▼ *Table 6.4. Selecting text*

To select this item	Do this
Characters	Click an insertion point, keep pressing the mouse button, and drag to highlight the characters you want.
Words	Double-click the word; extend selection by dragging.
Any range of text	Drag to highlight.
Text between two points	Click an insertion point; then hold down Shift and click another insertion point.
All the text in a unit	Triple-click in the text of the unit.

▼ *Table 6.5. Selecting units*

To select this item	Do this
One unit	Click its icon.
A range of contiguous units	Select the unit at the beginning of the range as an anchor; then hold down Shift and click the unit icon at the other end of the range.
Noncontiguous units	Select a unit; then hold down Ctrl as you click other unit icons. Only the units whose icons you click are selected.
A mix of contiguous and noncontiguous units	Select a range of contiguous units as above, and then add noncontiguous units to it by holding down Ctrl and clicking the units you want.
All units in the outline	Select a unit; then choose "Select all" from the Edit menu.

Deselecting Units in the Outline

Editing an Outline

You can deselect an entire selection by clicking outside the selected area the way you deselect anything in Windows. But you can also deselect part of a selection while retaining the rest.

To deselect a unit:

Hold down Ctrl and click the icon of a currently selected unit. You can deselect any unit this way, whether it is part of a range of contiguous units or not.

CHECK YOURSELF

1. In Practice.PR2, the presentation you created in the previous check section, select all of Slide 2.

2. Deselect only Slide 2's slide title.

3. Deselect everything and select Slide 1's title unit.

4. Now select only the text in Slide 1's title unit. Note the difference in highlighting between selecting the unit and selecting the text in the unit.

ANSWERS

1. In Practice.PR2 (use the "Open" command if you need to), click the Slide 2 title icon. Then, while holding down Shift, click the icon of the last text icon on Slide 2. All the units from the title to the last text unit are highlighted.

2. Hold down Ctrl and click the slide title icon for Slide 2.

3. Click the slide title icon of Slide 1.

4. Triple-click the text of Slide 1's title unit or drag to select the text.

Cutting, Copying, and Pasting

In Outline view, you can delete or move text, outline units, and entire slides with their chart data and graphics by using the standard editing commands in Windows: "Cut," "Copy," "Clear," and "Paste." Except for "Clear," these commands use the Windows Clipboard to store text or units temporarily.

Cutting or copying outline units is especially useful for moving an entire slide or group of slides within a presentation or to another presentation. When you select a slide title and all its subordinate text in the outline and cut or copy it to the Clipboard, you can paste it in a new location in that presentation or another, and the chart or graphics that may be on the slide or slides are transferred, as well as the outline units.

Editing Text or Outline Units

You use commands from the Edit menu to cut, copy, or paste text in the outline.

To delete text or units:

1. Select them. (See Tables 6.4 and 6.5 for information on how to select text or units.)

2. Choose "Cut" (Shift + Delete) or "Clear" (Delete) from the Edit menu.

If you choose "Cut," the selection—outline unit or text—is deleted from the outline and transferred to the Clipboard, where it stays until you either paste it somewhere or replace it on the Clipboard by choosing "Cut" again.

If you choose "Clear," the selection is deleted from the outline and can only be retrieved with the immediate use of the "Undo" command.

To place a copy of selected text or units on the Clipboard while leaving the original as it is:

Choose "Copy" (Ctrl + Insert) from the Edit menu.

To insert a selection in the outline:

1. Cick to create an insertion point where you want to add the text.

2. Choose "Paste" (Shift + Insert) from the Edit menu.

If you click a vertical insertion point, the text of the first selected outline unit is added at the insertion point, and the rest of the text is pasted into units at the same indent level.

If you click a horizontal insertion point, the selection will be pasted as new units, while maintaining the structure of the original units.

To replace existing text:

1. Select the text or units.

2. Choose "Paste" (Shift + Insert) from the Edit menu. The text or units currently on the Clipboard replace the selected text.

Dragging Units in the Outline

You can cut and paste outline units, as you've just learned, but dragging is the easiest way to move units in the outline.

To drag a unit from one place to another in the outline:

1. Select the unit or units you want to move.

2. Holding down the mouse button, point to them and drag to the place you want them; then release the mouse button.

As you hold down the mouse button and drag, the pointer turns into the pointing hand and the horizontal insertion point indicates the valid positions.

TIP

Keep in mind that you can drag units sideways as well as up and down. You can subordinate one unit to another by dragging it to the right one level. Notice how you can move units up as well as over, as shown in Figure 6.6.

▼ *Figure 6.6. Dragging units to a different level*

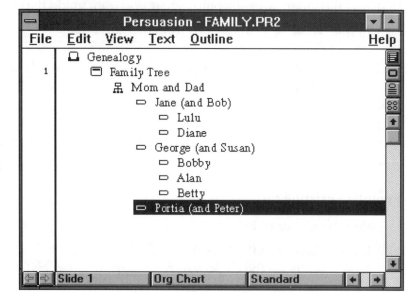

Portia is Jane's daughter, so her text unit needs to be dragged up and to the right.

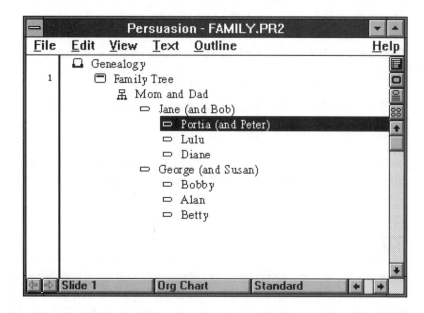

Now Portia and her husband are in the right place

CHECK YOURSELF

1. In Practice.PR2, move the text from Slide 2 and add it to Slide 1.

2. Now indent the text you just added one level.

ANSWERS

1. In Practice.PR2, click the text icon of the first text unit on Slide 2, hold down Shift, and click the last text unit icon to select all the text on Slide 2. Then point to the left of the selected block, hold down the mouse button, and drag the selection upward to Slide 1. (The pointing hand appears.) Release the mouse button when the horizontal insertion point is where you want the selection to go. A less desirable alternative is to select the text units and choose "Cut" from the Edit menu. Then click a horizontal insertion point where you want the units to go, and choose "Paste" from the Edit menu. (One reason this is less desirable is that you can "Undo" only one action at a time, either the cut or the paste. In dragging, you can "Undo" the entire move itself and the units return to their original place.)

2. While the units are still selected (select them again, if necessary), point to the left of them, and, while holding down the mouse button, move the pointing hand to the right so that the horizontal insertion point is one level over. Release the mouse button. The selection moves one level to the right. Alternatively, while the units are selected, simply press Tab.

Copying, Cutting, and Pasting Slides within a Presentation

When you cut or copy a slide from the outline to the Clipboard, all its information—charts, data sheet, breaks, and so forth—goes with it. All that information is retained when you paste it to a new location within the presentation *if* you use the correct insertion point for indicating that location.

If you want to duplicate a slide within a presentation, perhaps to make some variation of it, you can copy it and then paste it where you want it. If you simply want to move a slide to a different location in the presentation, it is probably easier to drag it in the outline or in the slide sorter than to cut and paste, unless the presentation has a large number of slides. In a large presentation, cutting and copying—whether in Outline view or Slide Sorter view—would be easier.

To cut or copy and paste slides within a presentation:

1. Select all the units you want to copy (or cut).

2. Choose "Copy" (or "Cut") from the Edit menu.

3. Click an insertion point at the end of the unit above the place you want to add the copied slides, and press Enter (and Backspace as necessary) to create a new slide title unit. Select the empty new unit.

   Note: You can also click a horizontal insertion point below the unit where you want the pasted text to be inserted. This method is faster, but it limits the levels at which you can paste the cut or copied unit.

4. Choose "Paste" from the Edit menu. All the copied information is added at the selected place, starting with the first slide title. If you copied and pasted a chart unit, its data sheet is copied along with it.

TIP

You can cut or copy a slide from Slide Sorter view and then paste it in Outline view, but you cannot paste a slide from Outline view into Slide Sorter view. If you select an empty title unit before you paste the slide, any drawn graphics on the slide will also come with it.

Using the Slide Sorter to Rearrange Slides

The slide sorter is a visual version of your outline where you can see miniatures of your slides laid out in order (see Figure 6.7). Everything you do in the slide sorter you can do in Outline view, but the slide sorter appeals to individuals who prefer a right-brained approach to the way they work.

▼ *Figure 6.7. Nested slides in the slide sorter*

Slides displayed slightly offset are nested

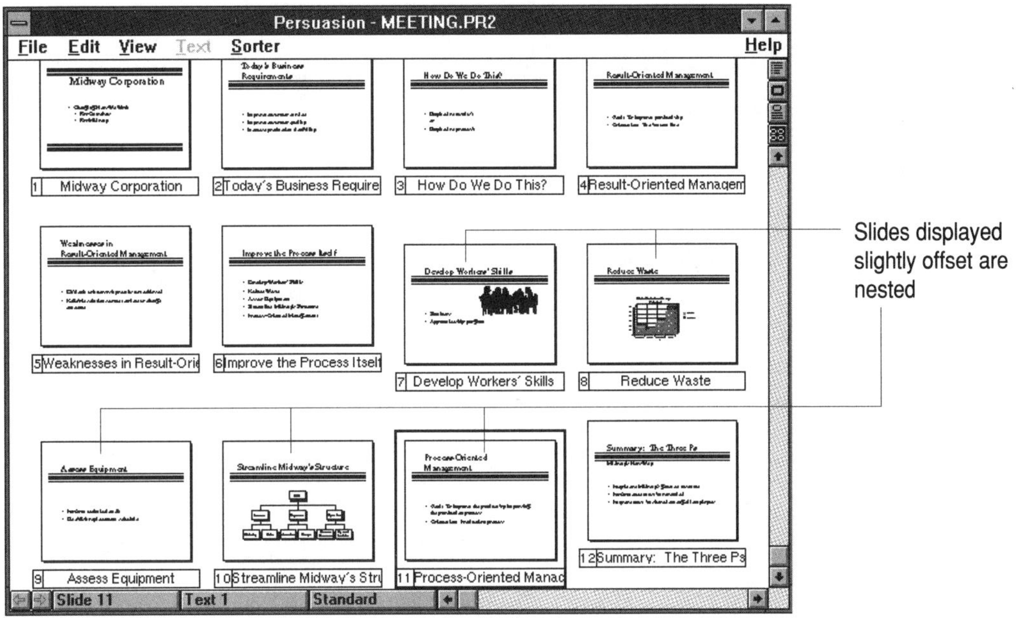

You can rearrange the order of the slides in your presentation at any time in the slide sorter by selecting and dragging one or more slides to a new location. If you select multiple slides, contiguous or not, they retain their order when you insert them elsewhere in the presentation. The rest of the slides fall into place according to the new arrangement.

To rearrange slides in the slide sorter:

1. Go to the slide sorter by clicking the Slide Sorter view icon in the upper-right corner of the window.

2. If you want to change the number of slides displayed in the window, choose "Normal size," "66% normal," "33% normal," or "20% normal" from the Sorter menu in the upper menu bar. The number of slides displayed on your screen varies according to the size of your window and the wide or tall orientation of your slides.

3. Select a slide by pointing within the slide miniature and clicking. Select adjacent slides by dragging a rectangle around

---

▼ *Figure 6.8. Rearranging slides in the slide sorter*

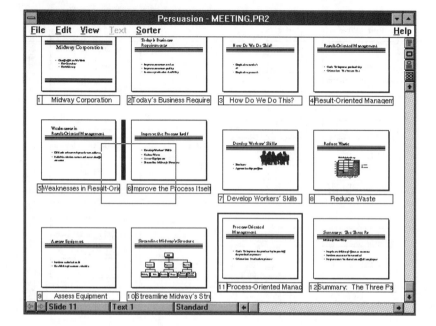

Vertical bar and box
show new location of
selected slide (slide 11).

the slides. Select nonadjacent slides by holding down Shift and clicking them. A box appears around the selected slide or slides. Remember to hold down the Shift key as you click additional slides to add them to the selection.

4. Point inside the selection and hold down the mouse button, dragging the slide or slides until the vertical bar is located where you want them to go. The vertical bar only appears at places where it's valid for slides to be inserted, as shown in Figure 6.8.

5. Release the mouse button to insert the slide or slides in the new position.

CHECK YOURSELF

1. In Practice.PR2, go to Slide Sorter view.

2. Copy the two slides in your presentation.

3. Paste them to the end of your presentation.

4. Move Slide 4 so that it follows Slide 1.

5. Delete Slides 3 and 4.

ANSWERS

1. Click the Slide Sorter view icon at the upper-right edge of the window.

2. Select the two slides by dragging a box around them or by clicking one, and, while holding down Shift, clicking the other. Then choose "Copy" from the Edit menu.

3. Select the last slide in the presentation, and then choose "Paste." The slides are pasted to the right of the selected slide.

4. Select Slide 4, point to it, and, while holding down the mouse button, drag it so the black vertical bar is between Slides 1 and 2. Then release the mouse button.

   Play with the vertical bar while you still have the mouse button held down. Notice that you can put it in a higher or a lower position between slides. The lower position subordinates the slide you are inserting so that it is "nested." (More information on nested slides is included in the next section.)

5. Drag-select Slides 3 and 4 and either press the Delete key or choose "Clear" from the Edit menu.

Changing Unit Types for Nested Slides, Charts, and Organization Charts

Changing a unit from one type to another allows you to nest a slide within a slide, to make text into a chart title with an accompanying chart, or to transform several levels of text into an organization chart.

To change unit type:

1. Select the unit you want to change.

2. Choose "Divider" (Ctrl + V), "Title" (Ctrl + L), "Text" (Ctrl + X), "Chart" (Ctrl + H), or "Org chart" (Ctrl + G) from the Outline menu. The selected unit changes to the new type and its icon is changed accordingly. If necessary, a new slide number is added in the left margin.

Nesting Slide Titles

The slide title icon marks the beginning of a new slide and usually is found in the leftmost position in the outline. However, this is not always the case.

When you have too much information to fit on one slide, you may want to break it into several slides that are introduced by an overview slide that prepares the audience for what's coming. In such a situation, you can subordinate the main points to the slide title of the overview slide, and, at the same time, make each main point a slide title. Nesting your slide titles makes it easier for your audience to follow the structure of your presentation.

To nest slides:

1. Enter each of the main points (and their subordinates) as slide text the way you usually do.

2. Change the text unit of each main point to a title unit, using the "Title" command from the Outline menu. If you do this, the overview slide will show only the list of its subordinate slide titles but not any of their subordinate text units. Each subsequent slide consists of one of those slide titles and its subordinates (see Figure 6.9).

CHECK YOURSELF

1. In Practice.PR2, add several subordinate points to each of the text units on Slide 2.

2. Make each of the superior text units into title units.

3. Look at each of the slides in your presentation.

ANSWERS

1. Click an insertion point at the end of the first text unit on Slide 2. Press Enter and then Tab. Type some text, press Enter, and type more text. Then click an insertion point at the end of the next main text unit on Slide 2 and repeat these steps until you have subordinate text units for each original text unit.

2. Click the first main text unit's icon and, holding down Ctrl, click the icons of the other original text units on Slide 2. Each main text unit should be highlighted. Then choose "Title" from the Outline menu. The icons for the selected units become slide title icons.

3. Click number 2 in the left margin to go to Slide 2. Note the text on the slide. Click the right-pointing arrow in the lower-left corner of the window to advance to the next slide; proceed through all your slides in this way.

Changing Unit Types for Nested Slides, Charts, and Organization Charts

▼ *Figure 6.9. Nested slide titles*

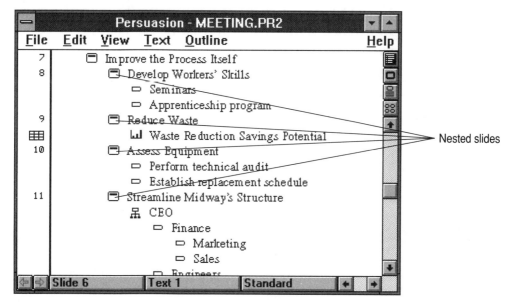

Creating Charts in the Outline

You can create a chart in either Outline view or Slide view. Essential to creating a chart is entering data in the data sheet and specifying the chart type and other details in the "Chart info" dialog box. Both the data sheet and the "Chart info" dialog box are available in Outline and Slide view. Thus, you can, for example, create a chart in Outline view, and if you want to change something about it when you see the chart drawn in Slide view, you can do so from there. Figure 6.10 shows how a chart looks in the outline and on the slide. You'll find a complete discussion of charts in Chapter 10.

To create a chart in Outline view:

1. Select a unit that is subordinate to a slide title—usually a text unit—and choose "Chart" from the Outline menu. The icon changes to a dimmed pie chart, and a dimmed data sheet icon is added in the margin to the left of the unit. The text in this unit becomes the title of the chart. (The slide title is the text in the slide title unit.)

2. With the unit still selected, choose a slide master containing a chart placeholder from the Master pop-up menu in the lower menu bar—usually "Graphic 1" or "Graphic 2." The icon changes to a darkened chart that illustrates the chart type of the placeholder on the assigned master. The data sheet icon remains dim.

3. Click the data sheet icon in the left margin. The data sheet opens and the "Chart info" dialog box appears behind it.

4. Enter the data for your chart in the data sheet by typing in the first cell. Use the arrow keys to move from cell to cell.

5. Click the "Chart info" dialog box to bring it forward, specify the format for your chart, and then click "OK." If you want to accept the placeholder's chart format, simply click "OK."

   If you want to change the chart's data or format at any time, click the data sheet icon (or click in the chart unit and choose "Chart info..." from the Outline menu) to display the data sheet and "Chart info" dialog box, make the changes you want, and click

▼ *Figure 6.10. Pie chart in Outline view and Slide view*

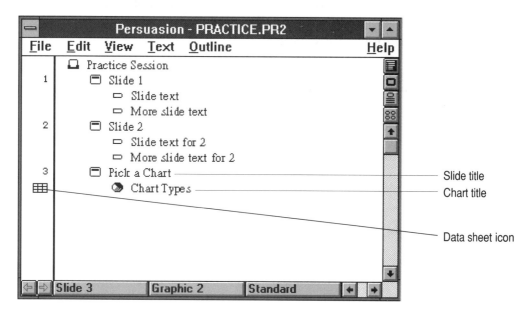

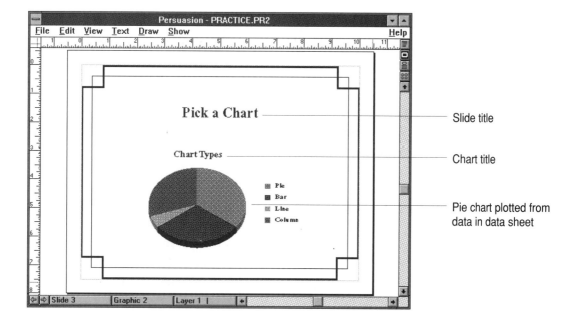

"OK." Whenever you click "OK" in the "Chart info" dialog box, the chart is replotted according to the new information. For more information on entering data in the data sheet or customizing a chart format, see Chapter 10.

CHECK YOURSELF

1. Add this new slide title to Practice.PR2: Pick a Chart.

2. Add this text unit under it: Chart Types.

3. Create a pie chart using this data:

Pie	35
Bar	30
Line	5
Column	30

ANSWERS

1. Click an insertion point at the end of the last text unit in your presentation. Press Enter and then press Backspace (or Shift + Tab) as many times as you need to get an empty slide title unit. Type "Pick a Chart."

2. Press Enter and then Tab. Type "Chart Types."

3. With an insertion point still in "Chart Types," choose "Chart" from the Outline menu. Then choose "Graphic 1" from the Master pop-up menu in the middle of the lower menu bar. Now click the dimmed data sheet icon in the left margin beside the chart title. Type "Pie" in the first cell, and, using the arrow keys, enter the rest of the data. Click the title bar of the "Chart info" dialog box to bring it forward. If necessary, choose "Pie" from the "Chart type" drop-down menu (you may have to scroll up to find it) and then click "OK." Click the Slide view icon at the upper-right edge of the window to go to Slide view and see your pie chart.

Creating Organization Charts

Changing Unit
Types for
Nested Slides,
Charts, and
Organization
Charts

Organization charts can be created only in Outline view. The levels of text units in the outline make up the hierarchy of your organization chart on the slide. The top unit of the organization chart is an "Org chart" unit.

If you were creating an organization chart for a company, the "Org chart" unit would contain the name of the CEO or president; the next level of subordinate text units would contain the names of the vice presidents; and the next indent level would contain the names of their assistants or support staff. Figure 6.11 shows how an organization chart looks in the outline and on the slide.

TIP

Just because an organization chart has that name does not mean that it can be used only for describing company structures. You can use the automatic diagramming capability of "Org charts" in Persuasion to draw any kind of hierarchical relationship—a parts list that shows how various pieces of hardware relate, an outline for the playoffs in a sports tournament, or the tasks required for a project and who must perform them. Let your imagination define the uses of an organization chart.

To create an organization chart:

1. Type the top level of your organization chart as a text unit, making it subordinate to a slide title.

2. Select the top unit of the organization chart, and choose "Org chart" from the Outline menu. The organization chart icon is beside the text that goes in the top box of your organization chart, but the icon is dimmed.

3. With the top unit still selected, choose a slide master containing an organization chart placeholder—usually "Org chart"—from the Master pop-up menu in the lower menu bar. The organization chart unit will darken.

4. Type the rest of the levels in the organization chart, making them subordinate to the organization chart unit.

▼ *Figure 6.11. Organization chart in Outline view and Slide view*

Slide title ——

Top level of ——
organization chart

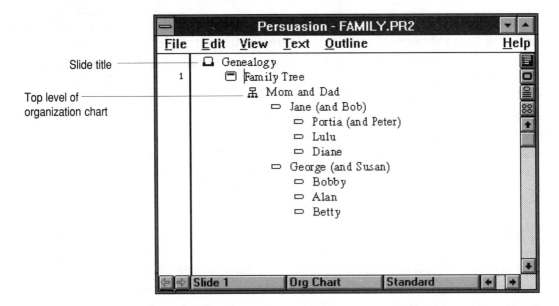

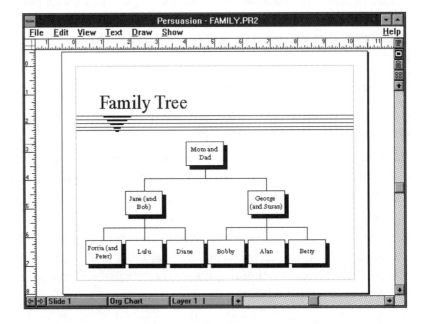

TIP

An alternative way of creating your organization chart is to type all the text first, indenting the levels appropriately, and then change the top level to an "Org chart" unit and assign a master with an organization chart placeholder.

CHECK YOURSELF

Create an organization chart that shows three generations of your family.

ANSWER

Create a new slide title unit (something like "Family Tree") and then press Enter and Tab. Type the text you want at the top level of your organization chart (maybe "Mom and Dad"). With the insertion point still in that text unit, choose "Org chart" from the Outline menu. Then choose "Org Chart" from the Master pop-up menu in the lower menu bar. Pressing Enter and Tab to create lower units and Shift + Tab to create higher units, type an outline that looks something like this:

    Mom and Dad
        Jane (and Bob)
            Lulu
            Diane
        George (and Susan)
            Bobby
            Alan
            Betty
        Portia (and Peter)

Click the Slide view icon when you finish typing to see what the organization chart looks like on the slide.

Inserting Breaks

Breaks tell the text in an outline which placeholder to do to when you have more than one text placeholder on a slide master. You can insert a break between text units in the outline to divert the text that follows the break to the next placeholder.

Most of the AutoTemplates that come with Persuasion have multiple text placeholders on their slide masters. In addition to the placeholder for the main text block, there's typically one for a subtitle as well. Another example of multiple placeholders in the Persuasion AutoTemplates is the "Text 2" master, which has side-by-side placeholders to create double-column text.

The placeholders on a slide master are numbered. The main text placeholder is usually numbered "1" so that the first text you enter for that slide is the main text block. The subtitle, on the other hand, is typically the text placeholder with the highest number. You need to be conscious of how many text placeholders are on the slide master you have assigned to the slide so that you can use breaks effectively. Figure 6.12 shows you what a slide with multiple text blocks looks like from Outline, Slide, and Master views.

Breaks in the outline consist of two parts: the break label and the break character. The break label indicates which placeholder the text that follows is diverted to and the number of the slide this text appears on. The break character is the down-pointing solid triangle to the left of the break label.

To insert a break in the outline:

1. Indicate where you want the break to occur in one of two ways:

    ▲ Click a vertical insertion point at the end of the text unit above the place where you want the break to occur.

    ▲ Click a horizontal insertion point between the two units where you want the break to occur.

2. Choose "Insert break" (Ctrl + Enter) from the Outline menu.

Charts and organization charts do not break text in the outline; only break units can do that. For example, if you want to put a

▼ *Figure 6.12. Breaks, multiple text placeholders, and text blocks on a slide*

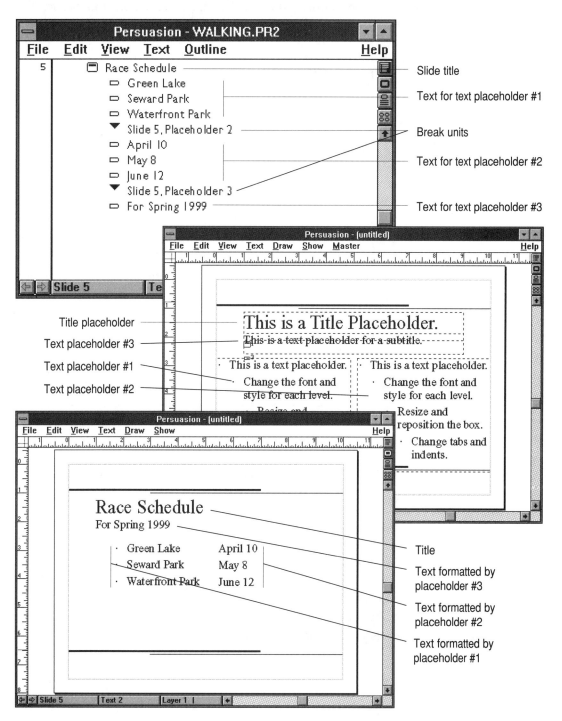

subtitle on a slide with an organization chart, you need to insert a break at the end of the organization chart text and before the subtitle.

CHECK YOURSELF

Add a subtitle to any slide in Practice.PR2.

ANSWER

If you are adding a subtitle to the last slide in the outline, click an insertion point at the end of the last unit on a slide and "Insert break" from the Outline menu. Type the subtitle you want. Click the Slide view icon to go to the slide and see your subtitle. If you want to add a subtitle to an earlier slide in the presentation, click an insertion point at the end of the last unit on the slide, and then choose "Insert break" from the Outline menu. Next, move the insertion point back to the break unit (press the Up arrow key or click an insertion point), press Enter to create a new line under the break unit, and type the subtitle. (Inserting the break unit *should* also insert the text unit for the subtitle, but as the design of the software does not yet permit it, this procedure will do the trick.

Collapsing and Expanding the Outline

Have you ever gotten mired in the details of a long outline? At times it is helpful to collapse the lower levels of an outline to see only the main units. Have you ever lost track of the flow of your presentation? By collapsing it, you can fit it on the screen to see where you've been as you continue to write.

Using the Unit Icon to Collapse and Expand

The shortcut for collapsing and expanding outline units is to double-click on the icon of the immediately superior outline unit. See Figure 6.13 for an illustration of collapsed units.

To collapse the subordinates of a unit:

Double-click the unit's icon. A left-pointing solid triangle beside the unit icon indicates that its subordinates are hidden. You can double-click a slide title icon, a text icon, or an organization chart icon to hide its subordinates.

To open a collapsed unit:

Double-click its icon again to display its subordinates. (If you collapsed by double-clicking at more than one unit level, some of the subordinates may still be collapsed.)

Using the Collapse and Expand Commands

Commands in the bottom section of the Outline menu let you collapse all the subordinates of a particular unit or collapse all the subordinate units in the entire outline at once. The Expand commands counter each of these Collapse commands. The procedure for expanding and collapsing units is similar to those for all the commands.

To use the Collapse/Expand commands, select the unit or units whose subordinate units you want to collapse or expand, and then choose the command appropriate to the results you want to achieve based on Table 6.6.

Collapsing and Expanding with the "Show levels..." Command

You can control the number of indent levels displayed in the outline quite easily by using the "Show levels..." command. For example, you could hide everything except for the far-left slide titles with only one command.

▼ *Figure 6.13. Collapsing and expanding the outline*

Before collapsing

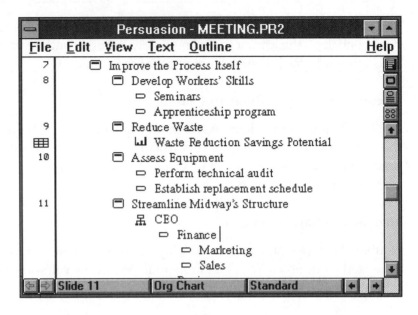

After collapsing

Indicates collapsed units

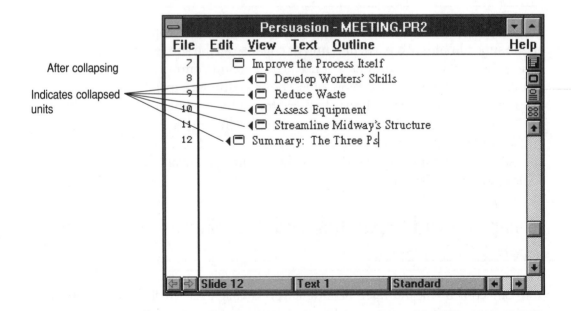

▼ *Table 6.6. Expand and collapse commands*

Command	Function
Expand (Ctrl + E)	Displays all the units subordinate to the selected unit
Collapse (Ctrl + C)	Hides all the units subordinate to the selected unit
Expand all	Displays all the units in the entire outline (Shortcut: Double-click the divider icon.)
Collapse all	Hides all the units in the entire outline in the divider unit (Shortcut: Double-click the divider icon.)

To specify the number of levels visible in the outline:

1. Choose "Show levels..." from the Outline menu.

2. In "Open to level," type the number of levels you wish to be visible. (Do not count the leftmost position where the divider unit is.)

Once you have used "Show levels...," you can treat the collapsed units as you would any collapsed units. For example, you can double-click them to open them. But if you want to return to the effect achieved when you first invoked "Show levels...," you need to choose it again.

QUICK COMMAND SUMMARY

In this chapter you have learned to do these procedures using these commands:

Commands	Procedures
Keyboard	Typing the outline
"Place..." (File menu)	Importing an outline
"Export..." (File)	Exporting an outline
Mouse	Selecting text and outline units
"Cut," "Copy," "Paste," "Clear" (Edit menu)	Editing an outline
Mouse	Moving outline units in Outline view
Mouse	Moving slides in Slide Sorter view

Commands	Procedures
"Title" (Outline menu)	Nesting slides
"Chart" (Outline)	Creating charts in Outline view
"Org chart" (Outline)	Creating organization charts in Outline view
"Insert break" (Outline)	Inserting breaks in the outline
"Expand," "Collapse," "Expand all," "Collapse all" (Outline)	Collapsing and expanding subordinate outline units
"Show levels..." (Outline)	Collapsing outline units to a certain level

PRACTICE WHAT YOU'VE LEARNED

In this exercise, you'll create a presentation, edit it, nest some slides, insert breaks to create double-columned text and a subtitle, and hide all but the slide titles in your presentation. If you want to practice charts or organization charts, do the tutorial in Chapter 7.

1. Open a copy of one of Persuasion's AutoTemplates.

2. Name the presentation file *Walking*

3. Type this outline:

    Racewalking
        Why?
        Where to go?
        What to wear?

4. Make the three units subordinate to the main title into nested slides and capitalize the first letter of each main word.

5. Add text to each of those four slides, giving specific points such as the following:

    Why?
        Low risk of injury
        Great aerobic benefits
    Where to go
        Out your front door
        Paved paths are best

What to wear?
    Running clothes
        Tights
        Shorts
        Sweats
    Good walking shoes

6. Add this subtitle to Slide 1: *A Sport for Life*

7. Add this title and text for Slide 5 of your presentation:

Race Schedule
    Green Lake
    Seward Park
    Waterfront Park
    April 10
    May 8
    June 12

8. Insert a break and assign a slide master that will format this text in two columns with the place names on the left and the dates on the right.

9. Add this subtitle to Slide 5: *For Spring 1991*

10. Collapse all subordinate text so that only slide titles are shown in the outline. (Because of the nested slides, you won't be able to hide the subtitle on Slide 1.)

ANSWERS

1. Choose "Open…" from the File menu, double-click [..], double-click [autotemp], and then double-click one of the AutoTemplates listed—for example, S08.AT2. Click "OK" in the "Slide setup" dialog box that automatically appears.

2. Choose "Save as…" from the File menu, type *Walking*, and then click "OK."

3. Type the text using the Enter, Tab, and Backspace keys to change indent levels. (Pressing Backspace erases letters unless it is used in an empty outline unit; then pressing Backspace moves the unit to the left.)

4. Click the text icon of the first text unit, "Why?" Hold down Shift and click the text unit of the last text unit, "What to wear?" Now all three units should be selected. Choose "Title" from the Outline menu to change all the units to slide titles. Click an insertion point after the g in "go," press Backspace, and type G. Alternatively, drag to select the w in "wear" and type W.

5. Add text to each slide by clicking an insertion point at the end of the slide title, and pressing Enter and then Tab to create a subordinate outline unit. Then type the text for that line and press Enter. Type the text for the next line, and press the down arrow key to move the insertion point to the end of the next slide title. Press Enter and then Tab, and continue as before. Remember that Tab moves the insertion point to the right; Shift + Tab (sometimes Backspace) moves the insertion point to the left.

6. This is tricky because of the nested slides under Slide 1. Click an insertion point at the end of Slide 4 ("Good walking shoes"), choose "Insert break" (Ctrl + Enter) from the Outline menu, and type *A Sport for Life*. Then press Shift while you select both the break unit and the subtitle unit, and continue to hold down Shift while you press Tab to move the break label and subtitle one level to the left (that is, out to the first level under "Racewalking"). Go to Slide 1 and see how the subtitle looks.

7. Click an insertion point at the end of the subtitle ("A Sport for Life"), and press Enter and then Backspace to create a new slide title unit. Follow the typing rules in step 3 or refer to Table 6.3.

8. Click an insertion point at the end of "Waterfront Park" and choose "Insert break" from the Outline menu (or press Ctrl + Enter). Now choose "Text 2" from the Master pop-up menu in the middle of the lower menu bar. Click the Slide view icon to see how the two side-by-side text placeholders on "Text 2" format the Slide 5.

9. Click an insertion point at the end of the presentation (after "June 12"). Choose "Insert break" from the Outline menu (or

press Ctrl + Enter). In the empty text unit, type *For Spring 1999*. Go to Slide view to see how the subtitle works on this slide.

10. Choose "Show levels…" from the Outline menu, click "Open to level," press Tab to highlight the text box, and type 2. Then click "OK." Now point to the title icon on Slide 5 and double-click to collapse everything under it. The subtitle on Slide 1 cannot collapse without hiding all the nested slide titles as well. To open the outline again, either use "Show levels…" and click "Show all levels," or double-click on each title unit icon with a left-pointing triangle beside it.

7

Tutorial: A Presentation Created from Outline View

This exercise will take approximately 45 minutes to complete. If you wish, you can shorten this time by omitting some of the text in the outline, but we encourage you to complete every task so that you gain an understanding of the process of creating and producing a presentation. We will be covering all but Step 5 from our eight steps to creating a presentation as discussed in Chapter 1.

In this tutorial, you will learn how to do the following:

▲ **Create a presentation using an AutoTemplate**

▲ **Type an outline**

▲ **Nest slides**

▲ Edit the outline text

▲ Rearrange slides in the slide sorter

▲ Reassign a master slide

▲ Add subtitles (by inserting breaks)

▲ Create a chart

▲ Create an organization chart

▲ Preview your presentation by running the slide show

▲ Print your overhead transparencies and handouts for the audience

Overview

As a middle manager at Midway Corporation, you are charged with the responsibility of communicating upper management's new philosophy to the employees in your department. Midway Corporation is hoping to change the orientation of their company from an emphasis on product to an emphasis on process. The changes that the company leaders envision require the cooperation and even the enthusiasm of employees. Though the company will demand more from its employees, the new business philosophy also translates into tangible benefits for them.

To explain your ideas and to begin eliciting support, you plan to meet with the 25 people in your department tomorrow morning. You want the atmosphere of this meeting to be informal, to nurture discussion. In this situation, you decide to give a simple overhead transparency presentation that you will also make available to your department as a handout. You can have it ready for tomorrow morning in less than an hour because all you need to do is type out your ideas, enter data for a chart, and print.

Opening a Copy of an AutoTemplate

In keeping with your purpose, you want to choose an AutoTemplate design that is simple, can handle a fair amount of text, has subtitle placeholders on its masters, and is easy to look at in hard copy. AutoTemplate OB15.AT2 seems to be a good choice, but let's preview some in the "Open" dialog box to be sure.

To preview AutoTemplates before opening a copy of one:

1. Double-click the Persuasion icon in the Aldus group window. The Aldus copyright appears for a short time.

2. Choose "Open…" (Ctrl + O) from the File menu. The "Open" dialog box appears, open to the PR2US\PRES directory.

3. In "Directories," double-click [..] and then double-click [autotemp] to see the files in the AutoTemplate directory.

4. Click to check "Show thumbnail."

5. Click different names in the list box to see the various Auto-Template designs in the preview box. A miniature of each AutoTemplate's default slide master appears in the preview box.

6. Click "OB15.AT2." Leave the "Copy" button on. If you click "Original," you open the AutoTemplate itself. The "Open" dialog box now looks as it does in Figure 7.1.

▼ *Figure 7.1. "Open" dialog box*

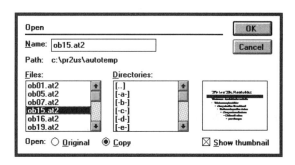

▼ *Figure 7.2. Outline view of untitled presentation*

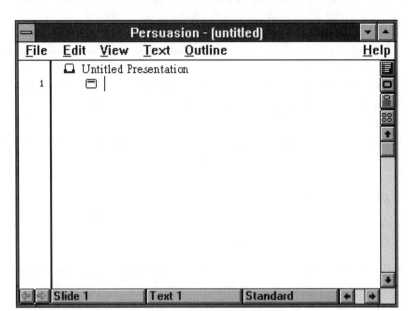

7. Click "OK." The "Slide setup" dialog box automatically appears.

8. Choose your printer for "Target device" in the "Slide setup" dialog box, and then click "OK" in the "Slide setup" dialog box. Persuasion opens an untitled copy of OB15 and places you in Outline view, as in Figure 7.2.

Saving and Naming Your Presentation

To give your presentation a name, change "Untitled 1" to the title you want by saving it as a presentation with its new name.

To name a presentation:

1. Choose "Save as…" from the File menu. The "Save as" dialog box appears, as in Figure 7.3.

▼ *Figure 7.3. "Save as..." dialog box*

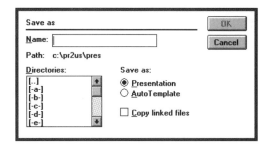

2. Type *Meeting*. Since you are creating a presentation, not an AutoTemplate, leave "Presentation" selected. Note that you are saving this to the "pr2us\pres" directory.

3. Click "OK." Now you see "MEETING.PR2" in the top border of the window.

Typing the Outline

This presentation is almost entirely text, so there's a bit of typing to do. The first thing you do is type the title in the top line with the divider icon beside it. The divider unit labels sections of your outline. Since the divider unit does not become a slide, but is displayed (or printed) as part of the outline, you can use it to add notes to yourself or to anyone else who may use this presentation.

To enter text into the outline:

1. Drag to highlight "Untitled Presentation." Type *Department Meeting* to replace "Untitled Presentation," as in Figure 7.4.

2. Press the down arrow key to put the cursor at the beginning of the line on the first slide. Type *Midway Corporation* as the slide title.

3. Press Enter to start a new line, then press Tab to type one level lower in the hierarchy. Type *Changing How We Work* and press Enter and Tab; type *For Ourselves* and press Enter; type *For Midway*.

▼ *Figure 7.4. Divider unit*

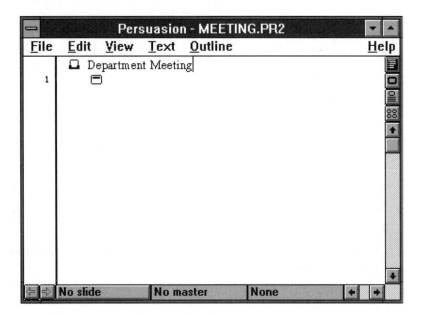

4. Press Enter and then the Backspace key twice to move the cursor back to the left margin to enter the next slide title. Type *Today's Business Requirements.*

5. Using Enter, Tab, and the Backspace key, continue typing the outline that follows until your outline looks like Figure 7.5. Save your work occasionally as you go (Ctrl + S).

```
Today's Business Requirements <Enter> <Tab>
    Improve customer service <Enter>
    Improve customer quality <Enter>
    Increase production flexibility <Enter> <Backspace>
How Do We Do This? <Enter> <Tab>
    Emphasize results? <Shift +Enter> or <Enter>
    Emphasize process? <Enter> <Backspace>
Result-Oriented Management <Enter> <Tab>
    Goal: To improve productivity <Enter>
    Orientation: The bottom line <Enter><Backspace>
Process-Oriented Management <Enter> <Tab>
    Goal: To improve the product by improving the
        production process <Enter>
```

```
    Orientation: Production process <Enter> <Backspace>
Weaknesses in Result-Oriented Management <Enter> <Tab>
    Difficult to know why results not achieved <Enter>
    Reliable solutions come too late to change outcome
        <Enter>
```

TIP

For a typeset apostrophe, type Alt + 0146 on the numeric keypad. For a full description of the special characters you can create, see the presentation installed in the PR2US\PRES directory called "XCHARSET.PR2."

▼ *Figure 7.5. Outline text, Part 1*

```
┌──────────────────────── Persuasion - MEETING.PR2 ────────────────────────┐
│ File   Edit   View   Text   Outline                                Help   │
│      ⌨ Department Meeting                                                 │
│  1      ▭ Midway Corporation                                              │
│            ⊐ Changing How We Work                                         │
│               ⊐ For Ourselves                                             │
│               ⊐ For Midway                                                │
│  2      ▭ Today's Business Requirements                                   │
│            ⊐ Improve customer service                                     │
│            ⊐ Improve customer quality                                     │
│            ⊐ Increase production flexibility                              │
│  3      ▭ How Do We Do This?                                              │
│            ⊐ Emphasize results?                                           │
│            or                                                             │
│            ⊐ Emphasize process?                                           │
│  4      ▭ Result-Oriented Management                                      │
│            ⊐ Goal:  To improve productivity                               │
│            ⊐ Orientation:  The bottom line                                │
│  5      ▭ Process-Oriented Management                                     │
│            ⊐ Goal:  To improve the product by improving the production process │
│            ⊐ Orientation:  Production process                             │
│  6      ▭ Weaknesses|in Result-Oriented Management                        │
│            ⊐ Difficult to know why results not achieved                   │
│            ⊐ Reliable solutions come too late to change outcome           │
│                                                                           │
│ Slide 6         Text 1          Standard                                  │
└───────────────────────────────────────────────────────────────────────────┘
```

Looking at Individual Slides

Once you have entered some of the text of your presentation you might want to take a look at a slide or two before typing the rest of the outline.

To go to Slide view from Outline view:

1. Point at one of the numbers in the left margin of the outline and click. The slide whose number you clicked appears, as you can see by its slide number in the lower-left corner of the window.

2. To go to the next slide, point to the slide number in the lower-left corner, and, holding down the mouse button, select the number of the next slide you want to see from the pop-up menu. When you release the mouse button, the slide you selected appears.

3. To go back to Outline view, click the Outline view icon in the upper right corner of the window.

Finishing Your Outline

Now finish typing the outline below so that it looks like Figure 7.6. Save your presentation again when you finish entering the text. This time use the "Save as..." command and save the file to the same name. This condenses the presentation file to its most recent version, whereas the "Save" command allows additional intermediate versions to accumulate in the presentation file.

```
Improve the Process <Enter> <Tab>
  Develop workers' skills <Enter> <Tab>
    Seminars <Enter>
    Apprenticeship program <Enter> <Backspace>
  Reduce waste <Enter> <Tab>
    Waste reduction savings potential: 15% <Enter> <Backspace>
  Assess equipment <Enter> <Tab>
    Perform technical audit <Enter>
```

▼ *Figure 7.6. Outline text, Part 2*

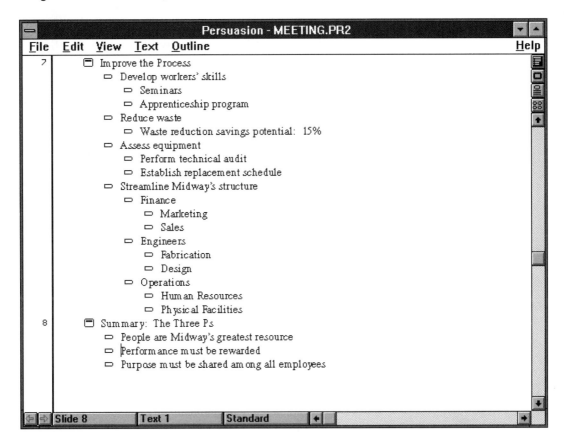

```
    Establish  replacement  schedule  <Enter>  <Backspace>
  Streamline  Midway's  structure  <Enter>  <Tab>
    Finance  <Enter>  <Tab>
      Marketing  <Enter>
      Sales  <Enter>  <Backspace>
    Engineers  <Enter>  <Tab>
      Fabrication  <Enter>
      Design  <Enter>  <Backspace>
    Operations  <Enter>  <Tab>
      Human  Resources  <Enter>
      Physical  Facilities  <Enter>  <Backspace  3  times>
Summary:  The  Three  Ps  <Enter>  <Tab>
    People  are  Midway's  greatest  resource  <Enter>
```

```
Performance  must  be  rewarded  <Enter>
Purpose  must  be  shared  among  all  employees
```

Now that all your text is entered, save your presentation by choosing "Save" (Ctrl + S) from the File menu.

Nesting Slide Titles

In the outline, look at Slide 7 for a moment; it contains too much information. If you look at Slide 7 in Slide view, you can see that the slide is a mess with information running off the edge. But we need all that information in the presentation. What can we do?

The basic information on Slide 7—four suggestions for improving the process—could be communicated more effectively if we first give an overview and then detail each item in particular. We can do that by nesting slides. In other words, we can do that by turning each of the suggestions for improvement into slide titles themselves, giving us five slides instead of one. Let's try it and then look at the results.

To nest slides:

1. In the Outline, click the text unit icon below Slide 7's title. The text unit "Develop workers' skills" is selected.

2. Hold down Ctrl, and click the text icons of the other three suggestions: "Reduce waste," "Assess equipment," and "Streamline Midway's Structure." All four suggestions are selected.

3. Choose "Title" (Ctrl + L) from the Outline menu. The icon for each of the four headings changes to the slide title icon. A number for each slide now appears in the left margin.

Now the four main units subordinate to Slide 7 are slide titles themselves, as in Figure 7.7. What does this mean?

If you view Slide 7, you'll see that it consists of five lines: a slide title and the four main points (the slide titles for Slides 8, 9, 10, and 11). Slide 7 provides an overview for Slides 8, 9, 10, and 11, each of

▼ *Figure 7.7. Nested slides in Outline view*

**Nesting Slide
Titles**

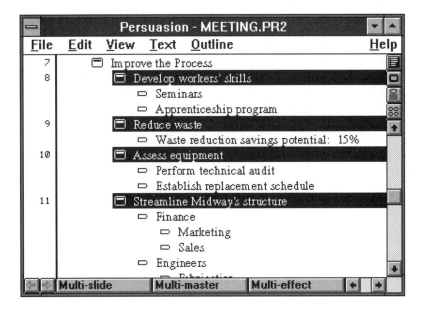

which go into more detail. As you might expect, Slide 8 through Slide 11 consist of their slide titles plus their subordinates (see Figure 7.8).

Editing the Outline

Standard Windows editing techniques are used to cut, copy, paste, insert, and replace text when you work in Persuasion.

Now that we have turned four text units into slide titles, we should capitalize the first letter of each word in the title.

To edit text in an outline unit:

1. Go to Outline view by clicking the Outline view icon.

2. In the title of Slide 8 in Outline view, drag to highlight the *w* in *workers'*, as in Figure 7.9.

3. Type W. Using the same technique, capitalize the *s* in *skills* as well. Finish capitalizing the words in the titles of Slides 9 through 11.

▼ *Figure 7.8. Nested slides in Slide view*

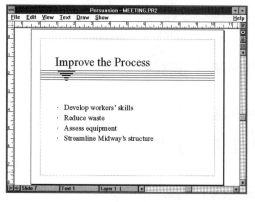

Slide 7

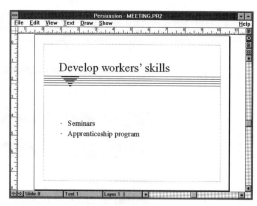

Slide 8

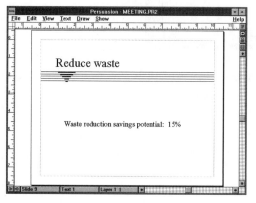

Slide 9

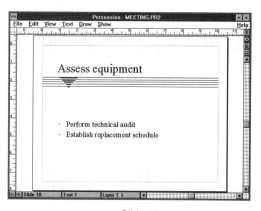

Slide 10

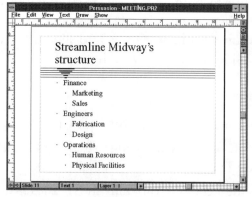

Slide 11

▼ *Figure 7.9. Editing in Outline view*

```
┌─────────────────────────────────────────────────────────┐
│  ─          Persuasion - MEETING.PR2              ▼ ▲    │
├─────────────────────────────────────────────────────────┤
│ File   Edit   View   Text   Outline              Help    │
├─────────────────────────────────────────────────────────┤
│   7        ⊟  Improve the Process                    ▤   │
│   8          ⊟  Develop workers' skills              ▣   │
│                 ▭ Seminars                           ▤   │
│                 ▭ Apprenticeship program             ▥   │
│   9          ⊟ Reduce waste                          ▲   │
│                 ▭ Waste reduction savings potential: 15% │
│  10          ⊟ Assess equipment                          │
│                 ▭ Perform technical audit                │
│                 ▭ Establish replacement schedule         │
│  11          ⊟ Streamline Midway's structure            │
│                 ▭ Finance                                │
│                    ▭ Marketing                           │
│                    ▭ Sales                               │
│                 ▭ Engineers                          ▼   │
├─────────────────────────────────────────────────────────┤
│ ⇦⇨│ Slide 8      │ Text 1      │ Standard     │ ◄ │ ► │  │
└─────────────────────────────────────────────────────────┘
```

To add text:

1. Position an insertion point by clicking after *Process* in the title of Slide 7.

2. Type *Itself*.

Rearranging Slides

The slide sorter displays miniature versions of your slides laid out in order. The number of slides in each row is dependent upon several conditions: the size of the window, the size of your view in the window (see the Sorter menu), the orientation of the slides (tall or wide), and the size of your monitor. You can easily rearrange the slides or reassign masters to them in the slide sorter.

To go to Slide sorter view:

Choose "Slide sorter" from the View menu, or click the Slide sorter view icon at the upper-right edge of the window. Slide miniatures of your presentation are displayed in rows, as in Figure 7.10. (You may have to scroll to see every slide.)

Notice as you look over the slides in Slide sorter view that slides 8 through 11 are offset slightly lower than the other slides (see Figure 7.11). This indicates that they are nested slides. They take their titles from the text on Slide 8, which introduces them.

As you examine your presentation, you realize that it makes more sense to place Slide 6 immediately after Slide 4. You are describing "Result-Oriented Management" in order to dismiss it in favor of "Process-Oriented Management," so insert Slide 6 ("Weaknesses in Result-Oriented Management") after Slide 4.

To rearrange slides:

1. Select Slide 6 by clicking inside it. Notice the box around Slide 6 and "Slide 6" in the lower-left corner of the menu bar, identifying the selected slide.

▼ *Figure 7.10. Slide sorter view*

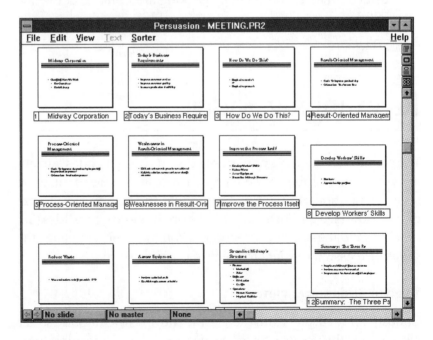

▼ *Figure 7.11. Nested slides in Slide sorter view*

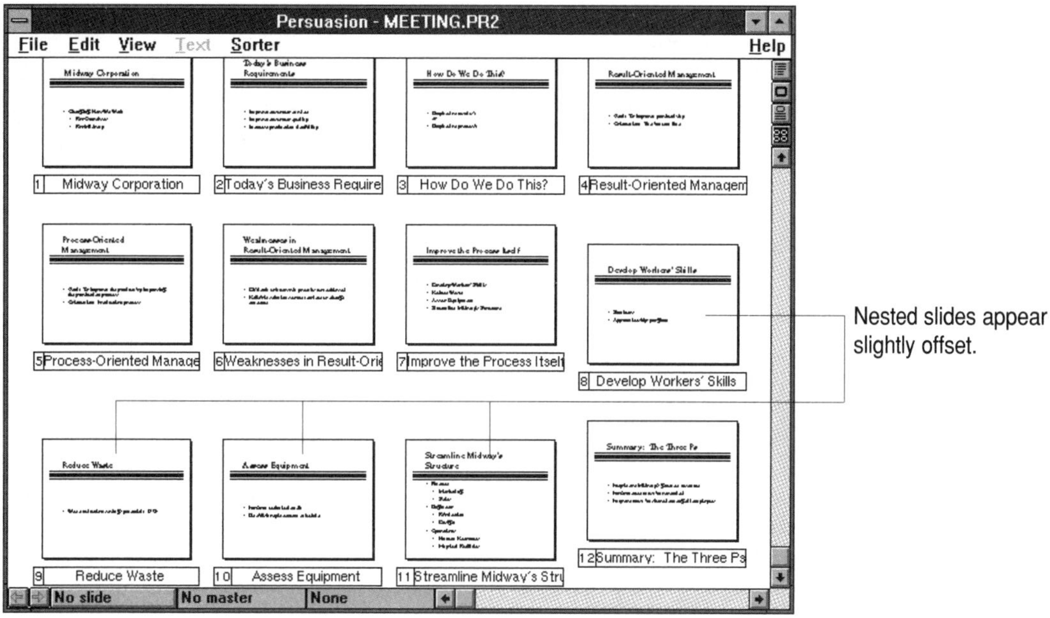

Nested slides appear slightly offset.

2. Point anywhere in Slide 6, and, keeping the mouse button down, drag Slide 6 to the place you want it—immediately after Slide 4. Notice the solid bar between Slide 4 and Slide 5 as you drag Slide 6. This indicates where Slide 6 will go (see Figure 7.12).

3. Release the mouse button. Slide 6 is now Slide 5, and the slides that follow are renumbered accordingly. The outline automatically reflects the new slide order.

Reassigning a Slide Master

Slide 1 should look different from the rest because it functions as a title for the whole presentation. To make Slide 1 appear distinctive, you can assign it the Title slide master, which gives more prominence to the title itself.

▼ *Figure 7.12. Rearranging slides in the slide sorter*

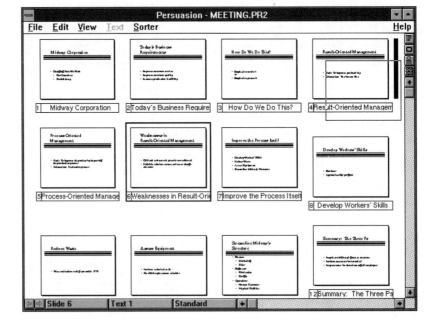

Vertical bar indicates
new position of slide.

To reassign a master:

1. In Slide sorter view, click on Slide 1 to select it. A box appears
    around the slide. Notice in the lower menu bar the slide number
    of the selected slide and, to its right, the name of the master
    assigned to it ("Text 1").

2. Select "Title" from the Master pop-up menu in the middle of the
    lower menu bar. Notice the change in the layout of your slide.

Inserting Breaks to Create a Subtitle

You can put a subtitle on any type of slide as long as you have a text
placeholder for it on the slide master that is assigned to that slide.
Most of the slide masters in the AutoTemplates that come with

Persuasion have a text placeholder located below the title. This "subtitle" placeholder is the highest numbered text placeholder on the master; therefore, the text for it needs to be entered in the outline as the last text on that slide. To differentiate the subtitle text from the main text, you must insert a break before it so the text that follows flows to the next placeholder.

On the summary slide in the Midway presentation, a subtitle could help to underscore the point of the presentation.

Inserting Breaks to Create a Subtitle

To a insert break for a subtitle:

1. In Outline view, click an insertion point at the end of the text on the last slide, right after the word *employees*.

2. Choose "Insert break" from the Outline menu, or press Ctrl + Enter. A break label appears, indicating the slide number and the number of the text placeholder that governs the following text.

3. Type *Midway's New Way*. Your outline should look like the one in Figure 7.13.

▼ *Figure 7.13. Inserting a break for a subtitle*

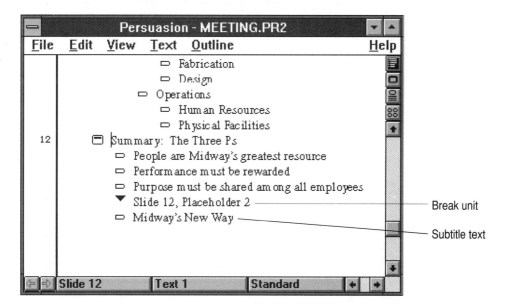

To see the effect of what you have done in Outline view, you must go to Slide view. Click the number for Slide 12 in the left margin to look at the summary slide. You should see a slide that looks like the one in Figure 7.14. Slide 12 looks the way it does because it is formatted by its slide master, Text 1, which is also shown in Figure 7.14.

▼ *Figure 7.14. Slide 12 and "Text 1" slide master*

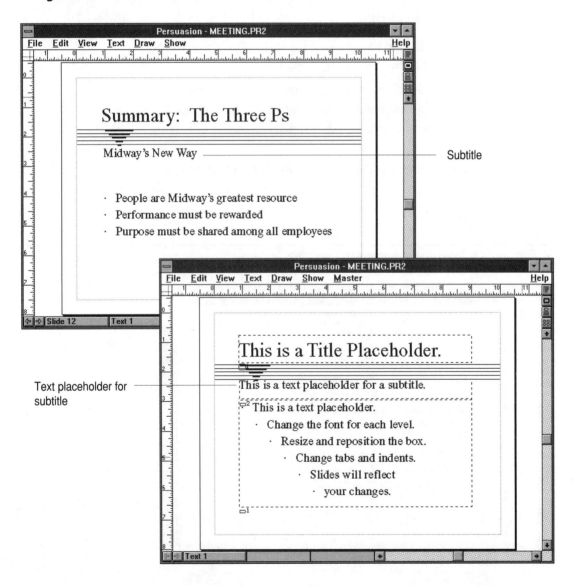

Subtitle

Text placeholder for subtitle

Creating a Chart

You can create a chart from Outline view by changing an outline unit to a chart unit. The text in the chart unit becomes the chart title. After you assign a slide master containing a chart placeholder to the slide, all you need to do is enter data for your chart and then plot it.

To create a chart from Outline view:

1. In Outline view, click an insertion point somewhere in the text unit for Slide 9, and choose "Chart" from the Outline menu. The unit icon changes to a dimmed pie chart.

2. Choose "Graphic 1" from the Master pop-up menu in the middle of the lower menu bar. Now you have assigned a master containing a chart placeholder. The chart icon darkens and reflects the chart type of the placeholder on the master, in this case a column chart.

3. Change the text in the chart unit to create this chart title: *Waste Reduction Savings Potential.* Specifically, you need to click an insertion point at the end of the chart unit and press Backspace five times to delete the colon, the space, and *15%*. Then drag to select the first letter of each word in the chart title and capitalize it. Slide 9 in Outline view now looks like Figure 7.15.

4. Click the data sheet icon in the left margin. Both the data sheet and the "Chart info" dialog box open. Since the data sheet is empty, it opens on top.

5. Drag to select the cells from A1 to C5. You can enter data without selecting the cells first, but selecting cells first makes entry easier. By pressing Enter after each entry, you systematically move down each column and to the top of the next until you are finished.

6. Press Enter to move the cursor to A2, type *Materials* and press Enter.

   Note: You can move a column divider in the data sheet by pointing to the column divider at the top, between the column heads. The cursor turns into the column-adjust marker with a double arrow. With the column-adjust marker, drag the column

▼ *Figure 7.15. Slide 9 in Outline view before data entry*

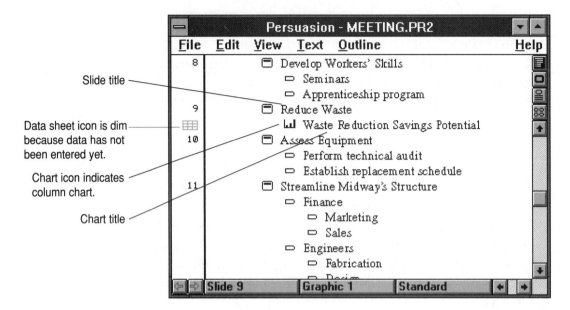

Slide title

Data sheet icon is dim because data has not been entered yet.

Chart icon indicates column chart.

Chart title

divider to the width you want as shown in Figure 7.16. Widening the column is optional; all the data you enter will be accounted for whether it is completely visible to you in the data sheet or not.

7. Continue entering data, pressing Enter after each entry, until the data sheet looks like the one in Figure 7.17.

▼ *Figure 7.16. Widening columns in the data sheet*

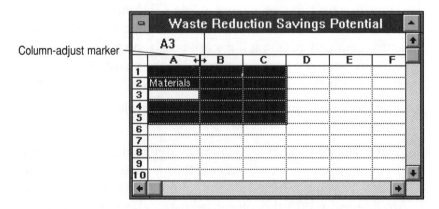

Column-adjust marker

▼ *Figure 7.17. Data sheet*

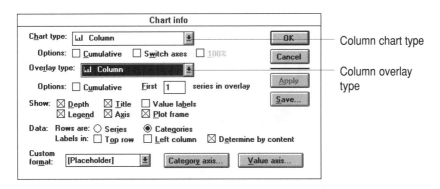

8. Click the title bar of the "Chart info" dialog box to bring it forward. In the dialog box, select "Column" from the drop-down menu for "Overlay type." The "Chart info" dialog box should look like Figure 7.18. The chart type is already Column.

9. Click "OK." Doing so in the "Chart info" dialog box plots the chart.

▼ *Figure 7.18. "Chart info" dialog box*

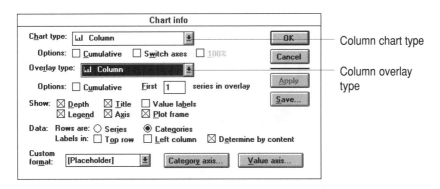

The chart you see in Slide view shows the first data series (Cost After) plotted on top of the second data series (Cost Before) in order to emphasize the ways in which waste reduction can shrink Midway's costs. This is called an overlay chart. Click the Slide view icon at the upper-left edge of the window to see your chart on the slide. It should look similar to the chart in Figure 7.19 (the chart in the illustration has been enlarged a bit).

Creating an Organization Chart

A quick look at Slide 11, "Streamline Midway's Structure," tells you that the text on that slide could be more easily digested if it were arranged as an organization chart. Your data in this case is already entered; it's the text on Slide 11. All you need to do is add a top level, change the unit to an org chart unit, and assign a master with an organization chart placeholder.

▼ *Figure 7.19. A column-on-column overlay chart*

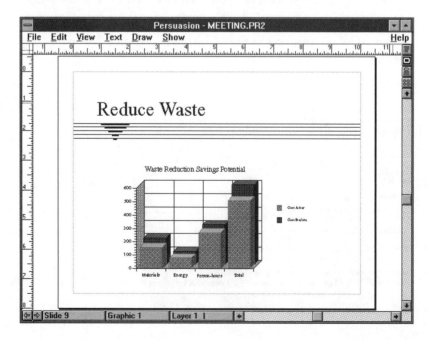

To create an organization chart:

1. In Outline view, click an insertion point at the end of the slide title for Slide 11, "Streamline Midway's Structure."

2. Press Enter, and then press Tab to create an empty subordinate text unit.

3. Type *CEO* to create the top level of your organization chart.

4. Subordinate the rest of the text on the slide. First select it (click the text icon for "Finance," hold down Shift, and click the text icon for "Physical Facilities"), and then press Tab. All the text under "CEO" shifts to the right one level.

5. Click an insertion point in "CEO," and choose "Org chart" (Ctrl + G) from the Outline menu. The icon for the text unit changes to a dimmed organization chart icon, and all the subordinate text units are dimmed because there's no organization chart placeholder on "Text 1."

6. Choose "Org Chart" from the Master pop-up menu in the middle of the lower menu bar to assign a master with an org chart placeholder. The organization chart icon in the outline darkens to show that an organization chart placeholder is in effect. It translates Slide 11's text in the outline into an organization chart on the slide, as shown in Figure 7.20.

Before you review your presentation, make sure you save it. Use either "Save as…" or "Save" (Ctrl + S) from the File menu.

Running the Slide Show

You can quickly preview your presentation before you give it by running the slide show. Since you have created an overhead transparency presentation, it helps to see each frame on the screen in succession as it will look when you use the overhead projector.

To run the slide show:

1. Choose "Slide show…" from the File menu.

▼ *Figure 7.20. An organization chart in Outline and Slide views*

Outline view

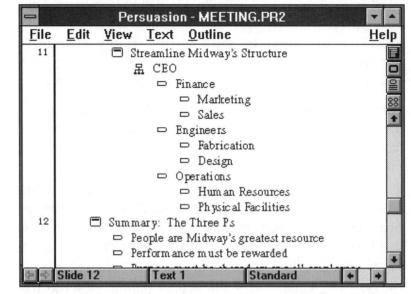

Slide view

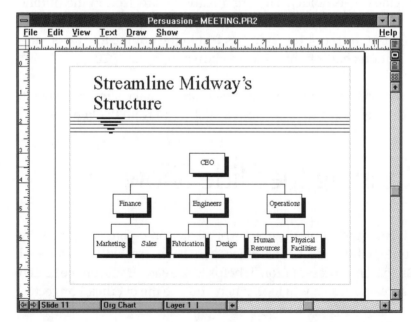

2. In the "Slide show" dialog box, click to uncheck "Continuous cycle." "Full screen" uses the whole screen to display the slides without showing the presentation window. "Automatic" moves from slide to slide in the increment indicated in "Delay between slides," stopping after the last slide. ("Continuous cycle" would have shown the slides in an ongoing loop.) The "Slide show" dialog box should look like the one in Figure 7.21.

3. Click "OK." The 12 slides in the presentation are displayed consecutively on your screen with a 2-second delay between each.

Running the Slide Show

Printing Your Presentation

You are ready to print your overhead transparency presentation, but you also want to print handouts. You can do both from the "Print" dialog box. However, because the slides are printed with a wide orientation and the handouts have a tall orientation, you need to print them in two batches, changing the printer orientation in between print sessions.

▼ *Figure 7.21. "Slide show" dialog box*

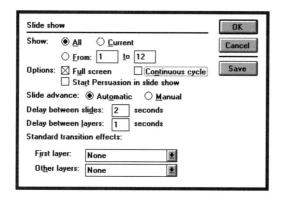

Save your presentation before you print; use the "Save as..." command from the File menu and save it to the same name. Using "Save as..." condenses the file size to the current version.

To set up for printing your handouts:

1. Choose "Notes setup..." from the File menu. The "Notes setup" dialog box appears, as in Figure 7.22.

2. In "Outline/Notes/Handouts printer," select the printer you'll use to print your handouts. Leave the other settings as they are.

3. Click "OK."

To print your handouts:

1. From Outline view, choose "Print..." (Ctrl + P) from the File menu.

2. Click to uncheck "Outline" and click to check "Handouts." Leave the other settings as they are. The "Notes printer" should match the one you specified in the "Notes setup" dialog box. The "Print" dialog box should look like the one in Figure 7.23.

3. Click "OK" to start printing.

   Note: If you get a message that page and paper orientations are different, click "Cancel" in the message box and check to make sure that your printer is set up for "Portrait" (that is, "Tall").

▼ *Figure 7.22. "Notes setup" dialog box*

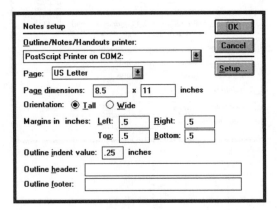

▼ *Figure 7.23. "Print" dialog box for handouts*

Printing Your Presentation

Print				OK
Copies: 1	**Pages:** ◉ **All** ○ **From** 1	**to** 1		Cancel
Print:				
□ **Outline** □ **Slides** □ **Builds**	□ **Notes** ☒ **Handouts**			Setup...
Graphics options:				
□ Reverse order □ **Proof print** □ **Print background**				
Outline options:				
□ Visible items only □ Current selection □ Print bullet characters				
Slide printer:		**Notes printer:**		
PostScript Printer on COM2: ⬇		PostScript Printer on COM2: ⬇		

Click the "Setup..." button in the "Print" dialog box, select "Portrait," click "OK," and continue to print.

Your handouts, each page containing four miniatures of slides from the presentation, are ready to be copied for the 25 people expected at the meeting.

You can print your overheads on paper and then photocopy them onto transparencies, or you can print directly on laser printer transparency film. Be sure to check the documentation for your printer to see if it is advisable to print directly to transparency film.

To print your overhead transparencies:

1. From Outline view, choose "Print..." (Ctrl + P) from the File menu.

2. Click to uncheck "Outline" and click to check "Slides." Leave the other settings as they are. The "Slide printer" should match the one you specified in the "Slide setup" dialog box, which appeared when you first opened this copy of OB15.AT2. The "Print" dialog box should look like the one in Figure 7.24.

3. Click the "Setup..." button in the "Print" dialog box, select "Landscape," and click "OK." Because you just finished printing handouts to a "Portrait" or "Tall" orientation, you must change the paper orientation in the printer-specific dialog box shown in Figure 7.25 to print slides that are oriented to the width of the paper.

▼ *Figure 7.24. "Print" dialog box for slides*

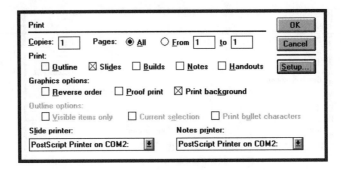

▼ *Figure 7.25. Printer-specific dialog box*

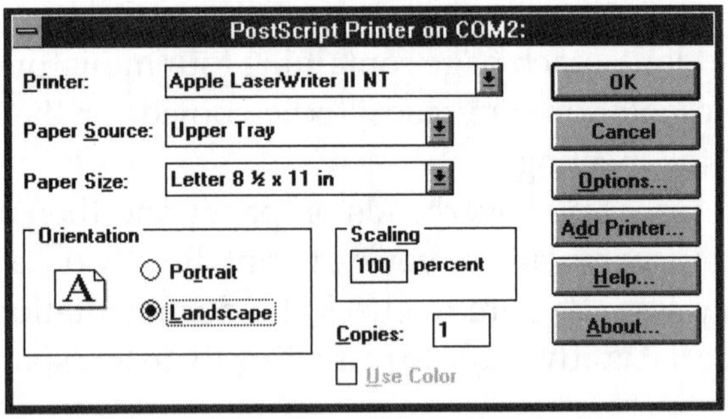

4. Click "OK" in the printer-specific dialog box, and then click "OK" in the "Print" dialog box to start printing. Your overheads are ready to be copied onto transparency paper.

Now you are ready. You have transparencies in-hand and a set of handouts to give your audience. You have done what you set out to do—without a hitch!

QUICK COMMAND SUMMARY

In this tutorial, you have learned how to do these procedures using these commands:

Commands	Procedures
"Open..." (File menu)	Starting your presentation
"Slide setup..." (automatic/File)	Defining size of your slides and targeting printer
"Save as..." (File)	Saving and naming your presentation
Keyboard	Typing your presentation
Icons	Moving between Slide view and Outline view
"Title" (Outline menu)	Nesting slides
"Slide sorter" (View menu)	Moving to Slide sorter view
Mouse	Rearranging slides
"Title" (Master pop-up menu)	Assigning a slide master
"Insert break" (Outline)	Inserting a break to create a subtitle
"Chart" (Outline)	Creating a chart unit
"Graphic 1" (Master pop-up)	Assigning a master containing a chart placeholder
Data sheet icon	Opening data sheet and "Chart info" dialog box
"Org chart" (Outline)	Creating an organization chart unit
"Org Chart" (Master pop-up)	Assigning a master containing an organization chart placeholder
"Slide show..." (File)	Running the on-screen slide show
"Notes setup..." (File)	Setting up printer to print handouts
"Print..." (File)	Printing your handouts, changing paper orientation, and printing slides

PART III

Working on a Presentation from Slide View

Enhancing the Text in Your Presentation

Suppose that you're happy with the outline you've entered and edited for the presentation you will be giving at your annual department meeting. However, when you view your slides, they strike you as a little dull. For instance, the word "Loss" would look better in red for emphasis. And the pic chart that illustrates your department's contribution to overall profits would have more impact if you could add the phrase "We met our goals!" next to it.

Let's face it. AutoTemplates are great for providing basic formatting for your presentations. And there's no denying that when you have a half-hour to throw together a presentation, they're the saving grace. But when you have a little more time, you may want to do more than simply enter your outline and assign predesigned slide masters.

This is the first of several chapters in this book that take you beyond the basics—that is, show you more about how to use Persuasion's powerful features to enhance your presentations. In this chapter you will learn how to do the following:

▲ **Control whether or not text on your slides is tied to your outline**

▲ **Apply formatting to text and paragraphs**

▲ **Use Persuasion's text ruler to set tabs and indents**

Entering Text: Placeholder versus Independent

"But wait," you say. "Didn't I learn how to enter text when I entered my outline in Part I?" The answer is, "Yes, you did." What you learned in Chapter 6 applies to working with text in any view in Persuasion. And the keyboard shortcuts for editing text are the same from view to view; but there's more.

Let's go back to your wish list that was described earlier—adding color to a word and adding a phrase next to a pie chart. Both of these enhancements add emphasis to your presentation but are not present in your outline. Persuasion allows you to add text to your presentation that will not flow back to the outline and to add text formatting that is not reflected in the outline.

There are two categories of text in Persuasion: placeholder text and independent text. Placeholder text is text from the outline that is placed and formatted on the slide by a placeholder on the assigned slide master. You can enter or edit placeholder text in either Outline or Slide view. Independent text is text that you add outside placeholder boundaries in Slide view. (You can add independent text to slide masters or notes as well.) Changes to placeholder text in Slide view are reflected back in your outline; independent text is not. Furthermore, text added to placeholders in

Slide view takes on the formatting characteristics of the placeholder, whereas for independent text, you must apply formatting yourself. Figure 8.1 provides an example of a slide with both independent text and placeholder text.

To enter or edit placeholder text in Slide view:

1. In Slide view, select the text tool.

2. Click an insertion point inside the placeholder boundaries (see Figure 8.2), or drag-select the text you want to replace.

3. Type your additions or changes.

To add new paragraphs to the placeholder text, click at the end of an existing line and press Return. Then use Tab to move the cursor to the heading level you want. Any new paragraphs you add will be reflected in the outline at the appropriate heading level. (Ctrl + Tab moves you from one tab stop to the next. For more information about using indents and tabs, see "Formatting Paragraphs with Tabs and Indents" later in this chapter.)

▼ *Figure 8.1. Slide with independent and placeholder text*

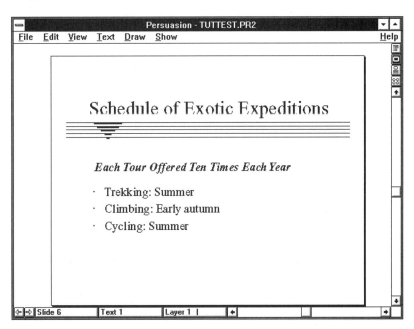

▼ *Figure 8.2. Slide with placeholder boundaries displayed*

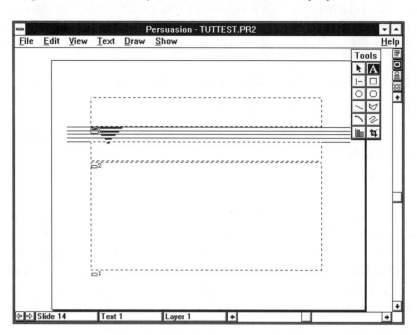

To add independent text to a slide:

1. In Slide view, select the text tool and click anywhere on the slide outside the placeholder boundaries. Persuasion creates a text block where you clicked, automatically calculating its size based on its position on the slide and its alignment based on the default alignment setting (see Figure 8.3).

2. Enter your text. Persuasion automatically wraps the text to fit the text block and applies the formatting characteristics—that is, font, point size, style, and so on—currently set for the text tool.

    Note: When you create a new text block in this fashion, Persuasion applies default text attributes—those set in "NEW.AT2," those set for the AutoTemplate you are using, or those that you have set for your presentation. If you want to change the default attributes before you create your new text block, you can use the text tool to choose commands from the Text menu or to click in some placeholder text that has the attributes you want. Either of these methods—when applied with the text tool active—sets temporary defaults for the text tool. For more information

▼ *Figure 8.3. Empty text block*

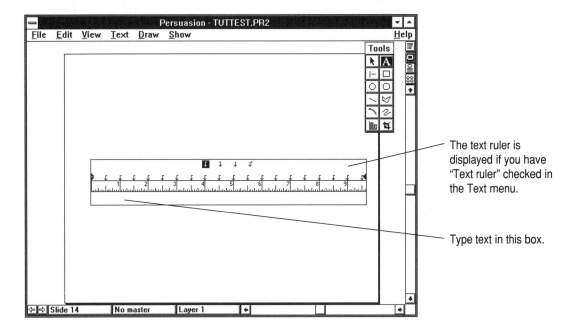

The text ruler is displayed if you have "Text ruler" checked in the Text menu.

Type text in this box.

about setting text attributes, see "Formatting Text," the next section in this chapter. For more information about setting defaults in "New.AT2," see Chapter 12.

TIP

To change the size of the text block after you've entered text, select the text block with the pointer tool and drag one of its handles just as you would any other object. For more information about resizing objects, see Chapter 9.

Formatting Text

When you use an AutoTemplate, Persuasion's text formatting features are almost invisible to you because the placeholders of the AutoTemplates have been defined to contain text formatting.

Characteristics such as font, type size, type style, text color, and alignment have been preset for you. If you want to change the predefined attributes of placeholder text or determine the look of independent text, you must know how to apply text attributes yourself.

In general, to apply any text attribute, use the pointer tool to select the independent text block or placeholder text block you want to modify, and then choose the appropriate command from the Text menu. (If you want to change only a portion of the text in the text block, use the text tool to select the text.) Table 8.1 provides an overview of the commands in the Text menu.

▼ Table 8.1. Text menu commands

Command	Function
Normal	Resets the text style to "none"—that is, without bold, italic, or other styles
Bold	Used for emphasis or in headings, and looks like this: **bold**
Italic	Used to stress a word in a sentence or for certain types of titles, and looks like this: *Moby Dick*
Underline	Used to underline text, and looks like this: <u>underline</u>
Shadow	Used to give text a three-dimensional effect and looks like this: shadow
Superscript	Used for scientific notations or formulas, and looks like this: $E = MC^2$ (the 2 is a superscript)
Subscript	Used in scientific notations or formulas, and looks like this: H_2O (the 2 is a subscript)
Bullet marks	Displays or hides bullets on a slide that you have specified with "Define bullets..." from the Master menu
Character...	Sets all available text formatting options from one dialog box
Paragraph...	Sets all available paragraph formatting options from one dialog box
Outline format...	Defines a text format for purposes of printing your outline (For more information about this command, see Chapter 14.)
Text ruler	Displays or hides the text ruler that lets you set tabs and indents for text blocks on a slide

Setting Text Characteristics

The top portion of Persuasion's Text menu contains all of the text style commands—"Normal," "Bold," "Italic," and so on. These commands, plus all of the additional attributes you would typically want to set for text, are also conveniently located in the "Character specifications" dialog box (choose "Character…" from the Text menu).

Font and Size

The typeface you select, as well as its size, largely determines the readability of your presentation. Therefore, it's important to be knowledgeable about how fonts work on the PC and on output devices such as printers and film recorders.

A font is a complete set of characters for a particular typeface and size, such as 10-point Times New Roman PS. On the PC, you probably installed fonts when you installed Windows, or you may have installed Adobe Type Manager (ATM), which provides PostScript fonts in all sizes for your screen and any other attached non-PostScript device. If you are using a laser printer to create overhead transparencies, it probably came equipped from the manufacturer with its own set of font files. Similarly, film recorders and other types of output devices usually come with a set of fonts that are designed for the resolution of that device. For more information fonts and type managers, see Chapter 2. You can also refer to the Windows documentation.

To set the font and style of existing text or the next text you enter:

1. Select the text tool and, if necessary, select the text you want to change.

2. Choose "Character…" from the Text menu. The "Character specifications" dialog box appears (Figure 8.4).

3. For "Font," select the name of the font you want.

4. For "Size," select the point size you want.

5. Click "OK."

▼ *Figure 8.4. "Character specifications" dialog box*

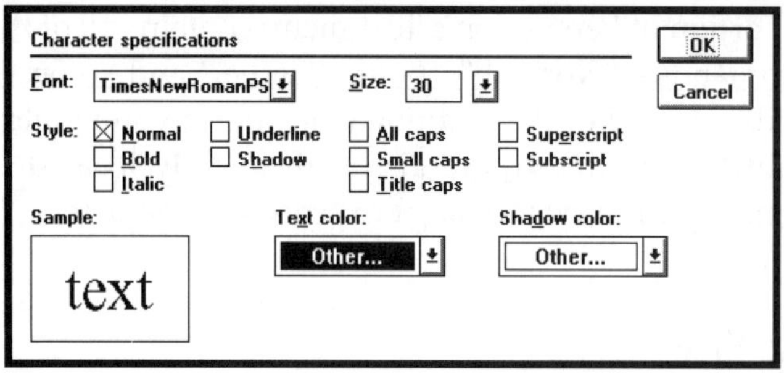

Style

If you have defined only the font and size of your text then you are, by default, using plain type style. For most slide text, plain style is fine. If you were to use another style, it would be harder to read. However, in headlines or labels, other styles can be used for special effect. Consider the following tips when deciding which type style to apply:

▲ Use bold in titles for dramatic impact, but not in slide text because bold text is harder to read, especially in smaller point sizes.

▲ On slides or overhead transparencies, italicized text may appear to be smaller than the text surrounding it. If you find this to be the case, try increasing the point size of the italicized word.

▲ Use shadow to give your text a three-dimensional effect. You can define the amount of text shadow offset by using the "Paragraph..." command from the Text menu.

▲ Use outline along with bold for special effect in larger point sizes.

Note: Text styles can be set cumulatively. For example, you can have text that is both outlined and shadowed. To set multiple text styles, simply choose from the submenu more than once. (Setting the style to "Plain" turns off all other styles.)

To apply one or more styles to your text:

1. Select the text you want to change.

2. Choose one or more styles from the top portion of the Text menu.

Note: You can also use the "Character…" command from the Text menu to set text styles.

Color

You can define the color of text just as you can any other object in Persuasion. Consider these points when applying color to text:

▲ In general, colored text is more difficult to read than black text on a white or light-colored background. Therefore, your best bet is to use color sparingly to give an occasional word emphasis.

▲ If you do apply color to all of your text, use a dark color for the text and a light color (preferably a lighter shade of the same color) for the background. Dark text on a light background is easier to read than light text on a dark background.

▲ Follow the rules for combining colors stated in Chapter 13.

To apply color to text:

1. If necessary, display the color palette by choosing "Colors" from the Show menu.

2. Select the text you want to apply color to. You can either use the pointer tool to select all the text or the text tool to select a range of text. Persuasion lets you apply color to only one character, if you want.

3. Make sure "Text foreground" or "Text shadow" is selected in the list box in the colors palette.

4. Choose the color you want.

Note: If you want to apply a color other than those in the color palette's working set, you can expand the palette to display additional colors. For more information about using Persuasion's color palette, see Chapter 13.

CHECK YOURSELF

Set default format attributes for the text tool and then create an independent text block on a slide.

ANSWER

If necessary, start Persuasion, open a new presentation, and go to a new slide in Slide view. Select the text tool. Choose "Character..." from the Text menu; in the "Character specifications" dialog box, select settings for font, size, style, and color, and then click "OK." Finally, click outside any existing placeholder boundaries and type some text.

Setting Paragraph Characteristics

How you format lines and paragraphs of text can dramatically affect the readability of your slide text when it is projected on a large screen. The "Paragraph specifications" dialog box, which you display by choosing "Paragraph..." from the Text menu, contains all the settings that affect lines and paragraphs as a whole.

Line and Paragraph Spacing

You can enhance readability of your slide text by setting different amounts of space between lines of a paragraph and between paragraphs. Typically, you should set paragraph spacing to be roughly twice as much as line spacing, but make preliminary settings, print one or two slides, and adjust for readability. Figure 8.5 provides examples of various spacing between lines and paragraphs.

To adjust the space between lines and paragraphs:

1. Select a text block on a slide—placeholder or independent text.

2. Choose "Paragraph..." from the Text menu. The "Paragraph specifications" dialog box appears (see Figure 8.6).

▼ *Figure 8.5. Spacing between lines and paragraphs*

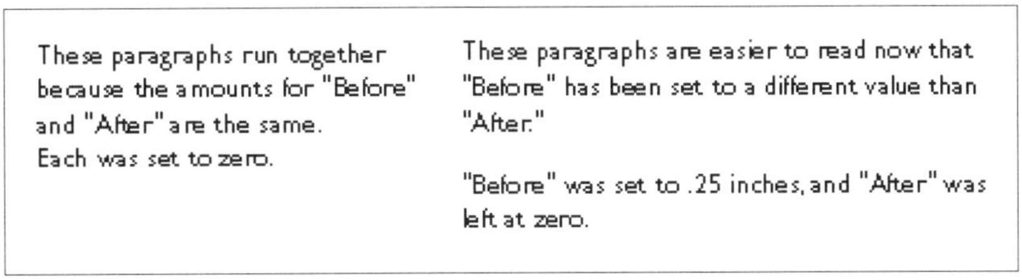

These paragraphs run together because the amounts for "Before" and "After" are the same. Each was set to zero.

These paragraphs are easier to read now that "Before" has been set to a different value than "After."

"Before" was set to .25 inches, and "After" was left at zero.

3. Under "Spacing," define the amounts of space you want between lines of a paragraph, before a paragraph, and after a paragraph.

4. Click "OK."

Note: Persuasion applies before- and after-paragraph spacing cumulatively. For example, if you set spacing both before and after a paragraph to be one-eighth of an inch, your paragraphs will be separated by one-quarter inch.

Letter Spacing

Fonts are designed to look best at a particular point size. For example, Gill Sans may have been designed so that the letters are perfectly spaced at a size of 30 points. Therefore, you may find that you want to tighten or loosen the spacing between letters of words once you see them projected on a large screen. Figure 8.7 shows the Gill Sans font at various sizes with standard letter spacing.

▼ *Figure 8.6. "Paragraph specifications" dialog box*

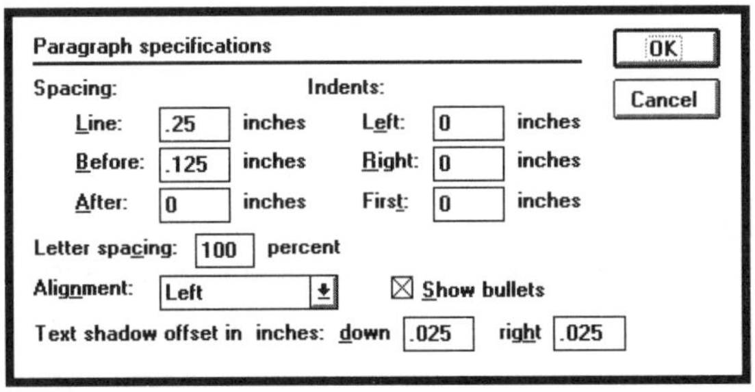

Paragraph specifications

						OK
Spacing:			Indents:			Cancel
Line:	.25	inches	Left:	0	inches	
Before:	.125	inches	Right:	0	inches	
After:	0	inches	First:	0	inches	

Letter spacing: 100 percent

Alignment: Left ▼   ☒ Show bullets

Text shadow offset in inches: down .025   right .025

▼ *Figure 8.7. Letter spacing at various point sizes*

This is Gill Sans at 18 points. Notice that the letters tend to run together.

At 30 points, text is more evenly spaced.

But at 60 points, the spacing is wider than necessary.

To tighten or loosen letter spacing:

1. Select the text you want to modify.

2. Choose "Paragraph…" from the Text menu.

3. For "Letter spacing," enter a percentage, and then click "OK." Percentages less than 100 (considered "normal" spacing) will delete space from, or tighten, the text; percentages greater than 100 will add space to, or loosen, the text.

Bullet marks

Bullet marks, along with their font and color, are defined as part of a text placeholder on the slide master. However, once they are defined, you can control whether or not they are displayed by selecting the text block and choosing the "Bullet marks" command from the Text menu. (You can also choose "Paragraph…" from the Text menu and select the "Show bullets" option.) If the command is checked in the menu, bullet marks will be displayed.

Alignment

Of the alignment options available in Persuasion, the two most commonly used for slide text are "Left" and "Centered." If you have long lines of text that may wrap, "Left" is the best choice; "Centered" is best for lines that don't wrap. Use "Right" under more unusual circumstances—either to line up a text block next to a graphic that borders it on the right or for columns of numeric

▼ *Figure 8.8. Alignment styles*

Formatting Text

Left-aligned text has an even border on the left but a ragged one on the right.

Right-aligned text is the opposite of left-aligned--it has an even border on the right but a ragged one on the left.

Text that is centered flows out from the middle as you type; each line is centered in the text block.

Justified text has even borders on both the left and right.

figures. Use "Justified" when you are placing text inside an object and you want it to extend to each side of the object. Figure 8.8 provides examples of alignments.

To apply an alignment style:

1. With either the pointer tool or the text tool, select the text you want to align.

2. Choose "Paragraph…" from the Text menu.

3. For "Alignment," select the alignment option you want, and then click "OK."

Text Shadow

You can apply shadows—black or colored—to your text for special effect. Keep in mind that this type of text format can be hard to read, so use it sparingly for emphasis (see Figure 8.9).

▼ *Figure 8.9. Shadowed text*

To apply text shadow:

1. With the text tool, select one or more words that you want to apply shadow to.

2. Choose "Paragraph…" from the Text menu.

3. For "Text shadow offset in inches," enter the amount of shadow you want. Positive numbers apply shadow down and to the right of the text; negative numbers apply shadow up and to the left.

4. Click "OK."

5. Choose "Shadow" from the top portion of the Text menu.

TIP

If you don't see a text shadow, check to see what color is assigned to text shadow in the color palette. Some of Persuasion's AutoTemplates have white assigned as the text shadow color. For information about changing and applying colors, see Chapter 13.

CHECK YOURSELF

Set paragraph spacing and indent specifications for a text block on a Slide.

ANSWER

If necessary, start Persuasion. Open a presentation that has some existing text, and go to a slide in Slide view that has placeholder text (other than a title). With the pointer tool, select a placeholder containing text. Eight handles should appear around the place-holder. Next, choose "Paragraph…" from the Text menu. In the "Paragraph specifications" dialog box, select settings to alter paragraph spacing and indents, and then click "OK."

Formatting Paragraphs with Tabs and Indents

Formatting Text

In addition to the heading levels in the outline that flow to slide text as indented paragraphs, you can set tabs and indents for any text on the slide just as you would in any word-processing program. If the tabs and indents are set in placeholder text, the formatting is reflected in the outline. For example, a line of text containing a decimal tab such as the following would appear in the outline the same as it does in Slide view:

Price per manufacturing unit $500.00

In order to set tabs or indents for independent or placeholder text, you must have the text tool active, an insertion point in the placeholder text or the text block, and Persuasion's text ruler displayed. (If the text ruler is not showing, choose "Text ruler" from the Text menu.) For an example of a text ruler, see Figure 8.10. Note that Persuasion sets tabs by default at half-inch intervals. You can clear them, if you want, before you set your own tabs. Table 8.2 summarizes how to set tabs and indents from the ruler.

TIP

You can adjust the upper portion of the left indent marker separately to make the indent level for the first line different from that of subsequent lines (see Figure 8.11). Once you have tabs and indents set on the slide, use Ctrl + Tab to move from tab to tab, and Tab to move from one indent level to another.

▼ *Figure 8.10. Text ruler*

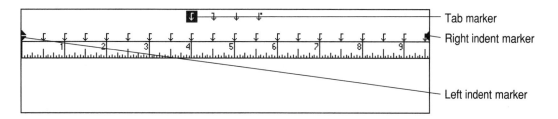

▼ *Table 8.2. Setting tabs and indents*

To accomplish this	Do this
Clear a tab	Click the tab marker you want to clear and drag it to the left, right, or bottom out of the ruler area.
Set a tab	Click the type of tab marker you want in the upper center of the text ruler, and then click where you want it in the ruler.
	The type of tab marker you choose determines the alignment of the text around the tab. Your choices are left, right, centered, and decimal (for aligning numbers around a decimal point).
Reset a tab	Click the tab marker you want to reset and drag it to its new position in the ruler.
Adjust indents	Click the left or right indent marker and drag it to where you want it.
Clear an indent	Drag its marker to the right or left edge of the ruler.

QUICK COMMAND SUMMARY

In this chapter you have learned to do these procedures using these commands:

Commands	Procedures
"Character..."	Set the font, size, and style of text
"Colors"	Display a palette in which you can set the color of text and text shadows
"Paragraph..."	Set paragraph and line spacing, letter spacing, and text alignment
"Bullet marks"	Display bullets next to text
"Shadow"	Display text shadow

▼ *Figure 8.11. Setting indents*

Indent marker set to be a hanging indent.

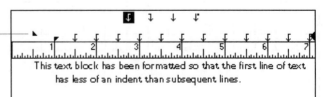

This text block has been formatted so that the first line of text has less of an indent than subsequent lines.

PRACTICE WHAT YOU'VE LEARNED

Create the slide in Figure 8.1.

ANSWER

Follow these steps:

1. If necessary, start Persuasion. Open a new presentation using a copy of OB15.AT2 (or any one of your choice), and then go to a new slide in Slide view. If necessary, choose "Text 1" from the Master menu in the lower menu bar. (The "Text 1" master contains the types of text placeholders you will need to complete this exercise.)

2. Select the text tool. (Placeholder boundaries should appear on the slide.) Click inside the title placeholder at the top of the slide, and type "Schedule of Exotic Expeditions."

3. Make sure "Bullet marks" is checked in the Text menu. Click inside the text placeholder and type the following three lines:

   Trekking: Summer
   Climbing: Early autumn
   Cycling: Summer

   As you type the text, bullets will appear in front of each line.

4. Select the pointer tool, and then select the placeholder text you just entered. Drag it further down on the slide. Refer to Figure 8.1 for approximate placement.

5. Select the text tool. Choose "Character…" from the Text menu. In the "Character specifications" dialog box, select the following settings and then click "OK":

   Font: Times New Roman PS
   Size: 18 points
   Style: Italic
   Alignment: Left

6. Click in between the title and the text placeholder, and then type "Each Tour Offered 10 Times Each Year." Select the pointer tool and adjust the placement of the independent text block to match Figure 8.1.

9

Creating and Importing Graphics

Diagrams and illustrations go a long way toward making a presentation visually appealing—even persuasive! Most of us already know the value of a well-designed graphic in a presentation but do not know how to get from a graphic idea to a fully realized illustration. This chapter cannot claim to bridge that gap, but we can present the variety of ways in which Persuasion helps you to get good-looking graphics on your slides. Your growing awareness of the design possibilities in Persuasion should nourish your own ideas for ways to illustrate your presentations and solve your individual design problems.

This chapter explains how to use Persuasion's drawing tools, palettes, and commands to do the following:

▲ **Set up your drawing environment**
▲ **Draw basic shapes**

▲ Modify and enhance objects

▲ Import images and clip art from other sources

Persuasion's Drawing Environment

You can draw in any view, except Outline view and the Slide sorter. In other words, Persuasion's palettes, the Show menu, and the Draw menu are available in Slide view, Notes view, and all the master views—Slide master, Notes master, and Handout master. To aid you in drawing and working with objects, you can display rulers, magnify the view, and use various commands to restrict drawing to the precise measurements of the Persuasion's layout grid. This section introduces you to the palettes and menu commands, and gives you tips on how to set up your drawing environment to best suit your needs.

The Show and Draw Menus

The Show menu, Draw menu, and the palettes function together. They are your means of creating and enhancing objects. Table 9.1 contains descriptions of the commands from the Show menu. From this menu you can control your drawing environment and display the various palettes. All of the commands, with the exception of the first one, are toggle commands; that is, you choose them to turn them on or off. When they are turned on, a check mark is displayed to the left of the command name.

The Draw menu contains commands that let you move, manipulate, and reshape objects. Table 9.2 defines the various commands of this menu. In practice the Draw menu is used in close conjunction with the Show menu. The objects you create with the drawing tools and edit with the commands from the Draw menu can be colored and filled in a variety of ways using the palettes from the Show menu.

▼ Table 9.1. Show Menu Commands

Command	Function
Fit in window, N% size	Displays the slide, note, master, or handout in a variety of sizes, from the whole slide visible within the Persuasion window ("Fit in window") to 400% magnification of normal size
Rulers	Displays rulers along the left side and top of the window (You can specify the type of measurement system for the rulers using the "Preferences..." command from the File menu.)
Snap to rulers	Causes objects you move or draw to be pulled toward (or snapped to) the intersections of the ruler increments
Zero lock	Locks the zero point of both rulers so that you don't inadvertently move them
Guides	Displays ruler guides that you can use to align the objects you draw or import
Snap to guides	Causes objects you move or draw to be pulled toward (or snapped to) a ruler guide
Lock guides	Locks the ruler guides in place so that you can't inadvertently move them
Toolbox	Displays Persuasion's set of drawing tools
Lines	Displays a palette of line widths and styles
Fills	Displays a palette of fill patterns
Colors	Displays a palette of colors

▼ Table 9.2. Draw menu commands

Command	Function
Bring to front	Moves an object to the front of all other objects in a stack
Bring forward	Moves an object one position forward in a stack of objects
Send to back	Moves an object to the back of all other objects in a stack
Send backward	Moves an object one position further back in a stack of objects
Group	Links several selected objects into a single object

(continued)

▼ *Table 9.2. Draw menu commands (continued)*

Command	Function
Ungroup	Breaks an object—a chart, a graphic, or a grouped object—into its individually selected parts
Regroup	Reassembles ungrouped objects
Align...	Lines up selected objects with each other or with the center of the slide—vertically, horizontally, or both
Rotate/Flip...	Moves objects in 90-degree increments in either direction and turns objects over vertically or horizontally
Element info...	Depending on the object—chart, table, or organization chart—you have selected, displays the appropriate dialog box in which you can alter its settings (For example, when you have a chart selected, "Element info..." becomes "Chart info..." and displays the "Chart info..." dialog box. This command is covered in other chapters that discuss creating charts (Chapter 10) and organization charts (Chapter 6).)
Rounded corners...	Sets the width and height of the corners on objects drawn with the rounded-corner, squared-corner, and ellipse tools
Shadow offset...	Sets the amount and direction of shadow offset for objects

Setting Tool Defaults

You can set temporary tool defaults for each drawing tool, just as you did for the text tool in Chapter 8.

To set drawing tool defaults:

Select the drawing tool you want to use from the toolbox, then choose from the other palettes (lines, fills, and colors) the line style, fill pattern, and color that you want the object to have. Anything you draw with the current drawing tool will possess the characteristics you have just selected. When you click another tool in the toolbox, the temporary tool defaults you just set will be lost.

Whenever you draw a shape or type text on the slide, it has a certain color, line weight, and fill pattern. These are the presentation defaults (usually set in the AutoTemplate), which can easily be reset. If you want to make your choices from the palettes the defaults for the presentation, choose them using the pointer tool with nothing selected. If you change your mind after you have drawn an object, you can select the object with the pointer and make different choices from the palettes. For more information about application and presentation defaults, see "Understanding Default Settings" in Chapter 12.

Persuasion's Drawing Environment

Zooming In and Out

You can magnify the display on your screen up to 400 percent by using the commands from the top of the Show menu ("Fit in window," "100% size," and so on).

Use the following keyboard shortcuts to zoom and pan the display as needed while you work:

▲ To zoom in, or magnify, the display, press Ctrl + Z repeatedly, moving from "Fit in window" by increments up to "400% size."

▲ To zoom out, or reduce, the display, press Ctrl + Shift + W, moving from "400% size" to "Fit in world" (which displays the slide as well as all of the pasteboard).

▲ To pan the display—that is, to move the slide around within the window frame—hold down Alt while you press the left mouse button. When the pointer turns into a hand, drag the hand in the direction you want the slide to move.

▲ To zoom in from "Fit in Window" to "100%," click the right mouse button on the place you want enlarged.

Using Rulers and Guides for Accurate Drawing

You can set up the drawing environment in Slide view, Notes view, or any of the master views to suit your tastes by using the commands from the Show menu. You can indicate whether you want rulers bordering the slide or an invisible background grid to work on. You can also create guides to aid in drawing and placing objects.

To set up your drawing environment:

1. Choose "Rulers" from the Show menu to display Persuasion's rulers along the top and left sides of the window. When you are working, dotted lines reflect your movements in these rulers, indicating the vertical and horizontal position of the cursor.

2. If necessary, choose "Preferences…" from the File menu and select a measurement system from the drop-down list box. You can choose from inches, decimal inches, millimeters, and picas. Click "OK."

3. If you want, reset the rulers' zero point (that is, the place on each ruler where zero occurs) by clicking where the dotted lines intersect in the top-left corner of the window and dragging the zero point to where you want it. "Zero lock" must be turned off in order to move the rulers' zero point. Once you have moved it to where you want it, be sure to select "Zero lock" to ensure that you can't move the zero point by mistake while you are working.

4. If you want, choose "Guides" from the Show menu and then drag vertical or horizontal guides from the edges of the rulers to the positions where you will be placing objects. As with "Zero lock," "Lock guides" must be turned off before you can adjust or create new guides. Be sure to select "Lock guides" when you are finished placing guides so that you can't move them while you are working.

5. If you want objects to be placed precisely on ruler increments or guides, make sure "Snap to rulers" and "Snap to guides" are checked in the Show menu.

CHECK YOURSELF

1. Open a copy of OB15.AT2 (one of Persuasion's AutoTemplates) and go to Slide view.

2. Make sure the zero point is in the upper-left corner of the slide margins and locked in place.

3. Set intersecting guides 3 inches down from the top slide margin and 2 inches in from the right slide margin.

4. Set up the window so that objects you draw or move will align perfectly to the guides.

ANSWERS

1. Choose "Open..." from the File menu, double-click "AUTOTEMP," and then double-click "OB15.AT2." Click "OK" in the "Slide setup" dialog box, and then click the slide icon in the upper-right corner to the window.

2. Notice that the zero marks in the rulers align to the upper-left corner of the slide. Choose "Zero lock" from the Show menu to lock them in place.

3. Make sure "Guides" is checked and "Lock guides" is unchecked in the Show menu. Drag a guide from the top ruler down until the dotted line in the left ruler is on the 3-inch mark. Drag a guide from the left ruler into the slide until the dotted line in the top ruler is on the 2-inch mark. Then choose "Lock guides" from the Show menu.

4. Choose "Snap to guides" from the Show menu.

Understanding and Using the Palettes

You will use Persuasion's four palettes—the toolbox, lines, fills, and colors—to accomplish most of your work on notes, slides, masters, and handouts. Each of these palettes displays in the Persuasion window in a predetermined default position, but you can drag them to the place that best suits your work habits. This section explains the contents of each palette as well as how you can use them to draw objects and apply special effects.

The Toolbox

Persuasion's toolbox contains the tools you need to add text, charts, and graphics to your slides. Typically, it is displayed by

▼ *Figure 9.1. Persuasion's toolbox*

default in any view except Outline and Slide Sorter views. If it isn't currently displayed, you can choose "Toolbox" (F9) from the Show menu. Figure 9.1 provides an illustration of the toolbox.

To use a drawing tool from the toolbox, click on the tool you want. As you move the cursor into the window, the cursor changes into a shape representative of what you use the tool for. For example, most of the drawing tools are represented by a crossbar cursor that helps you with precision drawing, whereas the text tool is represented by an I-beam (just as in Outline view). Using the crossbar cursor and the mouse, you can draw any of the shapes you see in the toolbox, plus additional shapes that become possible when you hold down the Shift key while drawing. "Creating Lines and Shapes," found later in this chapter, explains specifically how to use each tool.

The Lines Palette

The lines palette is displayed by default in the top-left corner of the window; it contains eight of the most frequently used line widths and styles. These eight lines comprise your working set, or the line styles you use most frequently. Figure 9.2 provides an illustration of the lines palette.

▼ *Figure 9.2. Persuasion's lines palette*

To apply a line style to the shape you will draw next choose that tool, then click on the style you want from the working set. To apply a line style to an object you have already drawn, select the object, and then click on the style you want from the palette. If you find that you apply line styles frequently that are not part of the default working set, you can edit the lines palette to contain the line styles you want.

Persuasion's Drawing Environment

To edit the lines palette:

1. Click "Edit..." at the bottom of the palette to expand it (see Figure 9.3).

2. In the working set, click the line you want to replace.

3. In the right side of the working set, select the style, weight, and line end you want, and then click "OK."

    Note: To close the palette and ignore the changes you made, click "Cancel."

The Fills Palette

The fills palette is displayed by default in the top center portion of the Persuasion window and has 12 fill patterns (including one called "None") as a working set. Figure 9.4 provides an illustration of the fills palette.

▼ *Figure 9.3. Expanded lines palette*

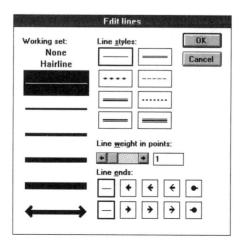

▼ *Figure 9.4. Persuasion's fills palette*

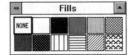

To apply a fill pattern to the shape you will draw next:

Select the tool and then click on the fill pattern you want from the working set. If you don't want the shape to be filled, click "None."

To apply a fill pattern to a shape you have already drawn:

Select that shape and then click on the fill pattern you want.

The fills palette also expands to provide additional fill patterns that you can assign. If you find that you are using some of these patterns frequently, it's more efficient to make them part of the working set so that you can work with the smaller version of the palette on the screen.

To edit the fills palette working set:

1. Click the "Maximize" button in the upper-right corner of the palette to expand it (see Figure 9.5).

2. With nothing selected on the slide, click the fill pattern in the top portion of the palette that you want to replace.

▼ *Figure 9.5. Expanded fills palette*

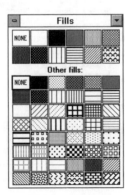

3. In the bottom of the palette—the section labeled "Other fills"—click the fill pattern you want to add to the working set.

    Persuasion replaces the fill pattern in the top portion of the palette, and then deselects it so that you don't inadvertently change it again.

4. Click the "Minimize" button in the upper-left corner of the palette to reduce it to its original size.

Persuasion's Drawing Environment

The Colors Palette

You use Persuasion's colors palette to apply colors to any text or graphic in your presentation. The palette is displayed by default in the lower-left corner of the window and contains the sixteen colors that make up the working set. Figure 9.6 provides an illustration of the colors palette.

You can set color defaults for the tools before you draw just as you would for line styles and fill patterns, or you can apply the colors after you draw the object. You can also apply color to text, portions of the text block surrounding the text, or the text shadow (if you have that style applied to the text).

To apply a color:

1. Select the tool you will be drawing with.

2. In the sample box in the lower-left corner of the colors palette, click the element of the shape you want to apply color to—such as the object's shadow.

3. Select the color you want to apply.

4. Repeat Steps 2 and 3 for each element of the object to which you want to apply color.

▼ *Figure 9.6. Persuasion's colors palette*

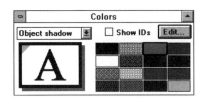

Note: If you set defaults and then don't see them when you draw the object check to make sure that you have the element in question chosen or displayed. For example, the current default for ovals might have no fill pattern. If so, you won't see the default colors you set for foreground and background fill until you choose a fill pattern.

Typically, the colors that make up your working set are pre-defined based on the AutoTemplate that you chose. However, you can modify those colors as needed. For more information on modifying the colors palette working set or defining your own color schemes, see Chapter 13.

CHECK YOURSELF

1. Open a copy of OB15.AT2 (one of Persuasion's AutoTemplates) and go to Slide view.

2. Make sure all four palettes are displayed.

3. Set up presentation defaults for all four palettes.

ANSWERS

1. Choose "Open…" from the File menu, double-click "AUTOTEMP," and then double-click "OB15.AT2." Click "OK" in the "Slide setup" dialog box, and then click the slide icon in the upper-right corner to the window.

2. Choose "Toolbox," "Lines," "Fills," and "Colors" as needed from the Show menu.

3. Select the pointer tool from the toolbox. Then, from each of the other three palettes, select the line style, fill pattern, and colors you want. (Remember, you can select each element of an object—its shadow, its fill foreground, and so on—and apply colors separately.)

Creating Lines and Shapes

The availability and types of tools may vary, but you draw with each tool in similar ways and with similar results. Likewise, using Shift while you draw gives you similar results with each of the tools.

The Basics

The following procedures provide directions for drawing basic lines and shapes.

To draw a curved or straight line:

1. Select one of these tools:

   ▲ The rule tool for a horizontal or vertical line

   ▲ The line tool for a straight line in any direction

   ▲ The arc tool for a curved line

   ▲ The freehand tool for a freeform line

2. Make sure the tool defaults you want are in effect. Check to see what is highlighted in the various palettes (use commands from the Show menu to display them, if necessary). If the defaults are not the ones you want, choose the line width, line style, and color you want from the "Lines" and "Colors" palettes. The crossbar cursor will hold these defaults until you choose a different tool.

3. Put the crossbar cursor where you want to start drawing.

4. Hold down the mouse button and drag to where you want the line to end.

   Note: You should use the rule tool to draw horizontal or vertical lines that you want to position adjacent to text or other objects; use the line tool for lines that you want to attach to other objects. Rules are placed so that they align on their edges and have square ends. Lines are placed so that they align on their centers and have rounded ends that attach smoothly to other objects.

To draw a shape:

1. Select one of these tools:

   ▲ The square-corner tool for rectangles or squares

   ▲ The rounded-corner tool for rectangles with soft corners

   ▲ The ellipse tool for egg shapes or circles

   ▲ The polygon tool for a many-sided shape

   ▲ The freehand tool for a freeform shape

2. Make sure the tool defaults you want are in effect.

   Check to see what is highlighted in the various palettes (use commands from the Show menu to display them, if necessary). If the defaults are not the ones you want, choose the line width, line style, fill pattern, and color you want. The crossbar cursor will hold these defaults until you choose a different tool.

3. Position the crossbar where you want to begin drawing.

4. Drag in any direction to:

   ▲ Form a rectangle or ellipse

   ▲ Draw any freeform shape, releasing the mouse button to fill the shape

   ▲ Start a polygon, then click to begin each new side, and double-click to end drawing the polygon

Using the Shift Key While You Draw

You can "regularize" the basic drawing shapes by holding down Shift while you draw. For instance, you can draw a circle with the ellipse tool or a line at exactly a 45-degree angle with the line tool. Whenever you draw in combination with the Shift key, you must be sure to release the mouse button first and then release Shift to achieve the desired effect.

CHECK YOURSELF

1. Open OB15.AT2 (Persuasion's AutoTemplate) and go to Slide view.

2. Draw a rectangle and a square with the same tool.

3. Draw a ellipse and a circle with the same tool.

ANSWERS

1. Choose "Open..." from the File menu, double-click "AUTOTEMP," and then double-click "OB15.AT2." Click "OK" in the "Slide setup" dialog box, and then click the slide icon in the upper-right corner of the window.

2. If necessary, choose "Toolbox" from the Show menu to display the drawing tools. Click either the square-corner or rounded-corner tool. Place the cursor anywhere on the slide, press the mouse button, and drag until you have a rectangular shape. Then, while holding down Shift, press the mouse button and drag until you have a square shape. Release the mouse button before you release Shift. (Note that no matter what direction you drag the mouse, Persuasion maintains the proportions of the square.)

3. Click the ellipse tool. Place the cursor anywhere on the slide, press the mouse button, and drag until you have an oblong shape. Then, while holding down Shift, press the mouse button and drag until you have a circular shape. Release the mouse button before you release Shift. (Note that no matter what direction you drag the mouse, Persuasion maintains the proportions of the circle.)

Modifying Objects

Objects in Persuasion can be composed of graphics, text, or a combination of both. Since you know some ways to manipulate text, this section may sound familiar because, for the most part, you treat graphics the same way. You can manipulate an object—graphics or text—in these ways:

▲ Move it on the slide

▲ Copy and paste it within that slide or to another slide

▲ Delete it

▲ Resize it

▲ Duplicate it

▲ Rotate or flip it (only graphic objects)

▲ Align it with other objects

▲ Center it on the slide vertically or horizontally

▲ Apply a shadow to it

Moving and Removing Objects

You can move an object within a slide or to another slide—or remove it altogether from any slide.

To move an object on a slide:

1. Select the object you want to move. To select more than one object, hold down Shift while you click each object.

2. Point within the selection and drag it to the location you want.

To move an object to another slide:

1. Select the object you want to copy.

2. Choose "Cut" (Shift +Del) from the Edit menu to remove the object from the slide and put it on the Clipboard. Choose "Copy" (Ctrl + Ins) from the Edit menu if you want to leave the original in place.

3. Go to the slide where you want to put the object from the Clipboard.

4. Choose "Paste" (Shift + Ins) from the Edit menu. The object appears in the middle of the slide.

   Note: You can avoid using the Clipboard altogether by dragging the objects onto the pasteboard, going to the other slide, and then dragging them onto the slide.

To remove an object from a slide:

1. Select the object you want to delete.

2. Choose "Clear" (Del) from the Edit menu. Choose "Clear" when you want to remove the object permanently or do not want to replace what is on the Clipboard; choose "Cut" when you want to temporarily move the object to the Clipboard in order to paste it elsewhere.

Changing an Object's Size, Number, and Orientation

You can resize graphic objects in the same manner that you resize text blocks, tables, or charts—by dragging a handle. You can also duplicate any type of object, but duplicating alters the identity of a chart, table, or text block: the duplicate is not longer tied to a placeholder. Rotating turns an object 90 degrees at a time, while flipping turns it over either horizontally or vertically. You can rotate or flip graphic objects, but not text.

To resize an object:

1. Select the object you want to resize.

2. Click a corner handle. As you press the mouse button, a four-headed arrow appears, indicating that you can resize in any direction. Dragging a side handle gives you a two-headed arrow, constraining your resizing to the left/right or up/down direction indicated by the arrow.

3. Drag to resize.

   Note: Press Shift while dragging to maintain the proportions of the object as you resize. Release Shift after you release the mouse button to retain the effect.

To duplicate an object:

1. Select the object you want to duplicate. This can be a text block or even placeholder text, but the duplicate of placeholder text

will not be tied to the outline. Duplicates of charts or tables are also no longer tied to their placeholders.

2. Choose "Duplicate" from the Edit menu. A copy of the selected object appears almost on top of the original (see Figure 9.7 for an example).

3. Drag the copied object to the place you want.

   Note: Be aware that a duplicated table or chart loses its tie to the data sheet.

You can use the "Duplicate" command to repeat a series of actions you take to enhance an object, as long as the object remains selected.

To duplicate a series of actions:

First duplicate an object; then apply the effects you want from the palettes and move it, resize it, or whatever. At the end, choose "Duplicate" again. Choosing "Duplicate" the second time repeats all the actions you took since the last time you chose it, as long as the object remains selected.

To rotate or flip an object:

1. Select the object you want to rotate or flip.

2. Choose "Rotate/Flip..." from the Draw menu.

3. Check "Rotate" and then the option you want to rotate the object to the right or left in increments of 90 degrees, or check "Flip" and then the option you want to flip the object horizontally or vertically.

   Note: To get rotated text, create the text as a bitmap with another application such as Windows Paint, import it, and then

---

▼ *Figure 9.7. Duplicated object slightly offset from the original*

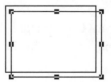

rotate it just as you would any other object. For information about importing graphics, see "Importing Graphics," found later in this chapter.

Changing the Shapes of Objects

In addition to resizing, you can change an object's shape. You can round the corners of a rectangle or square, and add or subtract sides as well as alter the angles of a polygon.

To round corners of a rectangle or square:

1. Select the object(s).
2. Choose "Rounded corners…" from the Draw menu (see Figure 9.8).
3. Select one of the corner shapes, and then click "OK."

   Note: You can round the corners of the boxes in organization charts. Shadows created by the "Object shadow…" command from the Draw menu will automatically reflect the shape of their boxes.

To reshape a polygon:

1. With the pointer tool, double-click the polygon to display its vertices.
2. To reshape the polygon, do one of the following:
   - ▲ Click anywhere on a side to add a vertex
   - ▲ Drag a vertex to move a side
   - ▲ Drag one vertex on top of another to delete a vertex

▼ *Figure 9.8. "Rounded corners" dialog box*

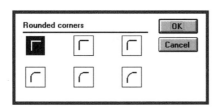

Aligning Objects

You do not have to rely on a steady hand to line objects up with each other, to the rulers, or to the center of the slide. In each case, one command can do the work for you.

To align objects:

1. Select one or more objects to be aligned. Text, charts, and tables can all be aligned with other graphic objects.

2. Choose "Align..." from the Draw menu (see Figure 9.9), and then select settings as follows:

   ▲ To align objects to the center of the slide, check "Up/down" or "Right/left," or both.

   ▲ To align objects to the rulers, click "To rulers."

   ▲ To align objects to each other, click "To each other," check "Vertical" or "Horizontal," and then click one of the following options.

   For vertical alignment:

   ▲ "Top" aligns the top handles of all selected objects.

   ▲ "Center" aligns the central side handles of all selected objects.

   ▲ "Bottom" aligns the bottom handles of all the selected objects.

▼ *Figure 9.9. "Align elements" dialog box*

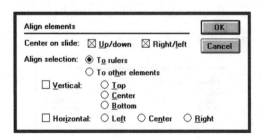

For horizontal alignment:

▲ "Left" aligns the left handles of all the selected objects.

▲ "Center" aligns the top center handles of all selected objects.

▲ "Right" aligns the right handles of all the selected objects.

3. Click "OK."

Note: If you want drawn objects to be automatically aligned to the rulers' grid, check "Snap to rulers" on the Show menu before you start drawing.

Applying Shadows to Objects

Persuasion lets you add a shadow to any object, including text. Text shadow is defined with the "Paragraph…" command on the Text menu. For more information about the "Paragraph…" command, see Chapter 8. For object shadow, you can determine which direction the shadow falls as well as how large (offset) the shadow is.

To create a shadow for an object:

1. Choose "Shadow offset…" from the Draw menu.

2. In the "Shadow offset" dialog box, check "Show object shadow" and then enter the measurements you want for the offset.

3. Click "OK."

Note: If you want the shadow to fall in a position other than down and to the right, enter negative values for one or both of the offset options.

CHECK YOURSELF

1. Open OB15.AT2 (Persuasion's AutoTemplate) and go to Slide view.

2. Draw a cross by drawing a rectangle, and then duplicating and rotating it.

ANSWERS

1. Choose "Open..." from the File menu, double-click "AUTOTEMP," and then double-click "OB15.AT2." Click "OK" in the "Slide setup" dialog box; then click the slide icon in the upper-right corner of the window.

2. If necessary, choose "Toolbox" from the Show menu to display the drawing tools. Click the square-corner tool. In the center of the slide, press the mouse button and drag until you have a rectangle that is about two inches high and one-half inch wide. Select the pointer tool and select the rectangle. Choose "Duplicate" (Ctrl + K) from the Edit menu.

   With the duplicate selected, choose "Rotate/Flip..." from the Draw menu. In the "Rotate/Flip figure" dialog box, check "Rotate." Leave "Right 90 degrees" selected, and click "OK." Add the original rectangle to the selection by clicking on it while you hold down Shift. Choose "Align..." from the Draw menu. Uncheck the options for "Center on slide" and click "To other elements." Select "Center" for both "Vertical" and "Horizontal." Then click "OK."

Importing Graphics

You can save considerable time if you are able to use graphics that are already created, such as drawings from a graphics or clip art library. Persuasion comes with a file on disk called the Art of Persuasion, which contains a collection of images chosen for their usefulness in presentations. To put one of these images or any others you may have onto a slide, you use the "Place..." command.

To import a graphic:

1. Go to the slide to which you want to import the graphic.

2. If you intend to replace an existing graphic with the imported one, select that graphic with the pointer tool.

3. Choose "Place..." (Ctrl + D) from the File menu (see Figure 9.10).

▼ *Figure 9.10. "Place' dialog box*

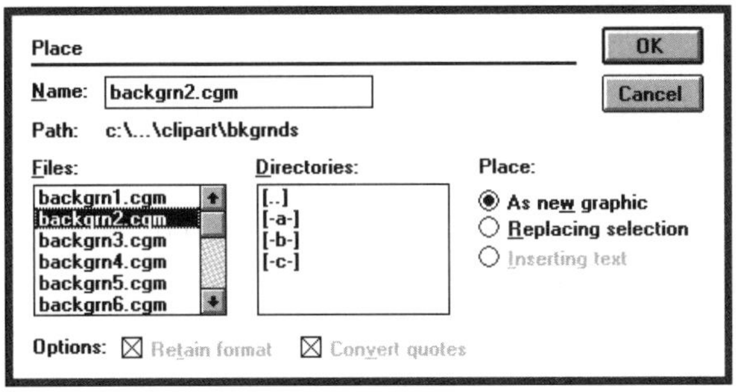

```
Place                                    [  OK  ]
Name:  backgrn2.cgm                      [ Cancel ]
Path:  c:\...\clipart\bkgrnds
Files:              Directories:    Place:
backgrn1.cgm   ▲    [..]            ● As new graphic
backgrn2.cgm   ▮    [-a-]           ○ Replacing selection
backgrn3.cgm        [-b-]           ○ Inserting text
backgrn4.cgm        [-c-]
backgrn5.cgm
backgrn6.cgm   ▼
Options:  ☒ Retain format   ☒ Convert quotes
```

4. In the list box, select the graphics file that you want to import. Alternatively, you can select an image from Persuasion's clip art collection from one of the subdirectories in the "CLIPART" directory.

5. Make sure the appropriate option is selected for "Place." If you have nothing selected, the default option is "As new graphic." If you have a graphic selected, the default is "Replacing selection."

6. Click "OK." The pointer turns into a loaded icon representing the type of graphic you are importing.

7. Click on the slide where you want the graphic to be placed. Persuasion places the graphic on the slide in its original size.

    Note: The "Place..." command uses a wide variety of graphics import filter programs that you can load when you install Persuasion. The filename extension of the file you want to import must be recognized by one of these filter programs. If it is not, the filename will not be displayed in the "Files" list box in the "Place" dialog box. If you cannot import the file you want, check to make sure you have installed the appropriate filter. (The filters you installed are listed in the "ALDUS.INI" file in the "USENGLSH" subdirectory of the "ALDUS" directory.) For more information about import filter programs, see the documentation that came with Persuasion.

    You can resize the imported graphic just as you would an object drawn with Persuasion's tools. You can also crop imported graphics.

To crop an imported graphic:

1. Select the crop tool from the toolbox.

2. Select the graphic you want to crop.

3. Click on one of the graphic's handles to trim the graphic as follows:

   ▲ To adjust one side of the frame around the graphic, click and drag the handle on that side.

   ▲ To adjust two sides of the frame at once, click and drag the corner handle between the two sides.

4. If necessary, adjust the graphic within the frame by clicking on the center of the graphic and dragging it. When you click in the center of the graphic, the pointer changes into a hand that you can then use to drag the graphic around within the frame.

CHECK YOURSELF

1. Open OB15.AT2 (one of Persuasion's AutoTemplates) and go to Slide view.

2. Import the world map from the Art of Persuasion, resize it to fill the lower portion of the slide, and then center it horizontally.

ANSWERS

1. Choose "Open..." from the File menu, double-click "AUTOTEMP," and then double-click "OB15.AT2." Click "OK" in the "Slide setup" dialog box, and then click the slide icon in the upper-right corner to the window.

2. Choose "Place..." from the File menu. In the "maps" directory under "CLIPART," double-click "FLATWRLD.CGM." When the loaded icon appears, click in the left center portion of the slide.With the world map still selected, drag the lower-right corner handle to enlarge the graphic. Choose "Align..." from the Draw menu. For "Center on slide," uncheck "Up/down" and leave checked "Right/left." Click "OK."

Grouping Objects

You often use several drawing tools to create a single illustration, yet each portion you draw is treated as a single object. For moving, resizing, or other modifications, it's advantageous to group these individual pieces together into a single unit. You can, in fact, group almost any text or graphics you've imported or added with the text or drawing tools, including the following:

▲ Text blocks created with the text tool

▲ Graphics drawn in Persuasion

▲ Imported text or graphics

You cannot, however, include any of the following in a group:

▲ Charts or tables

▲ Organization charts

▲ Placeholder text (connected to the outline)

Selecting One or More Objects

The first thing you must do to work with any object is to select it. Grouping objects requires that you make multiple selections.

To select an object or group of objects:

Click the object using the pointer tool. Hold down the Shift key while you click additional objects to add them to the selection. Handles appear around each object to indicate that it is selected. (See Figure 9.11 for an example.)

▼ *Figure 9.11. Selection of multiple objects*

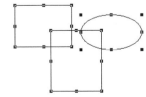

Grouping, Ungrouping, or Regrouping Objects

Grouping objects transforms them into a single selectable unit that can be moved, duplicated, or manipulated in a variety of ways.

To group objects:

Select two or more objects and choose "Group" from the Draw menu. Remember, you cannot group charts, tables, organization charts, or placeholder text.

You can combine a grouped object with other objects by using the "Group" command again, creating levels of grouping. Figure 9.12 shows objects after grouping. Note how the handles appear around the group, rather than around each object as in Figure 9.11.

To subselect an element within a group without ungrouping it:

Double-click on the element. Its own handles appear.

You can ungroup objects you previously grouped, and you can also ungroup charts, tables, organization charts, and imported graphics. However, ungrouping objects in the last category can have side effects that you don't want. For more information on ungrouping these types of objects, see "Ungrouping Charts and Imported Graphics" and "Organization Charts," found later in this chapter.

▼ *Figure 9.12. Grouped objects*

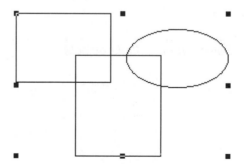

To ungroup an object:

Select it and choose "Ungroup" from the Draw menu. You can repeat the "Ungroup" command to ungroup additional levels of grouping.

To recombine the objects most recently ungrouped, choose "Regroup" from the Draw menu. You do not have to select the objects to regroup them. Persuasion automatically regroups the members of the previous group—and continues to regroup as you reissue the command until all previous levels of grouping are restored.

Ungrouping Charts and Imported Graphics

Certain objects—charts, tables, and imported Windows metafile graphics—lose their original identity when they are ungrouped. Ungrouping a chart or a table causes it to be treated as a graphic, disconnected from the outline or data sheet, and ungrouping a Windows metafile can cause its colors to map to Persuasion's color grid, thereby changing the colors in the graphic.

If you make changes to an ungrouped chart or table, the changes are not retained when you regroup it. Keep in mind that you do not need to ungroup to apply effects; you can double-click any part of a chart to subselect it for enhancement. Therefore, it is best not to ungroup a chart.

An imported Windows metafile graphic that is ungrouped is converted into Persuasion elements. Once you have ungrouped an imported metafile, you cannot use the "Regroup" command to change the graphic back into a metafile. If you want the graphic to revert to the original metafile, you must delete the ungrouped version and import the original one again.

Our best advice on ungrouping graphics is that you always try first to apply the effect you want by subselecting without ungrouping. Some effects, such as changing the shape of only one box on an organization chart level (see "Organization Charts" later in this chapter), can only be applied by ungrouping. But the potential problems caused by ungrouping can be time-consuming (and annoying) to correct, so beware.

Overlapping Objects and Layers

As you draw, each object is drawn in front of the previous one. Sometimes the most recently drawn object obscures an object you drew earlier. You can change this order without redrawing the objects in a different order. The objects you have drawn may overlap, but they are all on the same layer until you assign them a different one.

To change the order of overlapping objects:

1. Select the object you want to move. If the object is obscured by another and you are having trouble selecting it, hold down Ctrl while you click. Each time you do this, the next object down in the stack is selected.

2. Choose one of the following from the Show menu:

   ▲ "Send to front" puts the object in front of all the other objects

   ▲ "Send forward" moves the object forward one level

   ▲ "Send to back" puts the object behind all the other objects

   ▲ "Send backward" moves the object back one level

CHECK YOURSELF

1. Open OB15.AT2 (one of Persuasion's AutoTemplates) and go to Slide view.

2. Draw a square, a rectangle, and a circle, in that order, all on top of each other.

3. Put the circle between the square and the rectangle.

ANSWERS

1. Choose "Open..." from the File menu, double-click "AUTOTEMP," and then double-click "OB15.AT2." Click "OK" in the "Slide setup" dialog box, and then click the slide icon in the upper-right corner of the window.

2. If necessary, choose "Toolbox" from the Show menu to display the drawing tools. Select the square-corner tool. Draw a square and a rectangle. Then select the ellipse tool and draw a circle. (If you want the square and circle to be perfectly proportional, hold down Shift while you draw them.)

3. With the circle still selected, choose "Send backward" from the Draw menu.

Overlapping Objects and Layers

Assigning Objects to Layers

If you are drawing a graphic composed of several objects, it helps to put graphics you don't want to alter on layers other than the one you're currently working on. To avoid unintentionally moving or changing a nearby graphic, assign it to a lower layer and make that layer inactive.

Layering is useful as a drawing technique, but its primary purpose is to create slide builds for slide shows. For information on creating slide builds, see "Layering Individual Slides for Slide Builds" later in this chapter.

To assign an object to a layer:

Select the object or objects and choose a number from the Layer pop-up menu in the lower menu bar. The title of the pop-up menu then shows the active layer number on the right and the assigned layer number on the left.

To make layers visible or active:

1. Choose "Set…" from the Layer menu in the lower menu bar.

2. In the "Layer control" dialog box (shown in Figure 9.13), select the settings you want in each of the following areas:

   ▲ Drawing layer. Enter the number of the layer you want to affect in this dialog box.

   ▲ Active layers. Select the layers you want to be active. "Drawing layer only" makes the layer entered above the only active layer.

▼ *Figure 9.13. "Layer control" dialog box*

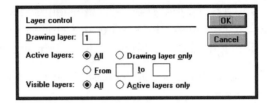

- ▲ Visible layers. Select the layers you want to be visible. Selecting "Active layers only" makes the layers you have chosen above in "Active layers" visible. (In other words, active layers will be visible, and inactive layers will be invisible.)

3. Click "OK."

CHECK YOURSELF

1. Open OB15.AT2 (one of Persuasion's AutoTemplates) and go to Slide view.

2. Draw a square, a rectangle, and a circle, in that order, all on top of each other.

3. Assign each to different successive layers.

ANSWERS

1. Choose "Open..." from the File menu, double-click "AUTOTEMP," and then double-click "OB15.AT2." Click "OK" in the "Slide setup" dialog box, and then click the slide icon in the upper-right corner of the window.

2. If necessary, choose "Toolbox" from the Show menu to display the drawing tools. Select the square-corner tool. Draw a square and a rectangle. Then select the ellipse tool and draw a circle. (If you want the square and circle to be perfectly proportional, hold down Shift while you draw them.)

3. Select the rectangle by holding down Ctrl and clicking until it is selected. Choose "2" from the Layer pop-up menu. Select the circle by clicking it, and then choose "3" from the Layer pop-up menu.

Overlapping Objects and Layers

Applying Special Effects to Objects

You can apply special effects before or after you draw an object. In fact, you can set your drawing tool to draw with certain special effects before or after you select it. For more information about setting tool and presentation defaults, see "Setting Tool Defaults," previously discussed in this chapter.

The following sections suggest some ideas for effects you can apply to various objects in Persuasion.

Text

You can use the palettes to define the bounding box of a text block in the ways listed below and illustrated in Figure 9.14.

▲ Outline the text block's borders (lines palette)
▲ Give the border a fill pattern (fills palette)
▲ Fill the text box with a background pattern (fills palette)

To apply special effects to a text box:

Select the text with the pointer tool and choose the effects and colors (for line color, fill background, or fill foreground) you want from the palettes.

▼ *Figure 9.14. Enhancing the bounding box of a text block*

Ten Years of Excellent Growth!

You can apply special effects to both independent and place-holder text. You can make enhancements to the text itself from either the palettes (text color and text shadow color) or the Text menu (font, size, style, color, alignment). For more information on using the Text menu, see Chapter 8.

Graphics

You can assign special effects to any object you draw in Persuasion. You can change the line style, fill pattern, or fill color of any tool you use to draw objects created with the square-corner, rounded-corner, ellipse, arc, freehand, and polygon tools. Experiment!

Organization Charts

The boxes and lines in an organization chart can be treated as any drawn object in Persuasion. You can change their line style and width, apply a fill pattern to the boxes, or give the boxes depth with a shadow. Initially, an organization chart appears according to the effects applied to its placeholder on the slide master. You can override those effects by making changes to the chart in Slide view. The locally applied characteristics override the ones in the placeholder.

You do not need to ungroup an organization chart to apply effects to a part of it. You can subselect any level of boxes or connecting lines in an organization chart by double-clicking it. In this way you can apply different effects and different text formats to different levels. You can also select individual boxes to apply effects by triple-clicking them. Text formats are applied by selecting the text with the text tool and choosing commands from the Text menu.

You can change the size of boxes by resizing the chart as a whole or by changing the point size of the text within the boxes. You cannot, however, resize individual boxes (within a level) without ungrouping the chart. An ungrouped organization chart becomes a set of objects and loses its dynamic link to the outline. If you change your mind and want the ungrouped organization chart to be connected to the outline, you must delete the organization chart graphics currently on the slide and change views. Persuasion will redraw the organization chart for you when you return to the slide.

Also, keep in mind that if you ungroup the organization chart and leave it on the slide, the next time you return to the slide you will have *two* organization charts: the ungrouped one that is now a set of objects and the redrawn one from the outline. To avoid having both organization charts show up, delete the text for the original in the outline after you have plotted and ungrouped it on the slide.

Applying Special Effects to Objects

If you are adding unusual special effects to an organization chart, you may find that you need to ungroup it. However, our advice is the same as for ungrouping charts, tables, and Windows metafiles: try first to apply the effect you want without ungrouping. If you must ungroup, beware of the potential ramifications.

You can use some of the commands from the Draw menu to further enhance an organization chart:

▲ Try the "Rotate/Flip" command to build the hierarchy from left to right or to invert it altogether.

▲ Use the "Rounded corners…" command to change the shape of the boxes.

▲ Choose the "Send to back" command to position an imported or drawn graphic behind the organization chart as a backdrop.

Charts and Tables

You can subselect the various parts of a chart or table by double-clicking them. Then you can apply various fill patterns, line widths and styles, and colors from the palettes, as shown in Figure 9.15.

▼ *Figure 9.15. Pie chart enhanced with fills*

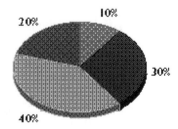

Consider the following suggestions for enhancing charts and tables:

▲ Use selections from the lines palette to enhance the lines in a line chart or the column dividers in a table.

▲ Use selections from the fills palette to enhance the pieces of a pie chart or the parts of an area chart, a column chart, or a bar chart.

Layering Individual Slides for Slide Builds

Creating slide builds is particularly useful for on-screen slide shows. Two paths are available for defining layers: You can define layers on a slide master or on an individual slide.

You may want to layer an individual slide rather than a slide master because you want different information on each layer than you can achieve on the slide master. For example, a layered organization chart is revealed layer by hierarchical layer in the slide show. You may want each box on the last level to be revealed individually and not as a group. You can do that for an individual slide using the Layer pop-up menu in the lower menu bar. For information about layering objects from the slide master, see Chapter 12.

To assign an object to a layer:

Select the object and choose a number from the Layer pop-up menu.

QUICK COMMAND SUMMARY

In this chapter you have learned to do these procedures using these commands and tools:

Commands	Procedures
Rulers, Zero lock, Snap to rulers, Guides, Snap to guides, Lock guides	Set up your drawing environment

Commands	Procedures
Toolbox	Display the toolbox so that you can draw circles, lines, squares, rectangles, polygons, and freeform objects
Lines, Fills, Colors	Display palettes so that you can apply line styles, fill patterns, and color to the objects you draw
Bring to front, Send to back, Bring forward, Send backward	Change the order of overlapping objects on a particular layer on a slide
Group, Ungroup, Regroup	Determine whether several objects are treated as one or separately
Align...	Align objects to the center of the slide or to each other
Rotate/Flip...	Rotate objects 90 degrees or flip them vertically and horizontally
Rounded corners...	Apply different corner shapes to squares, rectangles, and the boxes of an organization chart
Shadow offset...	Determine the depth of an object's shadow

PRACTICE WHAT YOU'VE LEARNED

1. Open OB15.AT2 (one of Persuasion's AutoTemplates) and go to the "Text 1" slide master.

2. Add two guides to the "Text 1" slide master: a vertical guide at 8 3/4 inches and a horizontal guide at 6 inches.

3. Import the clip art file "LITEBULB.CGM" from the "MISC" subdirectory.

4. Reduce it proportionally until it will fit in the lower-right corner between the guides and the slide margins. Use the guides to precisely position the graphic.

ANSWERS

1. Choose "Open..." from the File menu, double-click "AUTOTEMP," and then double-click "OB15.AT2." Click "OK" in the "Slide setup" dialog box. With the right mouse button, click the slide icon in the upper-right corner of the

window. Then choose "Text 1" from the pop-up menu at the bottom of the screen.

2. Make sure "Column guides" is checked and "Lock guides" is unchecked in the Show menu. Drag a column guide from the top ruler down until the dotted line in the left ruler is on the 6-inch mark. Drag a column guide from the left ruler into the slide until the dotted line in the top ruler is on the 8¾ inch mark. Then choose "Lock guides" from the Show menu.

3. Choose "Place..." from the File menu. In the "Place" dialog box, select "LITEBULB.CGM" in the "MISC" directory under "CLIPART." Click "OK." When you have a loaded icon, click in the middle of the slide to display the graphic.

4. With the graphic still selected, hold down Shift and drag one of the corner handles to reduce the size of the graphic. Then drag the graphic to the lower-right corner and position it between the guides and the corner of the slide margins.

Creating Charts and Tables

Persuasion's chart processor gives you the opportunity to prove your point visually. For instance, if your company profits have been soaring over the last five years and you've left the competition in the dust, don't *tell* your audience—*show* them with a chart like the one in Figure 10.1.

▼ *Figure 10.1. Charting your company's profits*

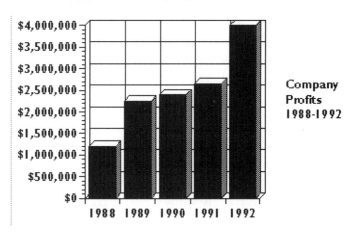

Creating effective charts and tables takes some thought and planning, but they're well worth the effort. Persuasion provides up to 10 different types of charts for illustrating your data, as well as overlay charts. In addition, you can access any of your company's spreadsheet data and plot all or a portion of it.

The first part of this chapter will introduce you to terms, concepts, and chart types, and also give you some advice for creating your own charts. If you are familiar with charts, you may want to skim this section.

The remainder of the chapter teaches you how to do the following:

▲ **Enter or import data into the data sheet**

▲ **Choose formatting options from the "Chart info" dialog box**

▲ **Create a chart with or without ties to the outline**

Overview of Charting Concepts and Terms

Creating a chart will be much easier if you're familiar with the terms used in many of Persuasion's dialog boxes. All chart processing programs use the same terms to describe the various parts of a chart, the sets of data you use to create a chart, and so on. This section explains the terms you will need to know for creating charts with Persuasion.

Axes

Most types of charts have two sets of data associated with them, and one set of data is usually dependent on the other. For example, if you are showing your company's profits over the last five years, the first set of data consists of the years 1987, 1988, 1989, 1990, and 1991; the second set of data is a list of net profit figures, for example, $1 million, $3 million, and so on. Because the graphic display of the profit figures is dependent on showing the trend over the years, the profits are said to be dependent on the years.

Chart processing programs plot these two variables, or data sets, along vertical and horizontal axes. For most chart types, the vertical axis, or *value* axis, plots the dependent data—in this case, the profits. The horizontal axis, or *category* axis, plots the independent data—the years. Column, stacked column, line, area, and high-low charts are plotted in this fashion. Bar and stacked bar charts reverse the data, plotting the dependent data along the horizontal axis.

Labels

The term *labels* refers to the values adjacent to data points in a chart. For example, you can display the percentages of each pie wedge, or the total value of a stacked column. Persuasion assumes for most chart types that you will only display labels as a special effect or for special emphasis. The values along the axes, of course, are displayed by default.

Legend

Frequently you will want to plot more than one *series* of data on a chart. For example, you may want to show sales volume for three company divisions over a period of five years. The sales volume for each company division represents a series of data. In such cases, each data series will be represented by a different shade or pattern in the chart. The chart's legend provides the key to understanding the chart by identifying each shade or pattern. Figure 10.2 shows a chart with a legend that identifies each data series with a different shade.

▼ *Figure 10.2. Column chart with legend*

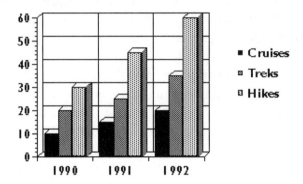

Symbols

Line, high-low, and scatter charts plot a series of data points—for instance, the average rain fall per month for a year. Each data point can be represented by a symbol such as a hollow or filled diamond. Symbols are used to visually identify the precise data point on a line, as well as to contrast one line of data with another. You can assign different symbols to each data series, much as you would use shades or patterns in a column chart. See Figure 10.3 for a line chart of the same data used in the column chart in Figure 10.2.

▼ *Figure 10.3. Line chart*

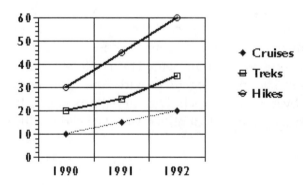

Choosing the Appropriate Chart Type

Once you've decided to prove your point in a chart, the obvious question is, "Which chart type is best?" Each chart type available in Persuasion is designed to display information in a way that your audience can immediately understand. The message you are trying to communicate as well as the data you are using to communicate that message determine the type of chart you will ultimately use. In this section, we'll review each chart format and give you advice on the kind of data that best suits each chart type.

Pie Charts

One of the simplest and most effective chart types, the pie chart is used to compare parts of a whole. The pie represents 100 percent, and each wedge of the pie is made up of one data value. It is more difficult to see the exact values of each part in a pie chart compared to, say, the columns in a column chart, but the comparison of parts to a whole is much clearer (see Figure 10.4).

The most important advice we can give you for creating a pie chart is not to have too many pie wedges. Try to limit the number

▼ *Figure 10.4. Pie chart*

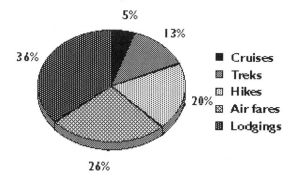

of segments to no more than eight, and five or six is better. If you have more, consider combining categories into one value for one pie chart, and then showing the breakdown of the combined categories on a second pie chart. You'll find this approach much more effective than trying to combine all of the segments in one chart. In addition, consider the following when creating your pie chart:

▲ Arrange your segments from the largest to the smallest in a clockwise fashion. (In other words, type the highest figure at the top of the column in Persuasion's data sheet, and type the descending figures below.) If you have several very small segments, combine them into a "Miscellaneous" or "Other" category and show them as one segment.

▲ Shade each segment of your pie chart to provide visual distinction between them. Use patterns that contrast well.

▲ If you have several series of data that you would like to show in a pie chart, create a pie chart for each (since pie charts can only show one series of data). Plot the data series logically, so that the pie charts lead to a conclusion based on the order in which they are presented. Each pie chart in the series of charts should be the same size; text for labels or legends should be formatted consistently across all the charts. Arrange the pie charts so that the space between them is approximately one-half the diameter of the pies.

Column Charts

The column chart format (see Figure 10.5) is the easiest method for showing how the value of an item has varied over a period of time—such as your department's growth over the last 18 months, quarter by quarter. Column charts have the advantage of showing precise measurements without being as daunting to a nontechnical audience as a line or a scatter chart would be. Keep the following guidelines in mind when creating a column chart:

▲ Don't try to show more than four series in one chart, or the chart will look cluttered and be difficult to decipher.

▼ *Figure 10.5. Column chart*

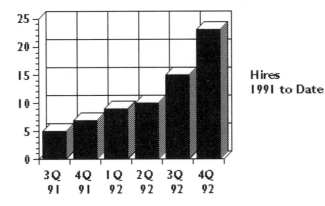

Hires
1991 to Date

Choosing the Appropriate Chart Type

▲ Select patterns carefully to contrast and differentiate series in a grouped column chart.

▲ Unless you have negative values to display, start your baseline at zero. If you have to start at a higher number because the columns would shoot off the page, do so, but tell your audience what you have done in a caption.

▲ If you have more columns than will fit across the chart reasonably, you are probably using the wrong chart format. Consider converting to a line graph. If you are adamant about illustrating your point with columns, consider a bar chart.

▲ If your column chart is crowded, stretch it horizontally as much as possible. This will insert white space between each group of columns. Hint: If you don't have enough room to stretch the chart, add an extra series of zero values to the data sheet.

Stacked Column Charts

Stacked column charts (shown in Figure 10.6) provide an alternative for grouping multiple series in a column chart. The data series are stacked on top of one another, instead of side by side. Each series can be judged based on its contribution to the whole as well. The stacked column chart combines the virtues of the column chart with those of the pie chart. Most of the advice we gave for column

▼ *Figure 10.6. Stacked column chart*

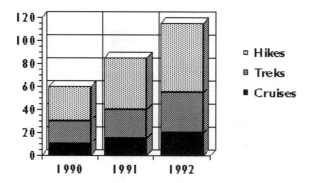

charts is also appropriate for stacked column charts. In addition, consider the following points:

▲ When plotting the series, plot the most important series on the bottom of the column. (In other words, enter the data in the first column after the label column in Persuasion's data sheet.)

▲ When shading each series, use the darkest shade on the bottom of the column, graduating up to the lightest at the top.

▲ If you want to emphasize the contribution of each series to the whole, check the "100%" option in the "Chart info" dialog box to have your data plot as parts of a whole adding up to 100%. (This dialog box is explained later in the chapter.)

Bar Charts

Whereas a column chart is used to show the variation over a period of time, a bar chart is used to compare different items at a specific point in time. For instance, if you want to show the growth of your department budget over 18 months, you would use a column chart. But if you want to compare the budgets of several departments at a specific point in time, say, at the end of the year, the bar chart is more appropriate, as shown in Figure 10.7.

▼ *Figure 10.7. Bar chart*

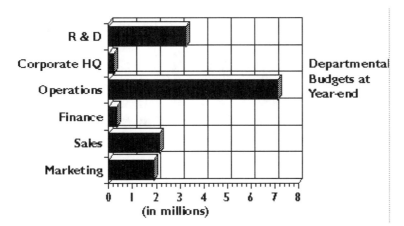

Bar charts can be used effectively to display data with larger value ranges that would cause the columns of a column chart to look too tall. And although it's relatively easy to clutter up a column chart with too many columns, you can have as many bars in a bar chart as you can fit on the slide. You should design bar charts as you would column charts; the advice we gave earlier applies. The following are a few more tips:

▲ Consider placing additional labels at the right end of each bar, identifying the exact value of the bar.

▲ Invert a bar chart using the "Rotate/Flip" command from the Draw menu so that the horizontal axis is at the top of the chart.

▲ If you have multiple series, stack the largest series on the bottom and shade it the darkest.

Stacked Bar Charts

Apply the same judgment to using a stacked bar chart as you would to using a stacked column chart. Is it important to show the total group's percentage contribution to the whole? If so, the stacked bar chart with the "100%" option is a good alternative to displaying grouped multiple series in a bar chart (see Figure 10.8).

▼ Figure 10.8. Stacked bar chart with "100%" checked

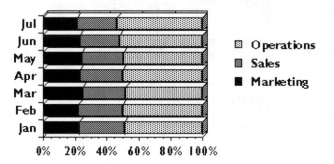

Line Charts

The purpose of a line chart is to present a large amount of information in a format that allows your audience to immediately understand a trend. The fluctuation of the line illustrates the variation in the trend, whereas the distance from the bottom of the chart indicates the quantity (see Figure 10.9).

Like a column chart, line charts indicate the change in values over a period of time. However, line charts provide a means of displaying quantities of data that would overwhelm a column chart. You can have multiple series in a line chart—each series is one

▼ Figure 10.9. Line chart

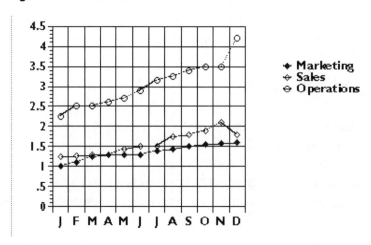

line, as shown in Figure 10.9. The intersections or gaps between those lines effectively illustrate the trends of the various series.

The one drawback to a line chart is that it can be more intimidating to a nontechnical audience. If you are planning to use a line chart with a general audience, plan the chart's design as simply as possible:

Choosing the Appropriate Chart Type

▲ Clearly identify the data points on each line with symbols such as diamonds or squares. Use a different symbol for each series or line.

▲ When plotting multiple series, use different line thicknesses or styles for each line to differentiate them. Label each line clearly, or display a legend.

▲ Be sure that you use captions that explain any information that the audience would not have the background to understand.

▲ Don't plot more than five series or lines; your chart can become too cluttered and difficult to read.

▲ If the audience is large and some distance from the chart, increase the line weight of each line for readability.

▲ If you are displaying multiple series, don't clutter up the chart by displaying the value of each data point on each line. This tactic is, however, effective if you have only one line with a reasonable number of data points.

Area Charts

If you are plotting a single data series, an area chart looks just like a line chart, except that the space below the line and above the horizontal axis is filled in. If you are plotting multiple series, the effect is the same except that the filled-in areas stack on top of each other as shown in Figure 10.10. The area chart is a good alternative to a stacked column chart if you have too much data to plot in columns.

As you might suspect, much of the advice you have been given about stacked column or bar charts and how to shade them applies to area charts. In addition, you can order the bands one of two ways:

▼ *Figure 10.10. Area chart*

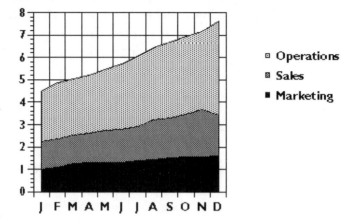

▲ By order of significance, with the largest, or most important area at the bottom of the chart.

▲ By stability, placing the band with the least variation (or most stability) at the bottom, graduating up to the least stable, most variable bands at the top, as shown in Figure 10.10.

Scatter Chart

There's always one exception to the rule, and scatter charts are it. Remember that we told you that the data for the value axis is usually dependent on the data of the category axis. For scatter charts, that's usually not true. Scatter charts are used to discover whether there *is* a relationship between two types of data, and, if so, whether that relationship is significant (see Figure 10.11). Because you are trying to judge the possible relationship between sets of data, special rules apply to the design of a scatter graph:

▲ Make sure that the horizontal and vertical axes are the same length. (For other types of charts, the vertical axis tends to be about three-fourths the length of the horizontal axis.)

▲ Show the plot frame, so that you have a visual "square" within which to judge the placement of data points.

▼ *Figure 10.11. Scatter chart*

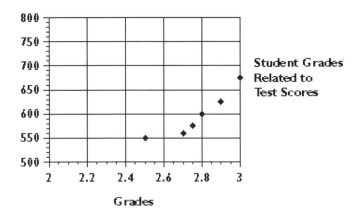

▲ Each axis should have a larger quantity of tick marks in finer increments than usual to make judgment easier; up to 15 increments is not unusual. In addition, each tick mark should be spaced far enough apart so that it is easy to identify the placement of data points on the grid.

▲ Label the tick marks on both axes clearly and specifically. In addition, use captions as needed to provide an explanation of the axes.

▲ Use different symbols to plot the data points for each series. Keep in mind that any one intersection of the horizontal and vertical axes can have two data points, one, or none. No lines are drawn between data points, so clear visual identification is mandatory.

High-Low Charts

A high-low chart is a variation of a line chart that you use to show the relationship between two sets of data over a period of time (see Figure 10.12). As the name suggests, the two sets of data are typically minimums and maximums. You plot the two sets of data, and Persuasion draws a line between them. Symbols identify the data points at each end of the line.

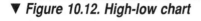

▼ *Figure 10.12. High-low chart*

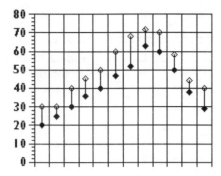

Temperature
Ranges for the
Year 1992

Tables

Persuasion considers tables to be a type of chart, primarily because the data for them is entered in Persuasion's data sheet. You can create tables from any number of rows and columns of text or numbers entered in the data sheet. You plot them just as you would a chart, choosing the chart type to be "Table." However, the similarity ends here. Category and value axes, symbols, and legends have no meaning in tables. Furthermore, tables can be edited on slides in more ways than charts in Persuasion, including moving the column boundaries and changing the data.

Some Final Advice

Now that you have been exposed to some general terms and concepts, as well as the types of charts from which you can choose to make your statement, consider the following when you get ready to create your chart:

▲ Remember that some chart types are far more exotic, and therefore more intimidating, than others. If your audience is being exposed to information for the first time and has little expertise in the subjects you are discussing, stick to pie, column, and bar charts. Scatter and line charts, as well as the more unusual designs of the bar and column charts, are for more sophisticated audiences.

▲ Use simple measurements, such as whole numbers or some multiple of 5 or 10 for the values on your axes. If possible, start from zero.

▲ Use labels and captions sparingly and only when necessary. Since your chart must be read from a distance, the less text cluttering up the space, the better. Try to put as much meaning as you can into as few words as possible.

▲ Don't use captions for the category axis when the values are self-evident, such as years.

▲ Conversely, don't leave out any information because it is included in the slide text. A chart should stand on its own and be completely self-explanatory.

▲ Leave enough white space around your chart to set it off visually on the slide. Don't crowd it with slide text.

▲ If you have more than one chart on more than one slide in your presentation, be consistent in your formatting. Use the same font and point size for text, the same series of patterns or shades from one chart to the next, and so on.

▲ Try to balance the elements on your slide effectively. Use slide text sparingly, and arrange both the slide text and chart under the slide title. Leave plenty of white space around each element.

Choosing the Appropriate Chart Type

Persuasion's AutoTemplates provide good models for arranging charts on slides: each AutoTemplate has one master (Graphic 1) that contains slide title and chart placeholders, as well as another master (Graphic 2) designed to contain a title placeholder, a text placeholder, and a chart placeholder. Look to these masters for guidance in your design.

Overview of Persuasion's Chart Processor

When you create charts and tables in Persuasion, you can work in either Outline view or Slide view, using the data sheet to enter data and the "Chart info" dialog box to design your chart.

In general, to create a chart, follow these steps:

▲ Decide what information you want to chart and the type of chart you want to use.

▲ From Outline view, create a chart outline unit and click the data sheet icon in the margin. Alternatively, from Slide view, select the chart tool from the toolbox, and double-click either inside a chart placeholder or anywhere else on the slide.

Note: You can create placeholder or independent charts, just as you can create placeholder or independent text. Placeholder charts are formatted by chart placeholders on the slide master and dynamically linked to the outline. Independent charts are formatted entirely by the values you enter in the "Chart info…" dialog box and are not linked to the outline. Placeholder charts have the advantage of already being formatted—you may be satisfied with how they look and not need to modify their formats at all. Independent charts, on the other hand, can be created anywhere except in the outline—on slides, notes, hand-outs, or masters. To create a placeholder chart, click inside the chart placeholder boundaries on the slide. To create an inde-pendent chart, simply drag-select the size you want with the chart tool anywhere on the slide (outside the chart placeholder boundaries), note, handout, or master.

▲ Enter or import data into the data sheet.

▲ Select options from the "Chart info" dialog box to format your chart, and click "OK." Otherwise you can rely on a chart placeholder from an AutoTemplate slide master (Graphic 1 or Graphic 2) to format the chart for you.

As with text, you can create placeholder charts in Slide view that are connected to your outline; independent charts, created outside of a chart placeholder, are not. You can also create charts directly from Outline view. For more information about creating charts in Outline view, see Chapter 6.

TIP

You create a table in Persuasion just as you do a chart. It is simply one of the chart formats you choose in the "Chart info" dialog box (explained later in this section). To practice creating a table, see Chapter 11.

Persuasion's Data Sheet

In essence, Persuasion's data sheet provides a work area that looks very similar to any other spreadsheet application. It consists of a series of rows and columns into which you can enter or import data using the standard data entry methods for spreadsheets. Each chart has its own data sheet.

Typically, each column in the data sheet represents a series of data. For example, three columns of data could be plotted as a column chart as shown in Figure 10.13. Unless you have specified otherwise with the "Switch axes" option in the "Chart info" dialog box, you should enter series labels in the first column of the data that you will use for the chart or table. Category labels should be entered in the first row. You can enter data from scratch or import data from an external file such as a spreadsheet. Table data is entered much the same as data for charts.

▼ *Figure 10.13. Three series for a column chart*

Categories —

Series —

	A	B	C	D	E	F
1		1990	1991	1992		
2	Cruises	10	15	20		
3	Treks	20	25	35		
4	Hikes	30	45	60		
5						
6						
7						
8						
9						
10						

This is the Chart Title

A1

To enter data from scratch into the data sheet:

1. In Slide view, select the chart tool from the Toolbox and double-click on the slide. Persuasion displays the data sheet and, in back, the "Chart info" dialog box (see Figure 10.16). If you want the chart you create to be a placeholder chart (tied to the outline), you must have a slide master assigned that contains a chart placeholder. "Graphic 1" and "Graphic 2" masters in Persuasion AutoTemplates contain chart placeholders.

2. In the data sheet, drag-select the group of cells you need to enter your data. For example, if you intend to enter three series of five values, you should drag-select cells A,1 through C,5 (or C,6 if you intend to enter a row of labels across the top). If you need to, enlarge the data sheet window by maximizing it (clicking the Maximize button in the upper-right corner). Each cell can hold up to 255 characters, and the data sheet can hold 256 rows by 256 columns of information.

3. Starting in cell A,1 and entering one column at a time, enter your data, pressing Enter to move from cell to cell.

TIP

If you are entering data that is wider than the default amount of space provided for each cell, click on the column boundary next to the column heading and drag to widen the column. To widen several columns at once, hold down Shift and click in the top area of each column you want to widen (where the letter is), and then drag one of the column boundaries to the width you want. (Persuasion accepts the information whether or not you widen the boundary, but it's easier to work with what you can see.)

Table 10.1 illustrates a variety of helpful ways in which you can select cells within the data sheet.

Once you have a selection of cells, you can enter your data row by row, from left to right, using Tab, or, as we described previously, column by column, using Enter. To reverse your direction, use Shift + Tab or Shift + Enter, respectively.

▼ *Table 10.1. Selecting cells in the data sheet*

To select this option	Do this
A group of cells spanning multiple rows or columns	Click in the top-left corner of the group you want to select, and, while holding down the mouse button, drag to the bottom-right corner of the group.
One row or one column	Click the row of column heading.
Multiple rows or columns	Hold down Shift and click each row or column heading.
The entire area of the data sheet that contains data	Choose "Select all" from the Edit menu.
All the data in the data sheet	Click in the upper-left blank box that separates the row numbers and column letters.

CHECK YOURSELF

1. Open a data sheet for a chart from Slide view.

2. Enter the following data, exactly as shown in this table:

	Sales $	Expense $
Q 1	100,000	75,000
Q 2	130,000	90,000
Q 3	100,000	150,000
Q 4	250,000	100,000

ANSWERS

1. If necessary, choose "Toolbox" from the Show menu to display the drawing tools. Select the chart tool and double-click on the slide to display the data sheet.

2. Click on the cell in the upper-left corner of the data sheet and, while holding down the mouse button, drag to cell C,5. Starting with the upper-left cell, enter the data, either row by row or column by column. Of you are entering data by rows, use the Tab key to move from one cell to the next. If you are entering data by columns, use Enter.

Enter versus Edit Mode

The last procedure showed you how to enter data from scratch in *Enter mode*. Enter mode is the mode that the data sheet is in when the cursor is active in a cell. You may have noticed that whatever you entered was reflected in the text box at the top of the data sheet. If you had made a mistake, you could have corrected it by clicking an insertion point in the text box and editing what you had typed. This is called *Edit mode*. These modes are the same as what you are used to working with in most spreadsheet applications.

Here are two tips to help you understand what mode you are in (although, for the most part, the data sheet functions intuitively and you will find that you can ignore what mode you are in):

▲ When the cursor is a cross and a cell is highlighted, you are in Enter mode. (The corresponding cursor that reflects your entries in the text box is a solid rectangle.)

▲ When the cursor is an I-beam in the text box, you are in Edit mode.

CHECK YOURSELF

In the data sheet you created in the last exercise, change the Q 4 sales figure to 275,000.

ANSWER

Click cell B,5. Drag to select 250,000, and then type 275,000.

Data Sheet Keyboard Actions

Persuasion utilizes the keyboard actions that you are accustomed to in the data sheet. Table 10.2 summarizes the key action for Enter mode (working in a cell).

Table 10.3 describes the keyboard actions that you can use in Edit mode (inside the text box).

▼ *Table 10.2. Keyboard shortcuts for data sheet enter mode*

Key	Action
Enter	Accepts what you typed in the cell
Esc	Cancels what you typed in the cell
Tab or Right arrow	Moves the cursor to the right one cell
Left arrow	Moves the cursor to the left one cell
Down arrow	Moves the cursor down one cell
Up arrow	Moves the cursor up one cell
Home	Moves the cursor to the cell in the first column of the same row
End	Moves the cursor to the cell in the last column containing data in the same row
Ctrl + Home	Moves the cursor to the top-left cell in the data sheet
Pg Up and Pg Dn	Moves the cursor up or down the data sheet by one data sheet page
Ctrl + Pg Up or Pg Dn	Moves the cursor horizontally in the data sheet by one data sheet page

Overview of Persuasion's Chart Processor

Importing Data

Persuasion accepts data imported in either spreadsheet file format or text-only tab-delimited file format (from word-processing programs). Text or data that is delimited with tabs is divided into columns and rows of the data sheet accordingly. Each paragraph represents a row, and each delimited section of data or text represents a cell's worth of data.

▼ *Table 10.3. Keyboard shortcuts for data sheet edit mode*

Key	Action
Enter	Accepts your changes
Esc	Cancels the changes you made
Left arrow or Right arrow	Moves the cursor one character at a time left or right
Home	Moves the cursor to the beginning of the text box
End	Moves the cursor to the end of the data in the text box

TIP

If you are working with a spreadsheet that saves data in a text-only file, make sure that the delimiters are tabs, not commas or spaces. If they are not, use a word-processing application such as Word for Windows or Windows Write to change the delimiters to tabs.

To import to the data sheet:

1. Click an insertion point in the data sheet, or select any existing data you want to replace. Make sure you have enough room for the data you intend to import. Persuasion will overwrite data if necessary.

2. Choose "Place…" from the File menu.

3. In the "Place…" dialog box, select the name of the file you want to import from the "Files" list box.

4. For "Place…," make sure the option you want is selected.

5. Click "OK."

The "Chart info…" Dialog Box

For the most part, you can create charts already formatted for you by using Persuasion's AutoTemplates. Each AutoTemplate contains two masters that have predefined chart formats. In fact, these masters are a good place to start when you need ideas for formatting your own charts. However, if you want to modify a chart formatted by an AutoTemplate or create chart formats of your own, you must understand the contents of the "Chart info…" dialog box. Figure 10.14 provides an illustration of the "Chart info" dialog box. You can display the "Chart info" dialog box in a number of ways:

▲ By selecting a chart unit in the outline and choosing "Chart info…" from the Outline menu

▲ By selecting a chart or table with the pointer tool on a slide and choosing "Chart info…" from the Draw menu

▲ By holding down Ctrl and double-clicking on a chart or table with the pointer tool

Overview of Persuasion's Chart Processor

▼ Figure 10.14. "Chart info" dialog box

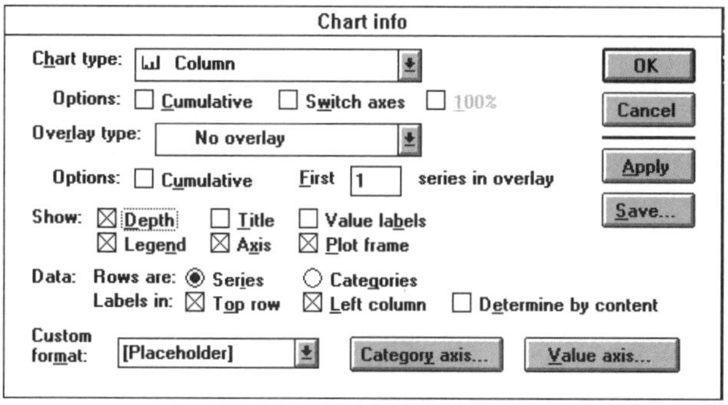

- ▲ By double-clicking on an existing chart in Slide view with the chart tool
- ▲ By clicking on the data sheet icon for a chart unit in Outline view

All options display both the data sheet and the "Chart info…" dialog box for the chart or table. If you have not yet entered data in the data sheet, it will be displayed in front of the dialog box. You can bring the dialog box in front of the data sheet by clicking on it.

The "Chart info…" dialog box contains many formatting options, some of which have their own dialog boxes that you get to by clicking a button. Table 10.4 describes how you can use the options in the dialog box to format your charts and tables. The secondary dialog boxes are described in tables that follow.

▼ Table 10.4. "Chart info" dialog box options

Option	***Description***
Chart type	A drop-down list box from which you can choose one of ten standard chart types, including "Table" (Use this to select the type of chart you want, unless you want to use a custom format.)
Options (for Chart type)	Three options that you can use to affect how your data is plotted (Depending on what chart type you have chosen, one or more of these options may be dimmed.)

(continued)

▼ *Table 10.4. "Chart info" dialog box options (continued)*

Option	Description
	Check "Cumulative" to plot your data as the sum of the values; check "Switch axes" to swap the axes on which the data and series are plotted; and check "100%" to have your data plotted as parts of a whole, the sum of which is 100%.
Overlay type	A drop-down list box from which you can choose the type of chart you want for an *overlay* chart (Persuasion lets you plot a portion of your data as a different chart type, which is overlaid on top of the other chart.)
Options (for Overlay type)	Two options that you can use to determine the content of the overlay chart (Check "Cumulative" if you want the data to be plotted as the sum of the values you entered. In the text box, enter the number of series from your data that you want plotted as the overlay chart.)
Show	A list of options that you check to affect how your chart is displayed (For example, you may want to show a grid behind a scatter chart.)
	Check "Depth" to give your chart a three-dimensional effect; "Title" to display the title you typed in the outline chart unit; "Value labels" to display the values of each data point plotted on the chart; "Legend" to display a key to each series in the chart; "Axis" to display the chart axes; and "Plot frame" to display the grid upon which the data is plotted.
Data, Rows are:	Two options that affect how your data is plotted (Select the appropriate one to tell Persuasion whether you entered your data series in rows or columns.)
Data, Labels in:	Two options that affect how your data is plotted (Select the appropriate one to tell Persuasion whether you entered your labels in the top row or the left column of the data sheet, or whether you want Persuasion to make its own determination based upon the content of the data sheet. For example, if all of your cells contain numbers except the left column, which contains words, Persuasion will choose the words automatically as labels.)

Overview of Persuasion's Chart Processor

▼ Table 10.4. "Chart info" dialog box options (continued)

Option	Description
Custom format	A drop-down list box of any custom chart formats that are available (All Persuasion AutoTemplates contain custom formats that you can choose. In addition, you can create your own using the "Save..." button.)
Category axis...	A secondary dialog box in which you format the category axis of your chart
Value axis...	A secondary dialog box in which you format the value axis of your chart
Apply	A button you can click to redraw the chart with the changes you have made (When you click "Apply," Persuasion redraws the chart without replotting the data from the data sheet. Any changes you made in the data sheet would not be reflected. To replot the data as well, click "OK.")
Save...	A secondary dialog box in which you can save the current settings as a custom chart format

"Category axis" and "Value axis" Dialog Boxes

The "Category axis" and "Value axis" dialog boxes are identical—one for formatting each axis of the chart. Figure 10.15 provides an illustration of the "Category axis" dialog box, and Table 10.5 provides a description of the options you can select.

▼ Figure 10.15. "Category axis" dialog box

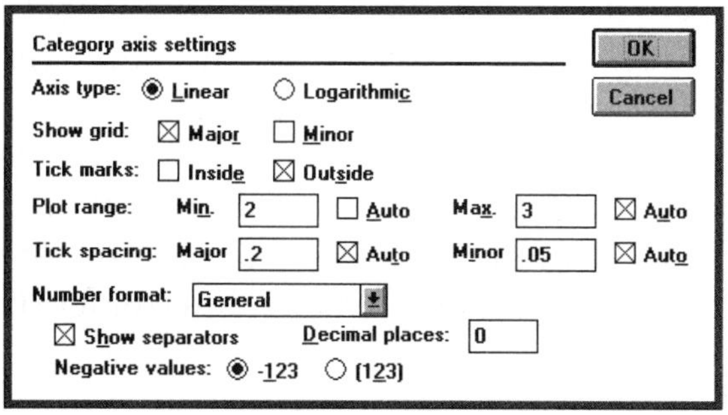

▼ *Table 10.5. "Category axis" and "Value axis" dialog box options*

Option	Description
Axis type	Two options that determine whether your data is plotted in a linear or logarithmic format
Show grid	Two options that you can use to display either major or minor intersections of the grid on which the data is plotted
Tick marks	Two options that you can use to display the axis tick marks inside or outside the plot frame
Plot range	Options that you can use to set the value range of the plotting area (If you choose "Auto," Persuasion will calculate the plot range automatically based on the chart's data.)
Tick spacing	Two options you can use to determine the spacing of tick marks, based on either major or minor increments (Checking "Auto" causes Persuasion to determine it for you.)
Number format	Options and a drop-down list box that you can use to determine that format in which numbers are displayed on the chart. (You can display numbers as they are entered in the data sheet ("General"), in scientific notation ("Scientific"), with a fixed number of decimal places ("Fixed," with the number of places entered for "Decimal places"), as percentages ("Percent"), or with the currency symbol for your country ("Currency"). Click "Show separators" to display commas as thousands separators. If you have negative values, you can display them as either preceded by a dash or enclosed in parentheses.)

"Save chart format" Dialog Box

You can save the selections you make in the "Chart info..." dialog box, as well as any special effects such as color that you apply, as a custom format with its own name. Once you have done so, the format shows up in the "Custom format" drop-down list box. You should consider doing this if you intend to use the same chart format more than once in a presentation. Custom chart formats can also be copied into other presentations. Figure 10.16 provides an illustration of the "Save chart format" dialog box. To save your chart format as a custom format, enter a name for it in the text box and then click "OK."

▼ *Figure 10.16. "Save chart format" dialog box*

Additional Formatting Options

There are three additional methods you can use to format your charts and tables:

▲ Custom chart formats, either from the current presentation or imported from another

▲ Enhancements made in Slide view

▲ Symbols for line, scatter, and high-low charts

Managing Custom Chart Formats

To rename, remove, or import chart formats from another presentation, use the "Chart formats..." command on the File menu. Figure 10.17 provides an illustration of the "Chart formats" dialog box.

To rename or remove a custom chart format:

1. Choose "Chart formats..." from the File menu.

2. In the "Rename" text box, enter the name you want the chart format to have (or, in the "Chart formats" drop-down list, choose the chart format you want to remove).

3. Click "OK."

▼ *Figure 10.17. "Chart formats" dialog box*

To copy chart formats from another presentation into the current presentation:

1. Choose "Chart formats…" from the File menu.

2. Click "Copy…." The "Copy chart formats" dialog box appears (see Figure 10.20).

3. In "Files" and "Directories," locate and double-click on the presentation filename that contains the chart formats you want to copy.

4. In "Chart format," select the format you want to copy. To select more than one format, hold down Shift while you click on format names.

5. If the chart formats you want have the same names as the ones already existing in your presentation, click either "Replace" to replace the formats with the new ones or "Append" to add the new formats with similar but altered names. If you are copying chart formats from one Persuasion AutoTemplate to another, they may very well have identical names. To ensure that you don't delete chart formats, you should use the "Append" option.

6. Click "OK."

CHECK YOURSELF

1. Open the Persuasion AutoTemplate OB15.AT2.

2. Add to its custom chart formats the one for pie charts from AutoTemplate OB20.AT2.

ANSWERS

1. Choose "Open…" from the File menu, double-click "AUTOTEMP," and then double-click "OB15.AT2." Click "OK" in the "Slide setup" dialog box.

2. Choose "Chart formats…" from the File menu. In the "Chart formats" dialog box, click "Copy…." In the "Copy chart formats" dialog box, click on "OB20.AT2" in the directory "AUTOTEMP." For "Chart formats," select "Pie Format."

Leave "Append" selected (although you aren't importing a duplicate name, in this case), and then click "OK." Click "OK" again in the "Chart formats" dialog box.

Modifying a Chart or Table on the Slide

You can edit the text in a chart or table as well as modify the look of chart and table parts directly on the slide. To do this, you must select the text or part you want to modify. Selection methods are explained in Table 10.6.

Once you have selected the part of the chart or table you want to edit, you can do the following:

▲ Move or resize a chart or table

▲ Move a legend or a piece of a pie chart

▲ Edit and format labels

▲ Edit text or data in a table

▲ Change a color or fill pattern

The methods you use to accomplish these tasks are the same as those you use for working with text and graphics. For more information, see Chapters 8 and 9.

Tables differ slightly from charts in that you can more extensively edit their data directly on the slide. Any changes you make will be reflected in the data sheet. Use the following methods to modify a table directly on the slide:

▲ To resize the width of a table column, drag the column boundary to where you want it.

▼ **Table 10.6. Methods for selecting portions of a chart or table**

To Select This:	*Do This with the Pointer Tool:*
The entire chart or table	Click once anywhere within the chart or table.
A portion of the chart or table	Double-click the portion you want.
A portion of an already selected part	Double-click that portion.

▲ To edit text or data in a table, select the text tool, click an insertion point or select some text, and then enter text or edit the selection.

TIP

Once you have edited text in a table, you may have to force Persuasion to redraw the slide (by going to another slide and coming back) before the format of the table will adjust to fit the new amount of text.

Defining Symbols for Scatter, Line, and High-Low Charts

Persuasion has a variety of symbols that you can select to identify the data point values for scatter, line, and high-low charts. The symbols are plotted on the chart grid to represent the data values in each series.

To choose a symbol for a data series:

1. Select the data series in the chart.

2. Choose "Symbols…" from the Draw menu.

3. Select the icon for the symbol you want to use, and then click "OK."

QUICK COMMAND SUMMARY

In this chapter, you have used these commands to accomplish these procedures:

Command/Function	*Procedure*
Data sheet	To enter data for a chart or table
"Place…"	To import data into the data sheet
"Chart info…"	To format a chart or table
"Chart formats…"	To rename, remove, or copy custom chart formats
"Symbols…"	To format the symbols for line, scatter, or high-low charts

PRACTICE WHAT YOU'VE LEARNED

Now that you know how to enter your data and format your chart, we will walk you through procedures for creating simple placeholder and independent charts. For each of these charts we will use the data from an earlier exercise. In both cases, we will use a bar chart format. For more practice on creating charts and tables, see the tutorials in Chapters 7 and 11.

1. Create a placeholder bar chart from Slide view, using a Persuasion AutoTemplate and the data in the table below.

	Sales $	Expense $
Q 1	100,000	75,000
Q 2	130,000	90,000
Q 3	100,000	150,000
Q 4	250,000	100,000

2. Create the same chart from Exercise 1 as an independent chart.

ANSWERS

1. Perform the following steps:

a. Choose "Open…" from the File menu, double-click "AUTOTEMP," and then double-click "OB15.AT2." Click "OK" in the "Slide setup" dialog box. Go to Slide view of the first slide by clicking its number in the left margin in Outline view.

b. To reassign the slide to a slide master that has a chart place-holder, choose "Graphic 1" from the Master pop-up menu at the bottom of the window.

c. If necessary, choose "Toolbox" from the Show menu to display the drawing tools. Select the chart tool and click inside the dotted boundaries of the chart placeholder.

d. In the data sheet, drag-select from cell A,1 to cell C,5. Type in the data from the table above, using either Enter or Tab to move from one cell to another.

e. Click in the "Chart info…" dialog box to bring it in front of the data sheet. If necessary, drag the title bar of the dialog box until you can see the entire box on the screen.

f. Verify that you have the following options selected:

Chart type	"Column"
Options	none checked
Overlay type	"No overlay"
Show	Depth, Legend, Axis, Plot frame; the rest unchecked
Data, Rows are	"Categories"
Data, Labels in	"Determine by content"
Custom format	"[placeholder]"

g. Click "OK" in the "Chart info..." dialog box.

2. The steps are the same, except there is no need to have a slide master containing a chart placeholder assigned to the slide. Once you select the chart tool in Step 3, make sure you click outside any existing chart placeholder boundaries. You also need to drag-select the area that represents the size you want the chart to be. Otherwise, Persuasion will by default draw the chart at a very small size.

Tutorial: An Enhanced Presentation with Graphics

As the sales manager at Exotic Expeditions, a company focusing on customized tours for the active traveler, your task is to prepare your sales staff to sell Exotic Expeditions' new package of tours for the coming year. You want them to understand the offerings fully, and you want them to be enthusiastic in their sales presentations to the public.

You decide to prepare a short presentation to introduce the new season to them. In addition to a description of the various tours, you want to impress upon the sales staff what makes Exotic Expeditions special. You also want to motivate them by making them feel part of this young, growing company and giving them some sales incentives. Showing the growth of the company since its inception four years ago is best accomplished in a chart, while a table clearly communicates the information about the various categories of bonuses.

Because your sales staff is small, you decide to give the presentation by running "Slide show" on your PC on the conference table at which the sales group is seated. In addition, you want to put a summary of what you've said in their hands, so you'll print handouts for them that contain miniatures of all the slides in your presentation.

This tutorial will take approximately one and a half hours to complete. Much of the work you will do will be from Slide view rather than Outline view. We present it in a flexible format so that you can cut tasks to save time or take extra time to experiment with the Persuasion features that are covered. From the eight steps to creating a presentation, you will be concentrating on learning Steps 4 through 6.

Starting Your Sales Presentation

You learned how to create a presentation using an AutoTemplate in Chapter 7. Let's begin this presentation in the same way: First open an AutoTemplate, and then type in the text of your presentation. To illustrate this presentation, which contains graphics, a chart, and a table, we'll choose a rather simple design, AutoTemplate OB15.AT2. Feel free to choose a different AutoTemplate—one in color, if you want.

Open the AutoTemplate

Open the AutoTemplate by choosing "Open…" from the File menu by double-clicking the directory "AUTOTEMP" and then double-clicking the AutoTemplate's filename. Alternatively, you can preview several AutoTemplates in the "Open" dialog box by checking "Show thumbnail" and then clicking on the names you want. Click "OK" in the "Slide setup" dialog box.

Name and Save Your Presentation

Once you have opened the AutoTemplate you want to use, save it under a new name, using "Save as…" from the File menu. (Review Chapter 7 if you need more help.)

Type the Outline

Because there is a fair amount of text on the slides for this presentation, we will still start by entering the outline from Outline view. (It is possible to enter all of the text in Slide view, but not as efficient.) The majority of the tutorial, however, will be done from Slide view.

You can enter the complete outline to reproduce the entire presentation, or you can abridge it to save time. At the very least, be sure to enter all the slide titles and some of the text—for example, up to the colons in the bulleted lists. The outline is divided into three parts and tips on entering each one are given.

Here are some general steps on how to proceed, but we assume you already know the basics about entering an outline. Refer to Chapter 7 if you need to refresh your memory on entering text in the outline.

First, enter the title of the presentation—and any other notes to yourself—in the divider at the very top. These entries, of course, do not appear on the slide; they help you keep organized.

After you have typed the first slide title, enter a break (Ctrl + Enter) and the subtitle *For the Active Traveler.* Select the break and subtitle, and copy them to the Clipboard (Ctrl + Ins). As you generate the text for each slide, click a horizontal insertion point below the last text unit's icon, and then paste (Shift + Ins) the break and text from the Clipboard to save yourself some typing.

For Slide 2, type the three main headings: "Trekking," "Climbing Adventures," and "Bicycling Excursions." To turn these headings into slide titles, select them (hold down Ctrl and click their icons) and choose "Title" from the Outline menu. Type the rest of the text indented under each of these headings. (Don't forget to add the subtitle at the end of each nested slide's text, as well as at the end of Slide 2. For each of the nested slides, you'll have to select the pasted break and subtitle text, and then drag them in one level.

Persuasion pastes break text at the level from which it was copied. When you drag them in, the number of the slide in the break text should change.) The first part of your outline should look like Figure 11.1.

Slides 6, 7, and 8 are straight text as shown in Figure 11.2. Note that Slide 6 doesn't have a subtitle; also, after Slide 7, the subtitles change. Slides 9, 10, and 11 contain a chart, a table, and a map. Figure 11.3 shows the outline for these slides. Other than the title and subtitle, the content of these slides will be created in Slide view. Slide 12, however, is a summary slide containing only text.

When you have finished, take a look at your slides. You can choose "Slide sorter" from the View menu to see miniatures of your slides for a quick overview of your presentation. You may need to

▼ *Figure 11.1. Outline for Slides 1 through 5 of "Sales Presentation"*

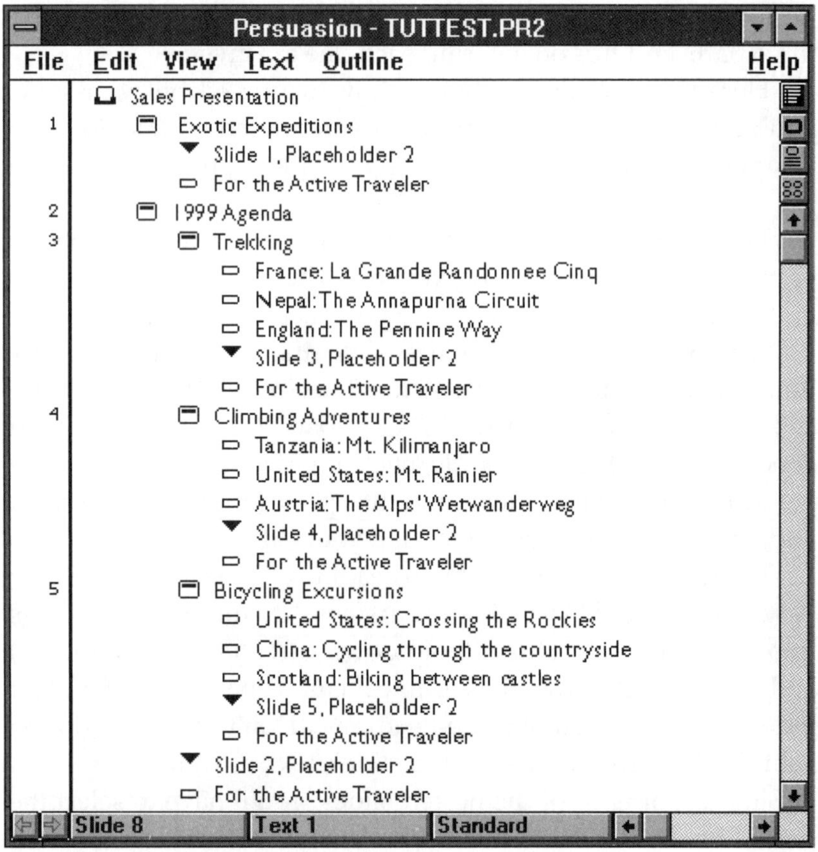

▼ *Figure 11.2. Outline for Slides 6 through 8 of "Sales Presentation"*

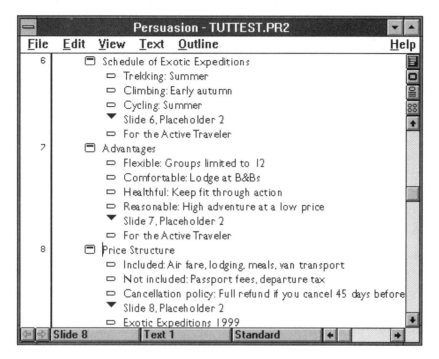

scroll in the window to see the entire presentation. Feel free to go to the Slide sorter at any time to look at several slides at once.

▼ *Figure 11.3. Outline for Slides 9 through 12 of "Sales Presentation"*

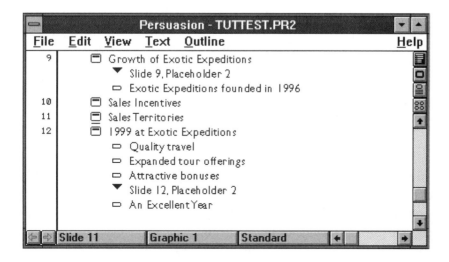

Importing and Enhancing a Graphic

Although Persuasion comes with a set of drawing tools, it also provides a drawing shortcut: clip art. This collection—as many others do—offers a number of images that add visual interest to your slides. Since Exotic Expeditions offers tours in several areas of the world, a map of the world would provide a dramatic opening for the title slide.

Before you import any clip art, do these tasks in preparation:

▲ Go to Slide 1 in Slide view.

▲ Change the slide master assignment from "Text 1" to "Title" by selecting "Title" from the middle pop-up menu in the lower menu bar. Note how the layout changes.

To import a graphic:

1. Choose "Place…" (Ctrl + D) from the File menu.

2. Locate the "CLIPART" directory. Then locate the "MAPS" subdirectory, and double-click the file "FLATWRLD.CGM". Once the file is imported, the cursor changes into a loaded icon.

3. Click to display the map in the center of the slide under the slide title.

4. Position the graphic by dragging it to a visually appealing position. If you want, hold down Shift and drag one of the handles to resize it proportionally. You can also use the "Align…" command ("Center on Slide,""Right/left" option) from the Draw menu to position the map on the slide. Your first slide will look similar to Figure 11.4.

In order to apply special effects to part of an imported graphic, you must break the graphic into selectable parts using the "Ungroup" command. An imported graphic, in fact, may consist of several groups of objects within a group. In other words, a graphic may support several levels of ungrouping.

▼ *Figure 11.4. Slide 1 for "Sales Presentation"*

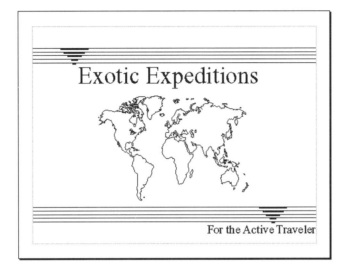

To ungroup and edit an imported graphic:

1. Select the world map on Slide 1.

2. Choose "Ungroup" from the Draw menu.

3. Subselect a part of the graphic by clicking outside the graphic and then clicking on the part you want. For example, you can subselect North America, Africa, or Europe.

4. Choose a fill pattern from the Fills palette. (If necessary, choose "Fills" from the Show menu to display the palette.) Highlight each general area that Exotic Expeditions tours by selecting it and choosing a muted fill pattern. If necessary, expand the fills palette so that you have more choices for fill patterns. Repeat this procedure until you have a map similar to the one in Figure 11.5.

Altering Slide Masters

The changes you make to a slide master are reflected in every slide to which you assign that master. The Text 1 master is already

▼ *Figure 11.5. Slide 1 enhancements*

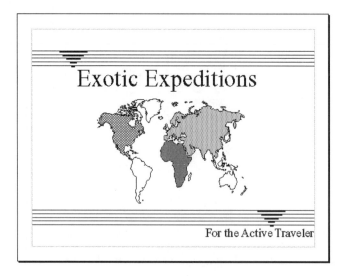

assigned to most of the slides in the presentation. Since we want all the Text 1 slides to have added graphic interest, we can add the graphic directly to the slide master.

On the Text 1 master, we want to make these changes so the master will resemble Figure 11.6:

▲ Add a small globe

▲ Change the bullets in the bulleted list

First, we want to add a small globe to the lower right corner of text slides. If we put the globe on the background master, it would appear on the title, graphic, and organization chart slide masters as well. These slides do not have room for another graphic. Thus, we'll put it only on the Text 1 master.

To import a graphic to a slide master:

1. Choose "Go to master" from the View menu, choose "Text 1" from the list of "Defined masters," and then click "OK."

2. Choose "Place…" from the File menu.

3. In the list box in the "Place" dialog box, double-click "GLOBE2.CGM" from the "MAPS" subdirectory.

▼ *Figure 11.6. Text 1 slide master*

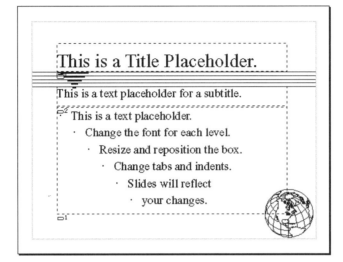

4. Click in the lower-right quadrant of the slide. Hold down Shift and drag one of the corner handles until the globe is approximately one-fourth its initial size. (Make sure you release the mouse button before you release Shift.) Then drag the graphic until it is positioned in the lower-right corner, abutting the slide margins.

To change the bullets in the text placeholder:

1. With the text placeholder selected, choose "Define bullets…" from the Master menu.

2. In the "Define bullets" dialog box, select all the bullet levels (using Shift + click), and then change the font to Gill Sans in the "Font" drop-down list box. Try other fonts. The display shows what the bullet looks like after each change. Try out combinations of fonts and colors for bullets on different levels. Or you may want to delete bullets on a single level. Experiment! Remember that if you want to eliminate bullets altogether, you can choose "Bullet marks" on the Text menu to uncheck it.

3. Click "OK." Save your work and return to Slide view to see what effect the changes on the slide master have made.

Adding a Text Block

The text you see on your slides comes from the outline and is formatted by the placeholders on the master slides. All of this text could have been added directly to the placeholders on the slides, but, for convenience, we had you use the outliner to enter it. You can also add independent text blocks to areas of the slide that are outside the placeholders. Naturally, text added in this way does not flow back to the outline.

On Slide 6, let's add a text block above the outline of the schedule to indicate how frequently each tour is offered. Before you add a text block, do these tasks in preparation:

▲ Go to Slide 6 by using the pop-up menu in the lower-left corner of the window.

▲ Spread out the title of the slide to fit on one line. Select it with the pointer tool and point on the right handle until it becomes a double-headed arrow. Then drag to the right to lengthen the text box. Release the mouse button. If the title still wraps to the second line, extend the text box even further until the text is on one line.

▲ Reposition the title by dragging it.

To add a text block:

1. Select the text tool.

2. Choose "Character..." from the Text menu.

3. In the "Character specifications" dialog box, select the text attributes you want from the various drop-down lists and check boxes. For the text block on Slide 6, the text attributes we chose are bold, italic, and 30 point Times New Roman PS.

4. Click "OK."

5. Click where you want to begin typing text (see Figure 11.7). Persuasion creates an empty text block that extends to the margin of the slide.

6. Type *Each Tour Offered 10 Times Each Year*. Slide 6 should look similar to Figure 11.7.

▼ *Figure 11.7. Slide 6 for "Sales Presentation"*

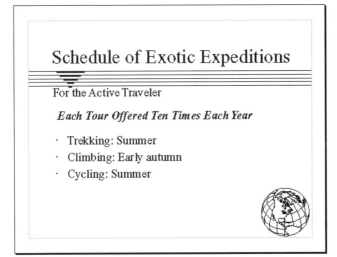

Framing Text

In Persuasion, you can easily create a frame around a text block or placeholder text without drawing at all. Let's try this on Slide 6 to emphasize the added text block, as shown in Figure 11.8.

To put a frame around placeholder text or an independent text block:

1. If necessary, go to Slide 6 and use the pointer tool to select "Each Tour Offered 10 Times Each Year."

2. Choose the third line style from the bottom in the lines palette. (If necessary, choose "Lines," F10, from the Show menu to display the palette. Then choose the command again to remove it.)

3. In the "Colors palette," select "Line color" from the drop-down list box, and then choose a gray color from the working set. (If necessary, choose "Colors," F12, from the Show menu to display the palette.) Persuasion automatically draws a frame in the chosen color and line thickness around the text.

▼ *Figure 11.8. Slide 6 with framed text*

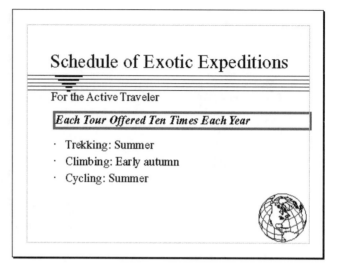

Creating a Chart

Persuasion automatically creates charts and tables for you by transforming the data you enter into each chart's data sheet. Once you have entered data, you select options such as chart type from the "Chart info" dialog box and click "OK." Persuasion draws the chart on the slide for you. Once you have created a chart, there are usually enhancements you'll want to make to it: You may want to enlarge the labels, resize and reposition the chart, or enhance the chart's components with different lines or fill patterns. Before you create a chart, perform these tasks in preparation:

▲ Go to Slide 9 using the pop-up menu in the lower-left corner of the window.

▲ Change the slide master assignment from "Text 1" to "Graphic 1" by selecting "Graphic 1" from the middle pop-up menu in the lower menu bar. The newly assigned slide master has a chart placeholder on it.

▼ *Figure 11.9. Chart of Exotic Expeditions' growth*

Creating a Chart

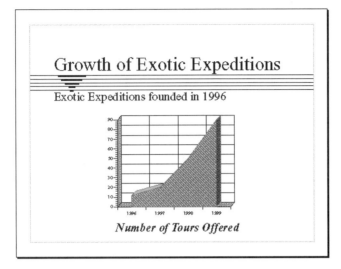

▲ Spread out the slide title, if needed, to fit on one line, as done on Slide 6.

Now you are ready to create the chart in Figure 11.9.

To create a chart:

1. Select the chart tool and click inside the placeholder boundary. The "Chart info" dialog box and the chart's data sheet appear.

2. In the data sheet, drag diagonally from the upper-left corner (cell A,1) to the lower-right corner of the area you'll need (cell B,5) to highlight it (see Figure 11.10).Selecting a portion of the

▼ *Figure 11.10. Data sheet for a chart*

data sheet confines your cursor to that area. After making an entry, you can press Enter to go to the next cell, repeating until your data is completely entered.

3. Enter your data to match the data sheet shown in Figure 11.11. Don't be concerned that you can't see all of the entry "# of Tours." You can enter more characters than will display in the default column width; if you want, you can resize the column by dragging the boundary next to the column heading to see the whole entry.

4. Click on the "Chart info" dialog box to bring it in front of the data sheet. (You may need to center the dialog box on the screen by dragging its title bar.)

5. Choose "Area" from the "Chart type" drop-down list box. Under "Show," make sure that "Depth," "Axis," and "Plot frame" are checked and the rest of the options are unchecked. The data in this chart shows the growth of Exotic Expeditions since its founding four years ago. Area charts and line charts are good choices for illustrating a trend over time. If you skipped this step and just clicked "OK" in the "Chart info" dialog box, the chart placeholder on the master slide would determine what chart type you would get.

6. Click "OK." The area chart illustrating your data appears on the slide. You may need to reposition and enlarge it. (Use the pointer tool to select it, and then, with Shift held down, drag one of the corner handles to enlarge it. Then point to the center of the chart and drag it to where you want it on the slide.) The text labels, however, are too small to read.

▼ *Figure 11.11. Chart data in data sheet*

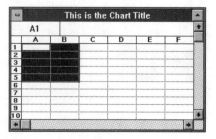

To enhance your chart:

1. Enlarge the labels on each axis by subselecting them with the pointer tool and applying a larger type size. First, double-click the labels of the chart to select them. Then choose "Character…" from the Text menu, select the point size you want, and click "OK." (We changed the point size to 12.)

2. Change the fill pattern in the area chart to one with more contrast. Double-click the filled area to select it, then choose an appropriate pattern from the "Fills" palette. Expand the palette by clicking the "Maximize" button in the upper-right corner.

You have already learned how to add a text block. Practice your skill by adding this caption in bold italic 30-point Times New Roman PS, below the chart: *Number of Tours Offered*. Center the chart on the slide using the "Align…" command from the Draw menu. Then center the caption underneath the slide.

Creating a Table

Tables let you extensively edit them on the slide in a way that charts do not. You can add information within a table and the box automatically adjusts to accommodate the new text. Furthermore, the text you add flows back to the data sheet. You can also move the column boundaries by selecting and dragging them. The information within the box is automatically reformatted to fit.

The preparatory tasks for creating a table are similar to those for the chart. Before you create a table, perform the following tasks:

▲ Go to Slide 10.

▲ Change the slide master assignment from "Text 1" to "Graphic 1" by selecting "Graphic 1" from the middle pop-up menu in the lower menu bar. The newly assigned slide master has a chart placeholder on it.

Now you are ready to create the table shown in Figure 11.12.

▼ *Figure 11.12. Table for Slide 10 (shown without fills for clarity)*

Sales Incentives

TOURS SOLD	CASH	BONUS
36 Int'l Treks	$100 or	An int'l trek
36 U.S. Climbs	$900 or	A U.S. climb
36 U.S. Cycle Trips	$800 or	A U.S. cycle trip
36 Int'l Climbs/Cycle Trips	$1200 or	An int'l climb or cycle trip

To create a table:

1. Select the chart tool and click inside the chart placeholder's boundary.

2. In the data sheet, drag diagonally to highlight the area you'll need for data entry: cell A,1 to cell C,5.

3. Using Figure 11.12, enter your data so that the data sheet looks like the highlighted data in Figure 11.13. After making an entry, press Enter to go to the next cell; repeat until your data is completely entered. Notice that you can type more in a cell than appears on the data sheet. Don't worry; all the information will appear in your table.

▼ *Figure 11.13. Table data in data sheet*

This is the Chart Title

A1	TOURS SOLD

	A	B	C	D
1	TOURS SOLD	CASH	BONUS	
2	36 Int'l Treks	$1.00 or	An int'l trek	
3	36 U.S. Climbs	$900 or	A U.S. climb	
4	36 U.S. Cycle T	$800 or	A U.S. cycle tri	
5	36 Int'l Climbs/C	$1.200 or	An int'l climb or	
6				
7				
8				
9				
10				

4. Click the "Chart info" dialog box to bring it in front of the data sheet.

5. Choose "Table" from the bottom of the "Chart type" drop-down list box.

6. For "Show," check "Depth." Make sure "Title" is unchecked, and then click "OK." The data in this table shows the incentives that Exotic Expeditions offers to its sales force. The table containing your data appears on the slide. Again, note that the text is too small to read, and the table itself is rather small.

To enhance your table:

1. With the pointer tool, resize the table by dragging a handle until the table is a more appropriate size for the space. Reposition the chart by dragging it to the middle of the open area on your slide.

2. Enlarge the text within the table by selecting the table and choosing "Character" from the Text menu. Select "18" for "Size," and then click "OK." This will change the height of your table, so you may have to play with its size and position as well.

3. Realign the data in the middle column. Select the data in the right column by double-clicking twice, and then choose "Paragraph…" from the Text menu. For "Alignment," choose "Left."

4. Boldface the text in the column headings. Select all three column headings by double-clicking, and then choose "Bold" from the Text menu. Make the categories in the left column bold as well.

Center the table from right to left on the slide using the "Align…" command from the Draw menu, and your table is finished.

Drawing on a Slide

Learning to draw on a slide takes practice and patience. We'll begin by outlining the territories assigned to each member of the sales team on a U.S. map. You may find tracing each territory difficult at first, but you can always choose "Undo" from the Edit menu and start that segment over again.

Before you draw your territories, these tasks should be performed:

▲ Go to Slide 11.

▲ Change the master assignment from "Text 1" to "Graphic 1."

▲ Import "USMAP.CGM" from the "MAPS" directory. Review the clip art import procedure detailed earlier in this chapter if necessary.

▲ Enlarge and drag the map to the center of the available area. You can use the "Align…" command from the Draw menu, if you want.

▲ Add four text blocks, one on each side of the map, and type the names of the four salespeople in 24-point Times New Roman PS (see Figure 11.14). For Lorraine Brewster's name, use Shift + Enter to break it into two lines. For Susan Weaver's name, you'll have to work around the title placeholder that is at the top of the map. Click elsewhere on the slide, type her name, select the pointer tool, and then drag her name into place. (Otherwise, Persuasion will think you are trying to add text to the title placeholder.)

▼ *Figure 11.14. U.S. sales territories of Exotic Expeditions outlined*

Now you are ready to outline each of the sales territories.

To draw on the slide:

1. Select the freehand tool. The cursor changes to a pencil when you move to the map.

2. Choose a line thickness with some substance from the "Lines" palette. Make sure "None" is selected in the "Fills" palette, and then trace the various territories on the map. Position the pencil on the perimeter of the map, and hold down the mouse button as you trace each area.

    It will be easier to trace the map lines if "Snap to rulers" (Show menu) is unchecked. Some thickness in the line style makes drawing easier because the line does not have to be as precise. However, if the line gets too thick, the map details will be obscured. Use your judgment.

3. Select the line tool. Choose a finer line style than you used for the outlining done earlier. Then draw individual lines from each name to the center of that person's territory.

Obviously, you have not used all the drawing tools in this exercise. But the best way to become adept at drawing in Persuasion is to experiment with all the drawing tools as you have time.

Changing the Organization Chart Master

Currently, you do not have an organization chart in your presentation, so you will need to enter the information in your outline and assign the Org chart master to it. Since you want the organization chart to have a list at the third level, you also need to change the current Org chart placeholder. It doesn't matter which task you do first, but your goal is to have a slide that looks like Figure 11.15.

▼ *Figure 11.15. Slide 12 organization chart*

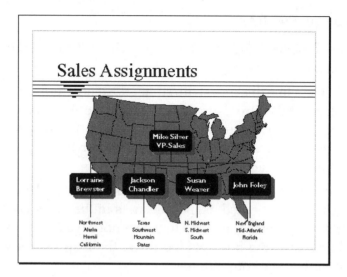

To change the organization chart placeholder:

1. Choose "Go to master" from the View menu. In the "Go to master" dialog box, choose "Org chart" from the bottom of the "Defined masters" drop-down list box, and then click "OK."

2. Select and delete the current Org chart placeholder. Also select and delete the Subtitle placeholder to give yourself more space to work with.

3. Choose "Add org. chart…" from the Master menu to display the dialog box in Figure 11.16.

4. In the "Add org chart placeholder" dialog box, specify the default number of levels (three), the default number of boxes (four), and the format of the information at the lowest level (List).

▼ *Figure 11.16. "Add org chart placeholder" dialog box*

Add org chart placeholder	OK
Default number of levels: 3	Cancel
Default number of boxes: 4	
Set lowest level as: List	

5. Click "OK." The new organization chart placeholder appears in the middle of the slide. Drag it to the location you want. Use the "Align…" command from the Draw menu, if you wish.

To create the organization chart on the slide, enter the names and territory assignments from Figure 11.17 in the outline after Slide 11. (You'll need to add a new slide with the title "Sales Assignments.") Be careful to use the same spacing as shown in Figure 11.17.

We offer some tips on entering the organization chart text:

▲ Assign the Org chart master to the slide by choosing "Org chart" from the middle pop-up menu in the lower menu bar.

▲ Type the first line of text (which will be the top box in the org chart) and then choose "Org chart" from the Outline menu.

▲ Use Shift + Enter to create a new line within an entry, such as with Mike Silver and VP—Sales.

▼ *Figure 11.17. Outline text for organization chart*

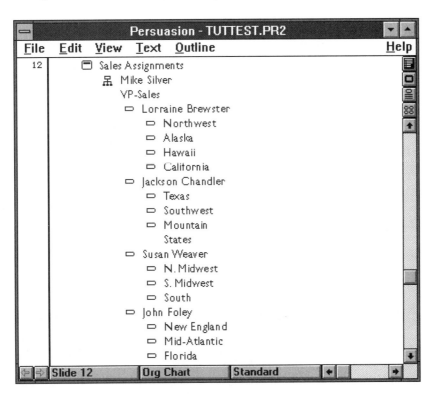

When you have finished entering your text, go to the slide to see what your organization chart looks like.

To modify the text and boxes in the organization chart:

1. Subselect (double-click) the top name box, choose "Character…" and apply these text attributes: Gill Sans, 18-points, bold, white. The text temporarily disappears against the white background.

2. While the box is still selected, do the following: Choose "Foreground color" from the drop-down list box in the colors palette, and then select black from the working set of colors. Then choose "Object shadow" from the drop-down list box and select a gray color. Now the white name appears on the black background with a gray shadow behind it.

3. Subselect the second tier of name boxes and make them look the same as the top box: Gill Sans, 14, bold, and white for the text; black fill foreground; and gray object shadow.

4. Subselect the bottom lists and make them Gill Sans, 14-points, plain, and black.

5. Select the entire organization chart and choose "Rounded corners…" from the Draw menu. In the "Rounded corners" dialog box, select right icon in the top row, and then click "OK."

6. With the organization chart selected, choose a heavier line width from the "Lines" palette. We chose the second line width from the top (not counting "None" and "Hairline"). Note how the lines connecting the boxes become slightly more pronounced and are better balanced with the darkness of the boxes.

Your organization chart is finished now—though we went on to enhance the slide with a background map of the United States.

To add a background map:

1. Choose "Place…" from the File menu.

2. In the "Place" dialog box, locate "USMAP.CGM" in the "MAPS" directory and click "OK." Then click on the slide to draw the graphic. The small map of the United States appears in the middle of your slide, on top of the organization chart.

3. Resize the map by dragging a corner handle. For proportional resizing, hold down the Shift key while you drag a handle.

4. While map is selected, choose "Ungroup" from the Draw menu. In order to change the fill, the imported graphic must be ungrouped.

5. Choose a muted gray fill from "Fills" palette.

6. Select and delete Alaska and all of the bits that make up the Hawaiian islands. (They will be in the way of the lists, otherwise.) Then choose "Regroup" from the Draw menu.

7. Now put the map behind the organization chart: With the map selected, choose "Send to back" from the Draw menu. If you need to adjust the map's size or position relative to the organization chart, you still can do so even though it's now behind the chart.

Changing the Organization Chart Master

This technique of adding a graphic and sending it to the background can be used successfully in a number of places. Keep it in mind as a way to enliven your slides.

Creating Slide Builds on the Master

The easiest way to create slide builds—that is, layered text or charts—is on the slide master. Since you'll be showing this presentation on-screen, displaying each new item of information one at a time can be more effective than displaying the whole slide at once.

To create slide builds in the organization chart and the body text placeholders on the slide master:

1. Go to the appropriate slide master (Org Chart or Text 1).

2. Select the Org chart or Text placeholder.

3. Choose "Build layers" from the Master menu. In the "Build layers" dialog box, specify which levels you want to appear

individually in the slide show. For the text placeholder, we checked "New layer for each ___ outline level" and chose "third," which should allow each level to display in succession. Check "Layer each level of org chart" to have each hierarchical level in the organization chart appear in succession during the slide show.

Applying Transition Effects

Another easy enhancement you can make for a slide show is to assign a transition effect to the way slides are displayed. The screen filling in from left to right or opening like a curtain, for example, is a transition effect. You can choose from 15 different transition effects and apply a different one to each slide in Outline view or Slide sorter view from the "Transition" pop-up menu in the lower menu bar. An effect applied locally (to an individual slide) over-rides the default global transition effect set in the "Slide show" dialog box. However, for our purposes, a global assignment from the "Slide show" dialog box is fine.

To set the transition effect default for the presentation:

1. Choose "Slide show…" from the File menu.

2. In the "Slide show" dialog box (shown in Figure 11.18), select the transition effect you want to apply to the way a slide opens from the "First layer" pop-up menu, and select the transition effect you want each subsequent layer on that slide to use from the "Other layer" pop-up menu. We chose "Wipe down" for the "First layer" and "Wipe right" for the "Other layers." These selections are now in effect for each slide that has "Standard" chosen as the local transition effect in the "Transition" pop-up Menu in Outline or Slide sorter view.

3. Check "Full screen" and "Start Persuasion in slide show." With "Start Persuasion in slide show" checked, you can automatically launch into the slide show from the Windows desktop by double-clicking the icon for this presentation in the File Manager.

▼ *Figure 11.18. "Slide show" dialog box*

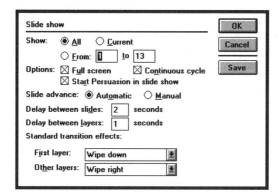

4. Select the other settings you want to save with the presentation for the slide show. We left the defaults as they were: "Automatic," 2 seconds between slides, and 1 second between layers. See Chapter 14, "Producing Your Presentation," for more information on slide shows.

5. Click "Save" to save the settings in the "Slide show" dialog box.

Finishing Your Presentation

You have now finished creating your presentation. However, before you print handouts, take a look at it by running the slide show. Choose "Slide show..." from the File menu, and let the show roll. Press Esc to stop the slide show at any time. If you are happy with what you see, you can save for the last time (Ctrl + S) and print (Ctrl + P).

Since you want slides and handouts printed, check those options in the "Print..." dialog box (see Figure 11.19) and verify that "Outline" and "Notes" are unchecked. The rest of the defaults can remain as they are. Once you click "OK," your handouts will begin printing.

Now you are ready to give your salespeople a pep talk to get them ready for the new season!

▼ *Figure 11.19. "Print" dialog box*

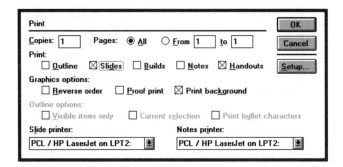

QUICK COMMAND SUMMARY

From doing this tutorial, you have experimented with a range of the special effects you can use in Persuasion. You now know how to do these procedures using these commands:

Commands/Tools	Procedures
Place...	Import graphics to both a slide and slide master
"Ungroup" and "Regroup"	Ungrouping, enhancing, and regrouping an imported graphic
"Fills" palette	Add fill patterns to parts of a graphic
Text tool	Add a text block to a slide
"Character..."	Set text attributes
"Paragraph..."	Set paragraph alignment
Lines palette	Frame a text block
Fills palette	Add fills to an imported graphic
Chart tool	Create a chart and enhance it
"Chart info..."	Apply special effects to a table; format a chart
"Add org chart..."	Change the Org chart master
Colors palette and "Rounded corners..."	Enhance an organization chart
Toolbox	Draw on a slide using Persuasion's drawing tools
"Build layers..."	Set up builds within a placeholder for items in a bulleted list and levels in an organization chart
"Slide show..."	Assign transition effects to slides and slide builds

PART IV

Creating Masters, Using Color, and Producing Your Presentation

On Your Own: Creating Masters

You can create a presentation in one of two ways:

▲ By drawing and writing directly on each slide as you go
▲ By using slide masters to give your slides a consistent design and format

If you choose the former, you'll bypass a great deal of the power of Persuasion and find yourself repeating many of the same actions from slide to slide. In that case, you do not need this chapter. If you choose the latter, you take advantage of Persuasion's unique ability to join form and content automatically, thereby saving time and avoiding inconsistency. In creating a master, you design the look of your slides once—not repeatedly.

Typing your outline into a copy of an AutoTemplate gives you a predesigned and formatted presentation. The slide masters in an AutoTemplate contain the information necessary to transform the words in the outline into a fully designed slide—a background pattern, repeated graphic elements, and instructions for formatting and placing type.

You have already learned how to create the content of a presentation—the words, the charts, and the drawings. Thus far, however, the slide masters in the AutoTemplate have been designed by someone else. Now you can take total creative control and learn how to make your own slide masters as well.

In this chapter you will learn how to do the following:

▲ **Set up your own AutoTemplate**

▲ **Create a background master**

▲ **Create a slide master and add placeholders**

▲ **Enhance your slide master with text, graphics, and other special effects**

▲ **Name and organize your masters**

▲ **Create speaker notes and handout masters**

Overview of Masters

Masters are like templates: Their design elements are copied on all the slides (or speaker notes or handouts) to which they are assigned. Although there are masters that specifically format the speaker notes page and handouts, we will first focus on creating slide masters and a background for them.

A slide master can provide two kinds of information:

▲ Format settings in the placeholder on the master

▲ Graphics or words drawn or entered on the master itself

When a master is assigned to a slide, the text from the outline flows to the slide according to the placeholder information on the master. Graphics and text from the slide masters are also transferred to the slide. Usually, however, most of the graphics and text that are repeated from slide to slide are located on the background master.

The background master can be composed of a background fill pattern, graphics, and text. It contains no placeholders—only design elements. A background master is associated with the slide masters that are in turn assigned to a slide. In this way, the characteristics of both the background and the slide master are communicated to the slide.

Overview of Masters

Master Views

The three master views correspond to the three types of masters and are available from the View menu:

▲ Slide master view (includes the background master)

▲ Notes master view

▲ Handout master view

In each of these master views, you establish the design or layout of the slides, notes, or handouts you produce. You create both slide masters and the background master in Slide master view. The Notes master lets you place a miniature of the slide on the notes page, as well as slide title, body text, and graphics. The Handout master lets you arrange the placement of the slide miniatures and slide titles on the handout and add any text or graphics you may want as static elements.

Master Menu

The Master menu, available in Slide master view and Notes master view, gives you the commands you need to create a master. These commands are described in Table 12.1.

▼ Table 12.1. Master menu commands

Command	Function
Add title	Adds a title placeholder to a slide master
Add text	Adds a body text placeholder to a slide master
Add chart...	Adds a chart placeholder to a slide master
Add org chart...	Adds an organization chart placeholder to a slide master
Add slide copy	Adds a placeholder for a miniature of your slide to the notes master
Renumber...	Renumbers placeholders consecutively on a slide master
Anchor...	Specifies the position of the text block in a title, text, chart, or organization chart placeholder
Build layers...	Designates what information will be on each subsequent layer for display in a slide show: the number of levels of body text, which axis of data on charts, or the number of levels of an organization chart
Set background...	Adds a pattern, color, or blend of colors to fill the slide master or the background master
Define bullets	Specifies the typographic characters that introduce each heading level of slide text
Define masters...	Lets you name, rename, or delete an existing slide master or create a new one

---

Quick Path to Creating a Master

Creating a master requires only a few basic steps, each of which will be elaborated on in the sections that follow:

1. Set up and name your new AutoTemplate.
2. Create a background master using the drawing tools and the "Set background..." command.
3. Create a slide master by adding placeholders that you position on the master and format.
4. Create optional enhancements:
   - ▲ Define bullet marks.
   - ▲ Add other text and graphics.

▲ Define slide builds.

5. Name the slide master using the "Define masters…" command.

Keep this outline of the basic steps in mind as you read the rest of the chapter. Pay attention to the steps you want more information on; skip the details that are not relevant to what you need to know.

Setting Up and Naming Your New AutoTemplate

You never start completely from scratch in Persuasion. At the very least, you are presented with Persuasion's original default settings when you open a new presentation or AutoTemplate. In fact, you have several possible starting points, depending on how empty or well-defined the AutoTemplate you begin with is.

Options for Starting an AutoTemplate

You can create a new AutoTemplate in either of two ways.

▲ Choose "Open…" from the File menu to open an existing presentation or AutoTemplate. You can now create a new AutoTemplate from an old AutoTemplate or presentation by saving it to a new name and modifying it. Remember to save it as an AutoTemplate if you want to get an untitled copy of it in response to the "Open…" command; save it as a presentation if you want to get the original.

▲ Choose "New" from the File menu. In the process of installing Persuasion, you had the opportunity to specify a default AutoTemplate. The AutoTemplate you chose, if any, became the file "NEW.AT2." If you did not choose an AutoTemplate during installation, choosing "New" opens the default AutoTemplate "OB37.AT2." To change your "NEW.AT2" file, see "Changing 'NEW.AT2'" at the end of this chapter.

TIP

If you specified a default AutoTemplate during installation and don't want to use it to create a new AutoTemplate, you can open a copy of the original "NEW.AT2" from the "PR2US" directory.

Setting Up Your Presentation

Once you have opened a new presentation, you need to set up the frame within which you are going to work: Will it be an overhead transparency, a slide, or the computer screen? Check the "Slide setup" dialog box to make sure that you have the correct medium and output device (laser printer or film recorder) selected. (If you are starting from another presentation or AutoTemplate that you intend to modify, it's best to start from one targeted to the appropriate device.) Consult Chapter 4 for advice on selecting the appropriate media for your purpose.

Setting up a new presentation is like stretching a new canvas to paint on—in doing so, you determine the shape of the area you have to work with. Although a 35 mm slide and an overhead transparency may seem relatively similar in shape, the differences are critical. The aspect ratio of each—that is, the relationship of height to width—differs significantly. If you arrange the elements within one frame to please the eye, switching to another aspect ratio will alter the visual appeal, if not the actual information, of the slide.

Naming and Saving Your AutoTemplate

You name and save your AutoTemplate as you would a presentation—with *one* difference.

To name and save an AutoTemplate:

1. Choose "Save as…" from the File menu.
2. Click "AutoTemplate" to save as an AutoTemplate rather than a presentation. The only difference between a file saved as a presentation and one saved as an AutoTemplate is its file

extension (.PR2 or .AT2) and the way it opens. When you open a presentation, the presentation itself appears; when you open an AutoTemplate, a copy of it appears, unless you specify otherwise.

3. Type the name of your new AutoTemplate in the highlighted text box in the "Save as" dialog box shown in Figure 12.1. Locate the directory in the list box in which you want to save your AutoTemplate. The file's extension—.AT2, which is automatically added by Persuasion—indicates that it is an AutoTemplate and helps you later to distinguish it from presentation files.

4. Click "OK." The next time you want to modify this AutoTemplate, remember that you need to click "Original" in the "Open" dialog box. You will automatically open an untitled copy of the AutoTemplate unless you click "Original."

Creating a Background Master

A background master contains the standard background elements you want repeated on some or all of your slides—graphics, text, or a fill pattern. You can apply the background master to any or all slide masters. It provides a way of having a consistent background that you create once for multiple slide masters. All Persuasion AutoTemplates have a background master design included, with the exception of OB37.AT2. If you open a new presentation based on OB37.AT2, a blank background master is available.

▼ *Figure 12.1. "Save as" dialog box*

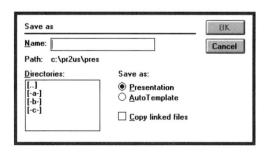

To edit the background master:

1. Choose "Go to master" from the View menu and "Background" from "Defined masters." The background master appears. It may or may not already contain fills and objects depending on what AutoTemplate is used for the basis of your presentation. If you want a blank background master to start from, select the objects on it and delete them using "Cut" (Shift + Del) from the Edit menu.

2. Choose "Set background..." from the Master menu to display the "Set background" dialog box, shown in Figure 12.2.

3. From the "Fills" submenu, choose the fill pattern you want. These patterns graduate from one color to another in the designated pattern on the background.

4. From "Color 1," choose the color of the foreground fill pattern, and from "Color 2," choose the color of the background. Use "Color 1" to specify a solid fill color other than white. You can see your color choices in their respective boxes and the effect of your color choices combined with your pattern choice in the sample box to the left of the lists.

5. Click "OK." Your chosen pattern and colors fill the background master.

6. Using the drawing tools and the commands from the Show and Draw menus, create the design you want as a background for some or all of your slides. You may want to import existing graphics, such as a company logo, rather than draw them yourself. Choose "Place..." from the File menu to import graphics to the background master.

▼ *Figure 12.2. "Set background" dialog box*

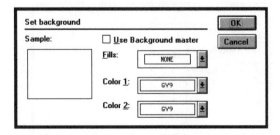

7. Using the text tool and the commands from the Text menu, add and format any text that you want to appear on every slide master and slide using this background master. To apply or remove the background master from a slide master, display the slide master and choose the "Set background…" command (the "Use Background master" option).

Creating a Background Master

Note: You can also use this command to create a background directly on the slide master that is unique to that master. Simply uncheck the "Use Background master" option and then define the background for that master using the previously described procedure.

CHECK YOURSELF

Change the background master of OB37.AT2 so that it has a diagonal graduated fill directly on the master.

ANSWER

Open a new presentation based on OB37.AT2. To go to master view, click the right mouse button on the slide icon in the upper-right corner of the window. Then choose "Background" from the pop-up menu in the lower-left corner of the window. Choose "Set background…" from the Master menu. Select one of the two diagonal graduated fill patterns from the "Fills" drop-down list box. Then choose colors for each of the drop-down list boxes. Click "OK."

Creating a Slide Master

Whether you opened a copy of an AutoTemplate or chose "New" to begin, you always have a slide master available. The procedure for creating slide masters is the same as that for creating background masters.

▼ *Figure 12.3. "New master" dialog box*

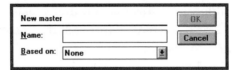

To add slide masters to an AutoTemplate:

1. Choose "Go to master" from the View menu and then click "New…" in the "Go to master" dialog box, or, if you are in a Master view, choose "New…" from the Master pop-up menu in the lower-left corner of the window. The "New master" dialog box appears as shown in Figure 12.3.

2. Type the name of your new slide master in the text box.

3. To base your new slide master on an existing one, choose the slide master you want to use as a starting point from the "Based on" drop-down list box. To start with a blank slide master, you can choose "None."

4. Click "OK." A copy of the slide master that you specified in "Based on" appears. You'll have to delete placeholders or other objects that you do not want before constructing the new slide master.

Adding Placeholders

Placeholders are the molds that shape the words and data poured into them from the outline and data sheet. Placeholders mark the location and indicate the format on the slide master of what becomes the text and charts on your slides.

You can choose from four types of placeholders in creating your slide master:

▲ Title
▲ Body text
▲ Chart
▲ Organization chart

The slide copy placeholder is available only for notes and handouts.

Defining Text-Type Placeholders

You will typically add title or text placeholders (or both) to slide masters. Additional text placeholders can be used for side-by-side text blocks, subtitles, footers, and so on.

To add a title or text placeholder:

1. Choose "Add title" or "Add text" from the Master menu. The appropriate placeholder is added to the slide master.

2. To specify the location of the placeholder, drag it to the place you want it on the slide master.

3. To change the size of the placeholder, point to a side handle and drag to the desired width. The text in the placeholder stretches or wraps accordingly. If you find that you can't achieve the desired size, use the text tool to edit or delete some of the sample text in the placeholder.

4. To change the font, size, style, or text color of the placeholder, use the commands from the Text menu. Text in the outline will take on the characteristics you specify for this placeholder when it appears on the slide, as will the placeholder itself.

5. To add a fill pattern, shadow, or color to the placeholder, use the palettes displayed in the Show menu.

Defining Chart-Type Placeholders

Because charts are a useful addition to most presentations, you'll typically want a slide master containing a chart placeholder.

To add a chart placeholder:

1. Choose "Add chart..." from the Master menu. The "Chart info" dialog box appears.

2. Specify the "Chart type" and its "Show" and "Data" characteristics in the "Chart info" dialog box (see Chapter 10 for a complete explanation of how to use this dialog box). For "Sample chart size," specify the number of series and categories for the default chart size. The numbers you enter for "Sample chart size" do not limit the number of categories or series you can have in your chart, but indicate to Persuasion

Creating a Slide Master

what size the placeholder should be to reserve adequate room for the chart. Categories usually appear as rows in your data sheet; their labels appear on the horizontal axis of your chart. Series usually appear as columns in your data sheet; series labels are taken from column headings.

3. Click "OK." A chart placeholder in the format just specified appears on the slide master.

4. To specify the location of the placeholder, point within the chart and drag it to the place you want it on the slide master. To change the size of the sample chart, point to a handle and drag to reduce or enlarge. You can resize the chart proportionally by holding down Shift as you drag. Be sure to release the mouse button before you release Shift. Also, you can use ruler guides to position chart placeholders consistently from one master to the next.

5. To add special fills and effects, subselect a chart part by double-clicking it, and then use the palettes from the Show menu.

6. To change the font and style of labels or text, subselect a group of labels by double-clicking them; then use the commands from the Text menu.

To add an organization chart placeholder:

1. Choose "Add org. chart…" from the Master menu. The "Add org. chart placeholder" dialog box appears (see Figure 12.4).

2. Type the number of vertical levels and the number of boxes at the lowest level you want, and select a format for the lowest level. Choose settings that are as close as possible to the number of levels and headings in the outline; otherwise, some distor-

▼ *Figure 12.4. "Add org. chart placeholder" dialog box*

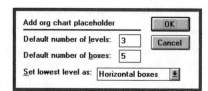

tion in the size of the boxes may occur when you create your organization chart.

3. Click "OK." You can drag the organization chart placeholder to the place you want it or modify it using the commands and palettes from the Text, Draw, or Show menus. Here are some suggestions:

    ▲ Change the line style of the box frames or other lines using the "Lines" palette from the Show menu.

    ▲ Use "Rotate/Flip" from the Draw menu to display the first level on the side or bottom.

    ▲ Round the corners of the boxes using the "Rounded corners..." command from the Draw menu.

    ▲ Change the font and size of the type using the commands from the Text menu.

CHECK YOURSELF

Create a slide master containing a title, a text, and a chart placeholder for a pie chart.

ANSWER

Perform these steps:

1. In a presentation, choose "Go to master" from the View menu and click "New...." Type in a name, click "None" for "Based on," and then click "OK."

2. Choose "Add title" from the Master menu, and drag the title placeholder to where you want it. Repeat this for the text placeholder using the "Add text" command.

3. Choose "Add chart..." from the Master menu. In the "Chart info..." dialog box, fill out the following options and then click "OK":

    ▲ For "Chart type," select "Pie."

    ▲ For "Show," check "Depth" and "Value labels."

▲ For "Sample chart size," enter "1" for the number of series and "5" for the number of categories.

4. Adjust the width of the text placeholder by pointing to one side and dragging to narrow the box, and then drag the chart placeholder so that it is positioned beside the text placeholder.

Anchoring Text within a Placeholder

You can anchor a text block to a certain position within a title or text placeholder. In anchoring the placeholder, you are defining its position relative to the placeholder boundary.

Anchoring text in a placeholder is particularly helpful when you have two adjacent placeholder boxes and you want to determine how the text in each will flow onto the slide with regard to the other. For example, suppose you want to ensure that the title will always be immediately above a subtitle at the same distance from it on each slide. You should anchor the text in the title placeholder to the center bottom of its box and anchor the text in the text (subtitle) placeholder to the top center of its box.

Do not confuse anchoring text within a placeholder with aligning text. Text is aligned with reference to the text block itself, but it is anchored with reference to its location in the placeholder box. For example, you can have center-aligned text that is anchored to the top left of the placeholder box.

To anchor a placeholder:

1. In Master view, use the pointer tool to select the title or text placeholder.

2. Choose "Anchor…" from the Master menu. The "Anchor placeholder" dialog box appears, as shown in Figure 12.5.

3. Click "Left," "Center," or "Right" and "Top," "Center," or "Bottom" to anchor the text within the placeholder. As you click each option, the sample text block in the dialog box moves to show you how text will be situated within the placeholder.

4. Click "OK." The text block in the placeholder shifts to the position you specified.

▼ *Figure 12.5. "Anchor placeholder" dialog box*

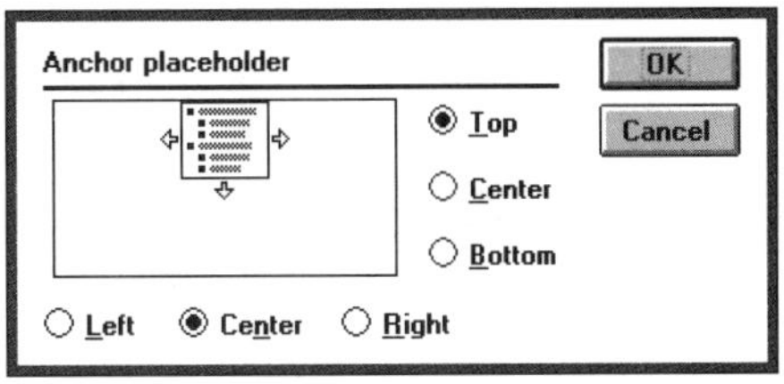

Anchor placeholder

OK

Cancel

◉ <u>T</u>op

○ <u>C</u>enter

○ <u>B</u>ottom

○ <u>L</u>eft   ◉ Ce<u>n</u>ter   ○ <u>R</u>ight

Creating a Slide Master

Enhancing Your Slide Master

In addition to formatting placeholders and establishing a background design, you may choose to enhance your slide master in a number of other ways. In fact, you may want to enhance some slide masters and not others so that you have a choice of fancy or plain when it comes to assigning masters to the slides in your presentation.

Defining Bullet Marks

You can specify the font, size, style, and color of the bullets in a body text placeholder by level. These attributes can only be defined in the placeholder on the master. (Bullets are displayed using the "Bullet marks" command from the Text menu.)

To define bullets in the placeholder:

1. Go to the slide master containing the body text placeholder whose bullets you want to define and select it.

2. Choose "Define bullets..." from the Master menu. The "Define bullet" dialog box appears, as shown in Figure 12.6.

3. In the "Define bullets" dialog box, select the bullet level you want to change. If you want to change more than one level, hold down Shift to select subsequent levels.

4. Select the font and size you want to apply from the "Font" drop-down list boxes. Different fonts have different bullets.

▼ *Figure 12.6. "Define bullets" dialog box*

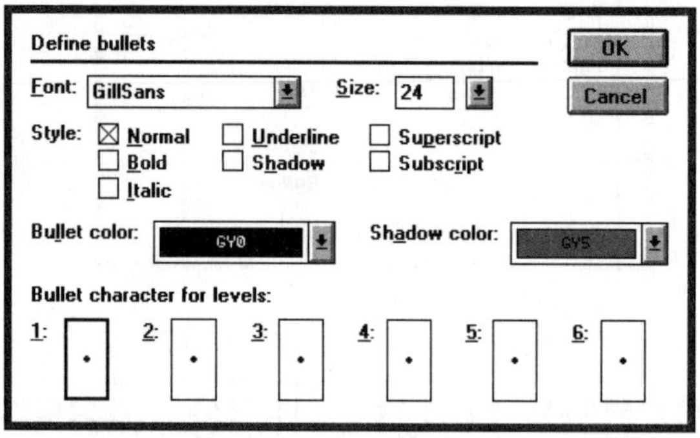

However, you can also type any other character you want from the selected font to replace the bullet.

5. Check the styles you want from the list under "Styles."

6. Select the colors you want to apply from the "Bullet color" and "Shadow color" drop-down list boxes. As you make a selection, you can see it take effect in the appropriate box or boxes for each level in the bottom half of the dialog box.

7. Click "OK." The body text placeholder on the slide master changes to the new color and font specifications for bullet marks. Slides with this master assigned to them will have the bullets displayed therein.

Note: To delete all the bullets in a body text placeholder, select the placeholder and choose "Bullet marks" from the Text menu. To delete the bullet for a single level, select the level you want to delete in the "Define bullets" dialog box and press the Delete/Backspace key.

Adding Other Text and Graphics

You can use the drawing tools and the text tool to add text and graphics to your slide master. You can also import a graphic or text. You may, for example, want to import your company logo. Keep in mind that the text and graphics you add to a slide master will appear on every slide to which the master is assigned. For more information about adding text and graphics, see Chapters 8 and 9.

Defining Slide Builds

When you assign different parts of a placeholder—levels in a body text placeholder, for example—to different layers on the master, you can have each layer displayed in succession when you give an on-screen slide show. Defining slide builds on the slide master will automatically create layers on the slide to which it is assigned. You can assign boxes in an organization chart placeholder, levels in a body text placeholder, or columns or rows in a chart placeholder to different slide layers.

You can also create slide builds directly on individual slides using the Layer pop-up menu. When you layer objects on a slide, you have more freedom in what you assign to each layer. For example, individual boxes in an organization chart rather than just levels of boxes (as on the master) can be assigned to different layers on a slide. Each of these layering methods—on the slide or on the slide master—achieve different effects.

To define slide builds on a master:

1. Go to the slide master.

2. Select the body text, chart, or organization chart placeholder for which you want to create a build.

3. Choose "Build layers..." from the Master menu. The "Build layers" dialog box appears, as shown in Figure 12.7.

4. Specify what is to be included in each layer:

    Text. The text number indicates how many of the text levels will be treated as individual layers. If you select "second" and have four levels of text on a slide, Level 1 will appear, and then Levels 2, 3, and 4 will appear together in the slide show.

▼ *Figure 12.7. "Build layers" dialog box*

Organization charts. If you check "Layer each level of org chart," each hierarchical level is displayed one at a time, starting with the highest.

Charts. Checking "Series" indicates that you want the data to display column by column from the data sheet, and checking "Categories" indicates that you want the data to display row by row.

5. Click "OK." To see the effect of what you have just done, choose "Slide show" from the File menu. You must, of course, have text in the outline or data in the data sheet with the appropriate masters assigned; otherwise, the slide show doesn't have slides to show. For more information on running a slide show, see Chapter 14.

CHECK YOURSELF

Using the slide master you created in the last "Check Yourself" section, set the pie chart up to build wedge by wedge.

ANSWER

On the master, select the chart placeholder with the pointer tool. Choose "Build layers..." from the Master menu. In the "Build layers" dialog box, check "Layer other charts by:" and select "Series." Then click "OK."

Naming and Organizing Your Slide Masters

You can save yourself some time and possible puzzlement by aptly naming your slide masters. Since you see only the name in the Master pop-up menu when you assign them, it helps if the name is descriptive of the slide master's contents. In naming your slide masters, consider these factors:

▲ What is the primary function of the placeholders on the slide master?

▲ Are slide builds defined on the master?

▲ Do you want to follow the naming pattern established in the Persuasion AutoTemplates so that importing masters results in replacement rather than addition?

You can use the "Define masters…" command on the Master menu to rename, delete, and add slide masters. Basically, "Define masters…" lets you keep track of your slide masters and clean house when you need to.

To rename or remove a slide master:

1. Choose "Define masters…" from the Master menu to display the "Define masters" dialog box, illustrated in Figure 12.8.

2. Select the master you want to remove or rename from the drop-down list box.

3. To remove the master, click "Remove."

4. To rename the master, drag to select the name in the "Rename" text box, and then type the name you want in the text box.

5. Click "OK."

   Note: The "New…" option in the "Define masters" dialog box is the same as choosing "Go to master" from the View menu and clicking "New…." For more information, see the "Creating a Slide Master" section, found earlier in this chapter.

Naming and Organizing Your Slide Masters

▼ *Figure 12.8. "Define masters" dialog box*

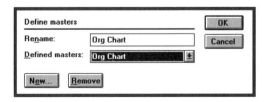

Creating a Speaker Notes Master

You can print your speaker notes by producing a series of notes pages, one for each slide. In order to do so, you create a notes master that can contain a title placeholder, a miniature copy of the slide, and room for text. You can add notes using the text tool, or import text from another application.

To create a notes master:

1. Go to the Notes master using the "Notes master" command on the View menu. The notes master is blank if you opened the presentation without basing it on an AutoTemplate. If you began by opening an AutoTemplate, the notes master probably contains some placeholders already.

2. Choose either or both of these commands from the Master menu: "Add title" or "Add slide copy." (The commands are unavailable if you already have placeholders of this type on the master.) The placeholder or placeholders appear on the notes master.

3. Position the placeholders where you want them and resize them by dragging their handles, if necessary.

4. Format the title placeholder using commands from the Text menu.

5. Use the text tool and the drawing tools to add any additional information you want to appear on every notes page.

Creating a Handout Master

A handout in Persuasion is simply a printed version of the slides in your presentation in miniature form, with space for your audience to take notes. You define how many slides go on a page by the number of slide copy placeholders you add to the master.

To set up a handout master:

1. Choose "Handout master" from the View menu.

2. For each slide miniature you want to appear on a handout, choose "Add slide copy" from the Master menu.

3. Arrange the slide copy placeholders on the handout by dragging them to where you want them.

4. Use the text tool and the drawing tool to add anything you want to appear on every handout.

This is all you need to do to create handouts. When you produce your presentation using the "Print" command from the File menu, specify "Handouts" as one of your "Print choices," and they will be printed along with your slides or the other items you specify.

Creating a Handout Master

Understanding Default Settings

When you open a presentation or AutoTemplate—whether new or old—a set of defaults is always in effect. Defaults are of two types:

▲ Presentation defaults are any settings saved with a presentation or AutoTemplate that you open by choosing "Open..." from the File menu.

▲ Application defaults are any settings saved in an AutoTemplate with the specific name *NEW.AT2*, which you open by choosing "New..." from the File menu.

The "NEW.AT2" file is stored in the "PR2US" directory. Unless it is removed or overridden (by specifying an AutoTemplate as default at installation), a new presentation opens with the "NEW.AT2" defaults in effect.

Setting Presentation Defaults

Presentation defaults are specific to each presentation. You can set them in two ways:

▲ By setting certain options using the "Preferences" command

▲ By setting the options on menus and in dialog boxes using the pointer tool with nothing selected

Using the drawing tool or the text tool to make selections results in settings that apply only to the objects you then create with that tool—until you select another tool. These are called tool defaults and they override the presentation defaults.

When you select one or more objects with the pointer tool and then change their text or graphic attributes from menus or dialog boxes, those settings affect only the selected object or objects.

To set presentation defaults in the "Preferences" dialog box:

1. Choose "Preferences…" from the File menu. The "Preferences" dialog box appears, as shown in Figure 12.9.

2. Select a measurement system from the drop-down list box. Your choice here affects the rulers, tabs, indents, and margins displayed in several views and a number of the dialog box settings throughout the program.

3. Choose the slide master you want automatically assigned to new slides from the "Default slide master" drop-down list box, or choose "None" so that no master is automatically assigned to the new slides.

4. Select the option you want to apply when you reopen a presentation. These are your choices:

   ▲ "Outline," which always reopens the presentation to Outline view

   ▲ "Slide," which always reopens the presentation to Slide view

   ▲ "Last saved," which reopens the presentation to the view in which it was last saved

---

▼ *Figure 12.9. "Preferences" dialog box*

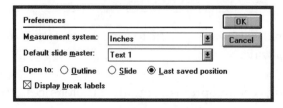

5. Check "Display break labels" to display the labels for breaks that you enter in the outline. For more information about break labels, see Chapter 6.

6. Click "OK." You can change these defaults any time. The new defaults are in effect for any action taken after "OK" is clicked, although previously created slides are not affected. Persuasion remembers the "Preferences" dialog box settings saved with the presentation the next time you open it.

To use the pointer tool to set other presentation defaults, choose the menus and commands you want to change with the pointer tool, without anything selected. Then specify the new default settings by checking or unchecking options in their dialog boxes. These settings will be saved with the presentation.

Changing "NEW.AT2"

Application defaults are saved in a presentation named "NEW.AT2," which is stored in the "PR2US" directory. These defaults are in effect when you start a new presentation by using the "New" command from the File menu. During installation, if you chose "No selection" for the default AutoTemplate, "NEW.AT2" is "OB37.AT2," a black-and-white AutoTemplate set up for overheads.

To change application defaults, edit the "NEW.AT2" presentation (open the original of "NEW.AT2" and edit it as needed). For example, if you want your new presentations to open in Slide view, you can specify that in "NEW.AT2" using the "Preferences..." command as previously described.

QUICK COMMAND SUMMARY

You have learned to use these command to accomplish these tasks:

Command	Task
"Set background..."	To create a background master
"Go to master..." ("New...")	To create a slide master
"Add title"	To add a title placeholder

Command	Task
"Add text"	To add a text placeholder
"Add chart..."	To add a chart placeholder
"Add org chart..."	To add an organization chart placeholder
"Add slide copy"	To add a slide miniature to a note or handout
"Anchor..."	To anchor text within a placeholder
"Define bullets..."	To define the style of bullet characters in a text placeholder
"Build layers..."	To define slide builds for slide shows
"Define masters..."	To name and manage slide masters

PRACTICE WHAT YOU'VE LEARNED

Create your own AutoTemplate with three slide masters—one for the title slide, one for text, and one for organization charts.

ANSWER

Perform the following steps:

1. Choose "New" to create a new presentation.

2. Name and save it as an AutoTemplate using the "Save as..." command and selecting "AutoTemplate."

3. Choose "Go to master..." from the View menu and click "New...." Type in the name "Title," make sure "None" is selected for "Based on," and then click "OK" in both dialog boxes.

4. Choose "Add title" from the Master menu. Drag the place-holder to a central position on the master and use commands from the Text menu to set its text attributes. (Gill Sans with a point size of at least 24 is a good choice.)

5. Choose "Set background..." from the Master menu. Because you want a different background for the first slide in the presentation, make sure "Use background master" is

unchecked. Add whatever graphics you want to the background master, and, if you want a background fill, select a graduated fill pattern and colors; then click "OK."

6. Choose "Background" from the pop-up menu in the lower-left corner of the window. Use "Set background" to define the background master fill and colors for the other two masters that you will create.

7. Choose "New…" from the Master pop-up menu at the bottom of the window. Type the name "Text" in the text box, choose "Title" for "Based on," and click "OK." Choose "Add text" from the Master menu, and then drag the placeholders to where you want them. Format them with commands from the Text menu.

8. To create the chart master, use the "New…" command and name the master "Chart," basing it on the "Title" master. Choose "Add chart" from the Master menu. Fill out the "Chart info…" dialog box and then click "OK." Position the placeholder where you want it.

9. Choose "Save" from the File menu to save your new AutoTemplate.

Using Color in Your Presentation

Welcome to the wonderful world of color! Persuasion offers up to 200 colors (160 predefined colors, 20 custom colors, and 20 scheme colors) that you can use to apply color to your overhead transparencies or slides. With Persuasion's color features, you can create truly memorable presentations that will remain in your audience's mind long after they leave the auditorium.

However, without a little planning, you can also create some truly memorable disasters. Commercial designers study the complexities of color theory for years before they become proficient in the use of color. Persuasion's AutoTemplates and color schemes will help you take shortcuts in the learning process, but you still need to know some of the basics of color theory and application.

We'll start this chapter by teaching you about color models and giving you advice for applying color to presentations. Then we'll concentrate on the following topics:

▲ **Persuasion's colors palette**
▲ **How to apply color to text and graphics**

▲ How to customize the palette's working set of colors
▲ How to set color defaults that can apply to all text and graphics you create

Color Theory and Color Models

One key concept about color will help you understand many of the issues you are about to face when creating a color presentation: The color you see on your computer screen is not the same as the color you see when your slides or overhead transparencies are printed. It's merely a *close approximation*.

As you learned in seventh-grade science class, light is either transmitted or reflected. White light transmitted from a light bulb differs fundamentally from the reflected white of a blank piece of paper—one is the opposite of the other.

Typically we perceive transmitted light as white. But in fact, light is made up of three primary colors: red, green, and blue. Light from a light bulb looks white to us because all three colors are being transmitted at full intensity. If you were to change the intensity of one of the primary colors, the color of the light would change. And if you were to mix two of the three primary colors in various ways, you would get the three secondary colors: cyan, magenta, and yellow. Still more colors can be created by mixing various levels, or intensities, of the various primary and secondary colors.

Color that is reflected, such as that from a page printed on a color printer, has primary colors that are the same as transmitted secondary colors (cyan, magenta, and yellow), and secondary colors that are the same as transmitted primary colors (red, green, and blue). With transmitted color, white is the combination of all primary colors, but the reflected color white is the absence of all colors.

Computer screens form colors by transmitting light at various levels from red, green, and blue light guns. Not surprisingly, there are color models that are used to define what you see on the screen. The most common model is the RGB model, or "red, green, blue," which defines a color in terms of percentages of red, green, and blue. Less common is the HSB or HLS model (hue, saturation, and brightness or lightness). Hue refers to a color's position in degrees on a color wheel. Saturation describes the intensity of the color, with 100 percent being the most intense and 0 percent being the least. Brightness, or lightness, is the percentage to which a color approaches white (100 percent is the closest to white).

Models developed for reflected color owe their origin to the commercial printing industry prior to the advent of desktop color. PANTONE colors (PANTONE Matching System) are defined by mixing inks in various combinations, printing color swatches, and then labeling those swatches based on the amounts of the various inks that were used to created the reflected color.

Persuasion allows you to define a color in terms of either the RGB or HLS models. If you import a graphic to Persuasion that has been defined for a color system such as PANTONE, Persuasion maintains those color assignments (even though they do not match Persuasion's color models) unless you ungroup the graphic. When that graphic is printed, the PANTONE colors are used, providing that the assigned color printer or film recorder is capable of doing so.

Using Color

Persuasion gives you three options for using color in presentations:

▲ Creating color overhead transparencies that can then be printed on a color printer—such as an inkjet printer—and reproduced onto transparencies with a color photocopier

▲ Creating color slides that can then be produced with a film recorder (that uses the RGB and HSB models) or at a slide service bureau

▲ Creating a color presentation for the computer screen that you display using "Slide show"

Each of these methods requires careful planning of the colors you will use in your presentation, selecting a color scheme for all of your slides, and designing the presentation to include color elements. When planning for color, the best place to start is with Persuasion's AutoTemplates and suggested color schemes, which were designed by professionals. However, if you decide to strike out on your own, the following general advice will help:

▲ Try to keep the number of colors on any one slide down to just a few—too many colors can present a message that is as mixed as too many different fonts and point sizes in the text.

▲ Use one color scheme throughout your presentation. Don't use one set of colors for the first slide, a second set for the next slide, and so on.

▲ Different colors have different effects on your audience. Use warm colors (such as reds and yellows) for impact in small doses; use cool colors (such as blues and greens) for background colors.

▲ Assign colors from the same range on the spectrum, such as a dark blue background and light blue objects. Colors that clash jar your audience.

▲ When slides are illuminated, their colors will seem brighter and more intense. Therefore, use darker colors when you create slides.

Above all, when applying color, print proofs of your slides so that you can judge the accuracy and effect of the colors you have defined. Then adjust your color scheme as necessary before printing the final product.

Applying Color in Persuasion

Persuasion gives you a variety of methods for adding color to your presentation. You can import color graphics or apply color to text and graphics as you create them in Persuasion. In this section, we'll show you how to do the following:

▲ Apply colors to text and graphics in your presentation

▲ Assign default colors that Persuasion will apply as you create objects

▲ Customize Persuasion's colors palette

▲ Import colors from another presentation

Applying Color in Persuasion

Applying Colors from Persuasion's Colors Palette

You apply colors to objects in your presentation by using Persuasion's colors palette. To display this palette, choose "Colors" from the Show menu in Slide view, Notes view, or any of the master views. Figure 13.1 provides an illustration of the colors palette.

This minimized version of the palette displays your presentation's *working set* of colors, as well as a sample box that you can use to specify which element you want to apply color to. The working set represents 16 colors from the palette that you use most frequently. If you want to modify the working set or create your own custom colors, you can enlarge—or maximize—the palette by clicking the "Maximize" button in the upper-right corner (see Figure 13.2).

A number of Persuasion's AutoTemplates come with color schemes already defined. This means that the working set has been defined to include colors that blend harmoniously when assigned to objects in your presentation. In addition, a color scheme (visible when you enlarge the palette) has been defined for the entire presentation.

In general, to apply colors from Persuasion's colors palette:

1. Select one or more objects, such as text or graphics, to which you want to apply color.

▼ *Figure 13.1. Persuasion's colors palette*

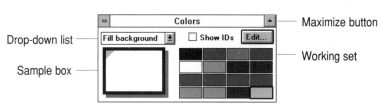

▼ *Figure 13.2. Expanded colors palette*

Standard colors

Scheme colors

Custom colors

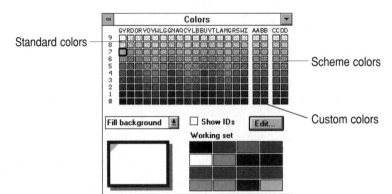

2. In the palette's sample box or from the drop-down list, select the element you want to apply color to. Choose "Fill background" to change to a solid color other than white or to change the white portion of a fill pattern to a color. Choose "Fill foreground" to change the black portion of a fill pattern to a color. For example, you might want to apply color to the object's shadow, text, the text's shadow, or whatever.

3. Choose a color from the working set, or, if necessary, enlarge the palette and choose a color from the color grid.

CHECK YOURSELF

1. In a presentation, create a new slide and go to it.

2. Draw a square and apply a fill pattern.

3. Apply colors from the working set to the white and black portions of the fill pattern.

ANSWERS

1. Choose "Go to slide" from the View menu, click "New," and then click "OK."

2. Select either the rounded-corner tool or the square-corner tool. On the slide, hold down the mouse button and drag until you have a square. Release the mouse button. In the "Fills" palette

(choose "Fills" from the Show menu), select a fairly distinctive fill pattern. (If there was a default fill pattern in effect when you drew the square, it may already be filled, but make sure the fill has a distinctive pattern.)

3. If necessary, choose "Colors" from the Show menu to display the colors palette. In the sample box, click on the center of the box and then select a light color for the fill foreground from the working set. Then click on the turned-down corner (the upper-left corner of the sample) and select a darker shade of the same color for the fill background from the working set.

Applying Color by Default

Persuasion allows you to set color defaults so that color is automatically applied to the text and graphics as you create them. For example, you can set a solid color for all filled objects—boxes, ovals, polygons—you draw in your presentation to green.

To set color defaults:

1. Select the pointer tool. Make sure that nothing is currently selected.

2. If necessary, choose "Colors" from the Show menu to display the colors palette.

3. In the sample box or drop-down list, select an element—such as "Fill background"—to assign a default color to.

4. Choose the color you want from the working set, or, if necessary, maximize the palette and choose the color you want from the color grid.

5. Repeat Steps 4 and 5 for each element that you want to assign a default color to.

Customizing the Colors Palette

The color AutoTemplates in Persuasion come with custom colors and color schemes designed to be complementary when you apply them to objects in your presentation. In addition, the scheme colors are designed to map to specific objects, such as the series of a chart. As a result, if you import a color scheme from another AutoTemplate to replace the existing one, the new scheme will map its colors in the same manner as the old—that is, old chart series colors will be replaced with new chart series colors. This method of applying colors provides consistency and good use of color across all of your presentations.

However, you may find that you want or need to design a color scheme of your own. For instance, it may be necessary to edit the working set to contain the colors of your corporate logo. To do this, use the "Edit..." button in the palette.

To edit the working set of the colors palette:

1. If necessary, choose "Colors" from the Show menu to display the palette.

2. Click the Maximize button in the upper-right corner.

3. In the working set, select the color you want to replace.

4. In the color grid, custom colors, or scheme colors, select the color you want to add to the working set. Persuasion replaces the color in the working set and then deselects it so that you can't inadvertently change it again.

5. Repeat steps 3 and 4 as necessary, and then click the Minimize button in the upper-right corner.

    Note: Persuasion does not change the color assignment of any objects that have old colors assigned to them.

You can also use this procedure to edit the 20 custom and 20 scheme colors in the colors palette and then assign them to objects in your presentation. To have the best of both worlds, leave the "Scheme colors" as they are so that you can benefit from the design expertise of Persuasion's AutoTemplate designers, but create the extra colors you want for the "Custom colors."

To create your own custom colors:

1. If necessary, choose "Colors" from the Show menu to display the colors palette.

2. Click "Edit…." The "Edit colors" dialog box appears, as shown in Figure 13.3.

3. In the portion of the color grid marked "Custom," select the color you want to edit. This section contains 20 colors that you can modify as you wish.

4. Choose the color model you want to use by clicking either "RGB" or "HLS." You can use either model to edit the color; both will provide the same quality of color. Pick the one you are most familiar with.

5. Either enter numerical values or drag the scroll bars until you have the color you want. The new color appears where you clicked in the "Custom" section of the color grid. The scroll bar pulses to show that it is the value—for example, hue, lightness, or saturation (HLS)—that you are currently editing.

6. Click "OK."

   Note: As long as you haven't yet clicked "OK," you can revert to the colors as they existed before you changed them:

   ▲ To change the color you just edited back to its original values, click "Reset current color."

   ▲ To change all the custom colors you have edited since you clicked "Edit…" back to their original values, click "Reset custom colors."

Applying Color in Persuasion

▼ *Figure 13.3. "Edit colors" dialog box*

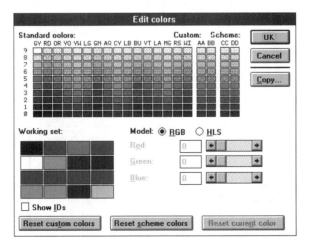

▲ To change all the scheme colors you have edited since you clicked "Edit..." back to their original values, click "Reset scheme colors."

Importing Colors from Another Presentation or AutoTemplate

Since professionals have gone to the trouble to create effective color schemes for you in Persuasion's AutoTemplates, you might as well take advantage of their expertise. This is made simpler by the fact that you can import color schemes from any presentation or AutoTemplate into your current presentation.

To import colors from another presentation or AutoTemplate:

1. If necessary, choose "Colors" from the Show menu to display the colors palette.

2. Click "Edit...."

3. In the expanded palette, click "Copy...." The "Copy colors" dialog box appears, as illustrated in Figure 13.4.

4. In the "Copy colors" dialog box, select the presentation or AutoTemplate you want to import colors from using the "Files" and "Directory" list boxes. Alternatively you can type the path and filename in the text box.

5. Select the portion of the color palette you want to import: "Scheme," "Custom colors," or "Working set."

▼ *Figure 13.4. "Copy colors" dialog box*

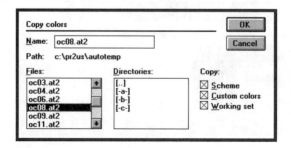

6. Click "OK" in the dialog box.

7. Click "OK" in the enlarged palette.

Applying Color in Persuasion

QUICK COMMAND SUMMARY

In this chapter, you have learned to use the colors palette to accomplish these procedures using these commands:

Command	Function
Colors palette	Apply colors to text or graphics and set default colors that apply to all text and graphics you create
Colors palette, "Edit..."	Edit the palette's working set of colors, custom colors, and color schemes
Colors palette, "Copy..."	Import colors from other presentations and AutoTemplates

PRACTICE WHAT YOU'VE LEARNED

In this exercise, we will alter a black-and-white AutoTemplate to include a color scheme from a color AutoTemplate, as well as the colors for your corporate logo. Then we'll set up the presentation defaults for the text and graphics you will create to be colors from the working set.

1. Open a copy of one of the black-and-white AutoTemplates and save it as a presentation.

2. Import the custom, scheme, and working set colors from a color AutoTemplate of your choice.

3. Modify the colors palette working set to include your corporate logo colors.

ANSWERS

1. Choose "Open" from the File menu. In the "Open" dialog box, select a black-and-white AutoTemplate, such as "OB15.AT2" from the "AUTOTEMP" directory. Click "OK." Choose "Save as..." from the File menu, name your file, and click "OK."

2. Go to Slide view by clicking the slide icon in the upper-right corner of the window. If necessary, choose "Colors" from the Show menu to display the colors palette. In the palette, click "Edit...." In the expanded palette, click "Copy...." In the "Copy colors" dialog box, select the name of a color AutoTemplate, such as "OC03.AT2," in the "AUTOTEMP" directory. Check "Scheme," "Custom colors," and "Working set," and then click "OK."

3. Perform the following steps:

   a. In the expanded palette, click the color in the custom colors you want to edit. Click either "RGB" or "HLS" for the color model. (Your corporate logo colors should be defined either in one of these models or in PANTONE colors. If it is defined in PANTONE, there are RGB equivalents available.) Type in the numerical values for the corporate logo color. Repeat this process for other colors, as necessary.

   b. In the working set, click the color you want to replace with a logo color. Then click the logo color you defined in the "Custom" section. Repeat this process for each logo color you defined. Then click "OK" in the expanded palette.

   c. Select the pointer tool. In the colors palette sample box, click the element you want to have a default color as you create your presentation—for example, text, text shadow, fill foreground and background, and object shadow. Click the color you want for a default in the working set. Repeat this process for each color default you want to set.

Producing Your Presentation

Once your presentation is created, you are ready to produce it—unless you've created an on-screen presentation. However, if you've created an overhead transparency presentation, you need to transform your "slides" into transparencies, and if you've created a slide presentation, you need to produce 35 mm slides.

Then there are the accompanying materials: Do you want to print handouts for the audience? Do you want to print speaker notes for yourself? Do you want to print the outline for your audience, yourself, or the record?

In this chapter, you will learn how to do the following:

- ▲ **Prepare your presentation for printing by spell checking**
- ▲ **Format text in the outline for printing**
- ▲ **Preview your slides in slide show or prepare your presentation to be run on-screen**
- ▲ **Produce your slides, overheads, speaker notes, audience handouts, or any combination of these**

Before You Print

Once you decide what items you want to print, you need to format them and make sure they are ready for others' eyes. If there are changes that need to be made at the last minute, you can use the "Find…," "Find next," and "Change…" commands to locate all the instances in your presentation of the changes you want to make—and have Persuasion make them. Using the spell checker is a safeguard against misspelled words, though it cannot substitute for careful proofreading. You can prepare the outline for printing by formatting it to look the way you want it; you can preview your presentation by looking at a slide show of it on-screen.

Using "Find…," "Find next," and "Change…"

You can search for and replace words in any part of your presentation: slides, notes, outline, or any combination. Any changes made in the outline are made on your slides, and any changes made in placeholder text on your slides are made in the outline. Use "Find…" to search for occurrences of a word, "Find next" to find subsequent occurrences of a word, and "Change…" both to search for and modify occurrences of a word. You can use "Find…," "Find next," and "Change…" from any view, including the master views, except Slide sorter.

To search for and replace a word:

1. If you want to search within a range of text, select it.

2. Choose "Change…" from the Edit menu to display the "Change" dialog box, shown in Figure 14.1.

3. In the "Find what" text box, type the word you want to look for.

4. In the "Change to" text box, type the word you want to substitute.

5. Check the parts of your presentation that you want to search: "Outline," "Slides," "Notes," and/or "Masters." Your options here may be limited if you have selected a range of text. For

▼ *Figure 14.1. "Change" dialog box*

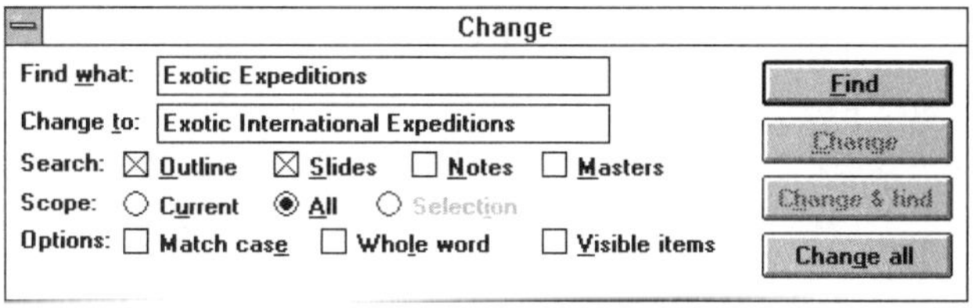

example, if you have a range of text selected in the outline, you won't be able to select any other parts of your presentation for Persuasion to search.

6. Select the scope you want for the search:

   ▲ Choose "Current" to search only the outline units associated with the currently displayed slide, or to search the currently displayed slide, note, or master.

   ▲ Choose "All" to search all of the outline, slides, notes, or masters.

   ▲ Choose "Selection" to search the currently selected text— contiguous outline units or text blocks.

7. Check whether you want to search for only whole words, as well as whether you want to search for words that have the same upper- and lowercase letters as your entries in "Find what."

8. Click one of the following:

   ▲ "Find" to search for the first occurrence and highlight it so that you can ignore it or change it

   ▲ "Change & find" to change the highlighted occurrence and then search for the next occurrence

   ▲ "Change all" to search for and change all occurrences

9. Double-click the Control menu in the upper-left corner to remove the dialog box from the screen.

The other commands—"Find..." and "Find next"—are limited versions of the functionality available in "Change...." "Find" searches for the first occurrence of what you type in, and "Find next" searches for the next occurrence. Neither of these commands lets you change what you find automatically.

Using the Spell Checker

You can use Persuasion's spell checker to check the spelling of words in any part of your presentation, including charts and tables. Persuasion comes with a set of dictionaries for 16 different languages, as well as a user dictionary that you can edit to include commonly used terms and acronyms from your field.

To check the spelling of the words in your presentation:

1. To check a range of text, select the text blocks or outline units.

2. Choose "Spelling..." from the Edit menu to display the "Spelling" dialog box, shown in Figure 14.2.

3. Choose the part of your presentation that you want to check for misspellings. Your options are similar to the options in the "Change" dialog box. See the preceding section.

4. Find the dictionary for the language you want to spellcheck, such as English, and start the spell check by double-clicking on the dictionary name. Alternatively you can select the dictionary you want and then click "Start."

5. As each unknown word is displayed, click the appropriate button as described in the following table:

To perform this task	Do this
Correct the spelling or change the word	Type the correction in "Change to" and click "Replace," or double-click the word you want from the "Suggestions" box.
Leave the unknown word as is	Click "Ignore" or press Enter.
Add the word to the user dictionary	Select either "Lowercase" to add the word in all lowercase letters or "As typed" to add the word exactly as typed, and then click "Add."

Note: If you plan to edit the user dictionary, keep a backup copy of it (go to the USENGLSH subdirectory under the ALDUS directory and create a backup copy). If you make an incorrect entry in your user dictionary, Persuasion doesn't allow you to make corrections to existing words. You must replace the current flawed dictionary (ALDUSN.UDC) with an earlier clean version to correct the situation.

▼ *Figure 14.2. "Spelling" dialog box*

Before You Print

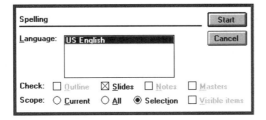

CHECK YOURSELF

Check the spelling of the presentation you created in Chapter 11.

ANSWER

Perform the following steps:

1. Choose "Open..." from the File menu and double-click the name you gave the presentation in the "PRES" directory. From any view except Slide sorter, choose "Spelling..." from the Edit menu.

2. In the "Spelling" dialog box, select all of the parts of the presentation—outline, slides, notes, and masters. For the scope, select "All." Click "US English" for the dictionary, and click "Start."

3. For each unknown word, select one of Persuasion's suggestions, ignore it, or change it by typing the new word in the text box and clicking "Replace."

Formatting Text in the Outline

Sometimes you'll want to print and distribute your outline to your audience. With Persuasion, you can define styles for the outline text that do not transfer to the slides, but that help you produce a good-looking outline in print.

▼ *Figure 14.3. "Outline format" dialog box*

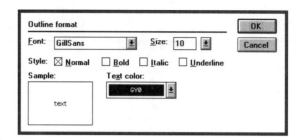

To define the text format for the outline:

1. In Outline view, choose "Outline format…" from the Text menu to display the "Outline format" dialog box shown in Figure 14.3.

2. In the dialog box, choose the font, size, color, and style that you want to appear throughout the outline. A sample of the text formatted as you specified is displayed in the window in the dialog box so that you can see what it looks like before you close the dialog box. You can easily change the type style and see how it looks before putting it into effect.

3. Click "OK" to apply this style.

   Note: You can also apply text styles by selecting the text or outline units and choosing the style you want from the upper portion of the Text menu.

Using the Slide Show to Preview or Present Your Slides

Before you part with your presentation or cast it into celluloid, you should preview it using the "Slide show" command. In fact, it's useful to look at a slide show of your presentation as you are building it. In addition, if you are presenting to a small audience, one of the least expensive and most effective ways to do so is to run your presentation on-screen. All you need to do is set up the presentation to launch directly into a slide show.

To run the slide show or set up the presentation to run in the slide show:

1. Choose "Slide show" from the File menu to display the "Slide show" dialog box, shown in Figure 14.4.

2. Select the settings you want in the "Slide show" dialog box:

   ▲ For "Show," click "All" to see all slides in the presentation, click "Current" to see only the selected slides, or type the range of slides you want to see.

   ▲ For "Options," click "Full screen" to see slides in a full-screen display rather than in the presentation window, and click "Continuous cycle" to display slides in a continuous loop.

   ▲ For "Slide advance," click "Automatic" to go from one slide to the next automatically, or click "Manual" to go from one slide to the next by clicking the mouse.

   ▲ For "Delay between slides," type the number of seconds you want to elapse before the next slide displays.

   ▲ For "Delay between layers," type the number of seconds you want to elapse before the next layer displays.

3. Click "Save" to save the dialog box settings with the presentation. This is particularly useful for automatically launching a slide show of your presentation from the Windows File Manager. Make sure that you checked "Start Persuasion in slide show" in the "Slide show" dialog box. When you double-click

---

▼ *Figure 14.4. "Slide show" dialog box*

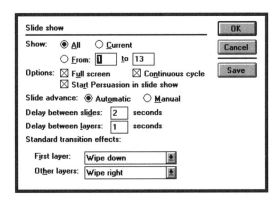

the icon for the presentation file, the slide show presentation begins immediately.

4. Click "OK" to run the slide show. To run the slide show manually, click the mouse to advance one slide, and double-click to back up one slide. To end the slide show at any time, press Esc.

Table 14.1 provides a helpful list of keyboard actions you can use to control a slide show in front of your audience.

Using Transition Effects

If you are planning to present your slides on-screen and are using a computer with adequate memory, transition effects can add a lot of pizazz to your show. You can move from slide to slide with no fanfare, or you can apply one of fifteen transition effects and attract the viewers' eyes from the moment the slide begins to open. However, you must keep in mind that you want to attract more than their eyes—ultimately, you want all of their attention. Thus, you shouldn't overdo transition effects, or they may detract from your presentation rather than lead your audience to the heart of the matter.

▼ *Table 14.1. Controlling the slide show with the keyboard*

Press this key	To do this
Right or Up arrow, or mouse button	Go to the next layer or, if no layer exists, the next slide
Shift + mouse button	Skip additional layers and go to the next slide
Shift + double-clicking mouse button	Go to the previous layer
Left or Down arrow, or double-click mouse button	Go to the previous slide
Space bar or hold down mouse button	Pause the slide show
Space bar or release mouse button	Resume the slide show

When you create a presentation, Persuasion applies a global default transition effect to each of the slides in your presentation. You can change the default transition effect using the "Slide show" command from the File menu, or you can apply transition effects locally to one slide or to several at a time in either Outline view or Slide sorter view from the "Transition" pop-up menu on the right in the lower menu bar. Any local application of a transition effect takes precedence over a global one.

In addition to applying a transition effect to a slide, you can apply a different transition effect to the layers that subsequently open on an individual slide. You can use one transition effect for the opening of the slide and one for the layers that follow: you cannot assign a different effect to each different layer.

To apply a transition effect locally to one or more slides:

1. In Outline view or Slide sorter view, select the slide or slides to which you want to apply a transition effect. The cursor can be positioned anywhere in any of the headings for a particular slide in Outline view for the effect to be applied to that slide.

2. Choose an effect from the "Transition" pop-up menu on the right at the bottom of the window. The different transition effects are described in Table 14.2. If you choose "Standard," you are applying the transition effects selected in the "Slide show" dialog box.

3. If you want to apply a transition effect to the layers on a slide, choose "Layers..." from the "Transition" pop-up menu. The "Layer transitions" dialog box appears, as shown in Figure 14.5.

4. In the "Layer transitions" dialog box, choose an effect from the "Other layers" drop-down list. You can also set the transition effect for the slide here, if you have not already done so.

   Note: You must have adequate memory for transition effects to be useful. If you don't have enough memory, Persuasion will not display transition effects. To regain memory, close any other Windows applications you currently have running or remove TSR (terminate and stay ready) DOS programs or drivers, such as your network connection. If you remove TSR programs or drivers, you'll have to reboot your system to regain the memory.

Using the Slide Show to Preview or Present Your Slides

▼ Table 14.2. Slide transition effects

Effect	Slide draws this way
Wipe left	From right to left
Wipe right	From left to right
Wipe up	From bottom to top
Wipe down	From top to bottom
To center	From the outside edges inward
Open curtain	From the center to the edges
Close curtain	From the outside edges inward
Blinds down	Horizontal "blinds" open
Blinds right	Vertical "blinds" open
Glitter right	Small squares cascade from left to right
Glitter down	Small squares cascade from top to bottom
Glitter across	Small squares cascade from top left to bottom right
Dissolve	Small squares randomly cover entire screen
Fade	The current slide fades out and the next slide fades in
Random	Persuasion applies transition effects in a random pattern

▼ Figure 14.5. "Layer transitions" dialog box

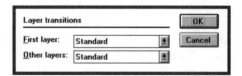

 ## CHECK YOURSELF

Set up the presentation from Chapter 11 to run as a slide show with a default transition effect of "Open curtain" for all but the last slide, for which you should use "Close curtain."

ANSWER

Perform the following steps:

1. Choose "Open..." from the File menu and double-click the name you gave the presentation in the "PRES" directory. From any view, choose "Slide show..." from the File menu.

2. In the "Slide show" dialog box, select "Full screen" and "Start Persuasion in slide show" for options, set the delay between slides and layers to zero seconds, and choose "Open curtain" for the "First layer" transition effect. Click "Save."

3. In Outline view, click an insertion point in one of the slides and choose "Select all" from the Edit menu. Select "Standard" from the Transition pop-up menu at the bottom of the window. Then click an insertion point in the last slide and choose "Close curtain" from the Transition pop-up menu. Save your presentation and close Persuasion.

4. From Windows File manager, double-click the presentation filename and let the show roll. Press Esc to terminate the show at any time.

Using the Slide Show to Preview or Present Your Slides

Producing Your Presentation

Whether you have decided on overheads or slides, the "Print..." command is central to producing your presentation. With "Print..." you can perform the following tasks:

▲ Create disk files that you can use to create slides

▲ Print transparencies of your slides

▲ Produce handouts for your audience or speaker notes for yourself

If you plan to print everything—slides, speaker notes, handouts, and outline—you may find that all you have to do is choose "Print..." from the File menu and click "OK." However, many of Persuasion's AutoTemplates contain slides that are landscape-oriented but notes and handouts that are portrait-oriented. If you have more than one orientation in your presentation, you'll have to print more than once.

Persuasion has default settings for printing that assumes that you are printing everything at once. For other situations—say, a copy of the outline with slide titles only—you must modify the settings in the "Print" dialog box. Table 14.3 lists each option for the "Print" dialog box (shown in Figure 14.6) and explains its use.

▼ *Table 14.3. Options for the "Print" dialog box*

Print option	*Description*
Copies	Enter the number of copies you want to print.
Pages	Choose "All" to print all slides (and corresponding notes, handouts, and so forth) in your presentation, or enter a range of slide numbers in "From" and "to" to print a portion of your presentation.
Graphic options	Choose from the following options: "Reverse order" to print slides from the last to the first; "Proof print" to print your slides with black text and white-filled objects (also faster) for proofing before final production; and "Print background" to print slides with or without their background fill (helpful for proofing your slides).
Outline	Choose among the following options: "Visible items only" to suppress printing of any collapsed items in the outline; "Current selection" to print only the currently selected outline heading and its subordinates; and "Print bullet characters" to print bullet characters to identify outline unit types ("o" for slide titles, "-" for slide text, and "*" for any other type of unit).
Slide printer	Temporarily specify, for proofing purposes, a printer that will override your selection in the "Slide setup" dialog box (see Chapter 4). This temporary override is useful if you are printing off-site; it does not affect the saved presentation.
Notes printer	Temporarily specify, for proofing purposes, a printer that will override your selection in the "Notes setup" dialog box (see Chapter 6). This temporary override does not affect the saved presentation.
Setup	Displays the printer-specific setup dialog for either the slide or notes printer (whichever one you currently have the cursor in). If necessary, you can modify settings of the temporarily chosen printer (or target printer). For the target printer, these settings are usually made when you first create your presentation. However, if you are temporarily reassigning a printer, you may need to adjust orientation or one of the other settings.

▼ *Figure 14.6. "Print" dialog box*

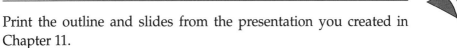

Note: If you are planning to print directly to transparency film (rather than print on white paper and create transparencies on a photocopying machine), be sure that you use the transparency film that is recommended for your printer. Consult your printer documentation. Transparency film can damage some printers.

CHECK YOURSELF

Print the outline and slides from the presentation you created in Chapter 11.

ANSWER

Perform the following steps:

1. Choose "Open..." from the File menu and double-click the name you gave the presentation in the "PRES" directory. From any view, choose "Print..." from the File menu.

2. Select "All" for "Pages," and check "Slides" for "Print." Make sure all the graphics options are unchecked. Click an insertion point in "Slide printer," and then click "Setup...." Make sure that the orientation matches that of your slides, and then click "OK" in both dialog boxes.

3. Once your slides are finished printing, choose "Print..." from the File menu. Select "All" for "Pages," and check "Outline" for "Print." Check "Print bullet characters" for "Outline op-

tions." Click an insertion point in "Notes printer," and then click "Setup…." Make sure that the orientation matches that of your outline, and then click "OK" in both dialog boxes.

Extra Notes for Producing 35 mm Slides

Remember that you can create 35 mm slides either by using a desktop film recorder or by sending your slides to a slide service bureau (see Chapter 2). Some desktop film recorders and slide service bureaus supply drivers that you can install. You can then select the film recorder or slide service bureau as a printer from the "Slide setup" dialog box. If the film recorder you will be using can't be selected in the "Slide setup" dialog box, you will have to export your slides rather than print them to disk. To determine this, check with your slide service bureau or read the documentation for your desktop film recorder.

To export your presentation for creating 35 mm slides:

1. From Slide view or the slide sorter, choose "Export…" from the File menu to display the "Export" dialog box shown in Figure 14.7.

▼ *Figure 14.7. "Export" dialog box*

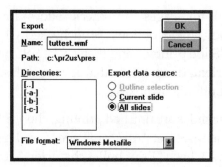

2. If necessary, type a name other than the one Persuasion has chosen for you in "Name." Persuasion, by default, exports each slide under the name of your presentation with a ".WMF" extension, indicating that it is a Windows metafile. Each slide is exported as a separate file, and the name is incremented. For example, if your presentation name is "Meeting," your exported slides will be in the form of "MEETING1.WMF," "MEETING2.WMF," and so on.

3. If necessary, choose "All slides." If you have slides currently selected in the slide sorter, "Selected slides" will be chosen by default. Choose "All slides" if you want to export the entire presentation.

4. Click "OK."

Note: Remember to produce a proof of at least one of your slides before attempting to produce all of them. Each film recorder and slide service bureau has slightly different requirements; the best way to discover those requirements and save yourself the time and expense of making corrections is to produce representative proofs prior to producing the entire presentation.

Extra Notes for Producing 35 mm Slides

QUICK COMMAND SUMMARY

You have learned to use these commands to accomplish these tasks:

Command	Task
"Find..."	To find an occurrence of a word
"Find next"	To find the next occurrence of the same word
"Change..."	To find and then change one or more occurrences of the same word
"Outline format..."	To format the text in your outline for printing
"Slide show..."	To preview or present your slides
"Print..."	To print slides, speaker notes, audience handouts, or the outline
"Export..."	To export your slides to send them to a slide service bureau

PRACTICE WHAT YOU'VE LEARNED

Print the slides, notes, and handouts from the presentation you created in Chapter 11.

ANSWER

Perform the following steps:

1. Choose "Open..." from the File menu and double-click the name you gave the presentation in the "PRES" directory. From any view, choose "Print..." from the File menu.

2. Select "All" for "Pages," and check "Slides" for "Print." Make sure that only "Print background" is checked for "Graphics options." Click an insertion point in "Slide printer," and then click "Setup...." Make sure that the orientation matches that of your slides, and then click "OK" in both dialog boxes.

3. Once your slides are finished printing, choose "Print..." from the File menu. Select "All" for "Pages," and check "Notes" and "Handouts" for "Print." Click an insertion point in "Notes printer," and then click "Setup...." Make sure that the orientation matches that of your outline, and then click "OK" in both dialog boxes.

A Guide to Persuasion's AutoTemplates

The following pages contain illustrations of each of Persuasion's AutoTemplates designs. Use the illustrations as a guide for picking the design that best suits your needs.

There are a total of 57 AutoTemplates shipped with Persuasion, but only 37 unique designs. Some of the designs are repeated for different mediums—for example, Design 05 comes in both black-and-white overheads and color slides.

We've used the last slide from the tutorial in Chapter 11 as the sample for the illustrations. Browse through the designs and choose the one you want. Then use the design number plus the following codes to find the AutoTemplate file in the "AUTOTEMP" subdirectory in the "PR2US" directory:

▲ "OB" = black-and-white overheads
▲ "OC" = color overheads
▲ "S" = slides

Note: Some of the designs that have a graduated color background appear overly dark and banded in our illustrations. The graduated fills, which look great in color overheads and slides, convert to bands of gray and black when printed on a black-and-white printer. However, we believe that you will find illustration of each design helpful, because the sample in the "Open" dialog box can be difficult to preview.

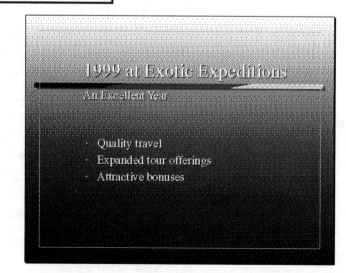

Design 01

Design 02

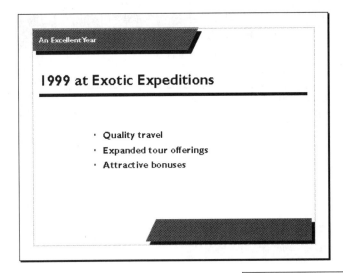

Design 03

Design 04

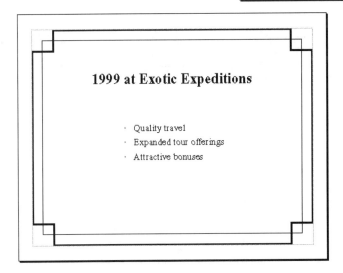

Design 05

Design 06

1999 at Exotic Expeditions

An Excellent Year

Quality travel
Expanded tour offerings
Attractive bonuses

1999 at Exotic Expeditions

- Quality travel
- Expanded tour offerings
- Attractive bonuses

Design 07

Design 08

1999 at Exotic Expeditions

An Excellent Year

- Quality travel
- Expanded tour offerings
- Attractive bonuses

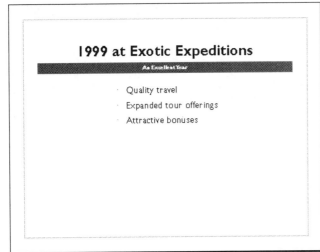

Design 09

Design 10

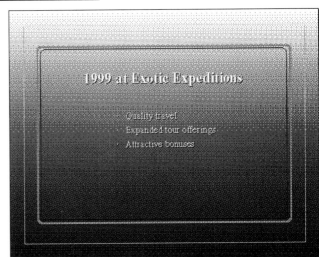

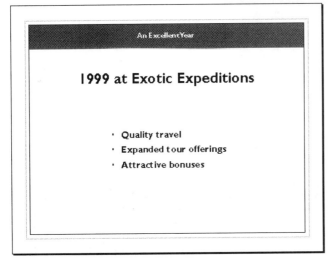

Design 11

337

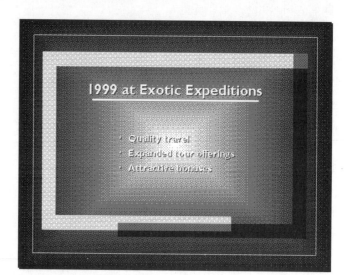

Design 12

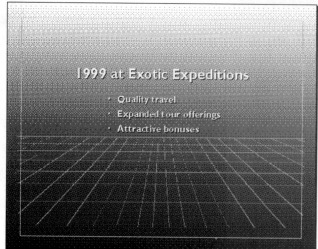

Design 13

Design 14

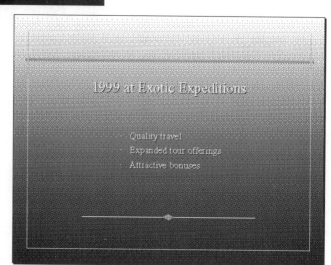

1999 at Exotic Expeditions

An Excellent Year

· Quality travel
· Expanded tour offerings
· Attractive bonuses

Design 15

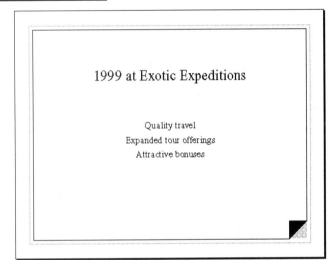

Design 16

1999 at Exotic Expeditions

Quality travel
Expanded tour offerings
Attractive bonuses

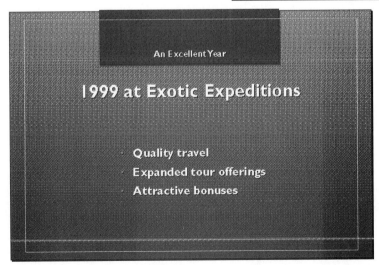

Design 17

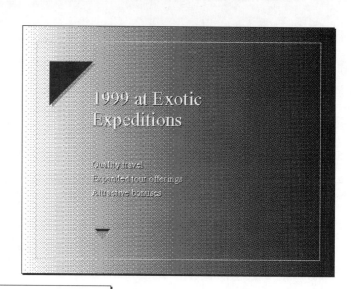

Design 18

1999 at Exotic Expeditions

- · Quality travel
- · Expanded tour offerings
- · Attractive bonuses

An Excellent Year

Design 19

1999 at Exotic Expeditions
An Excellent Year

- · Quality travel
- · Expanded tour offerings
- · Attractive bonuses

Design 20

1999 at Exotic Expeditions

· Quality travel
· Expanded tour offerings
· Attractive bonuses

Design 21

Design 22

1999 at Exotic Expeditions

An Excellent Year
· Quality travel
· Expanded tour offerings
· Attractive bonuses

1999 at Exotic Expeditions

· Quality travel
· Expanded tour offerings
· Attractive bonuses

Design 23

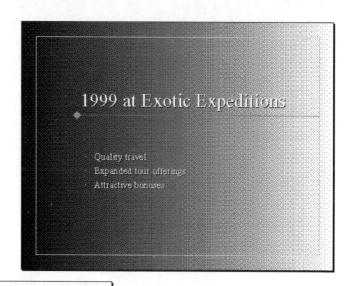

Design 24

Design 25

Design 26

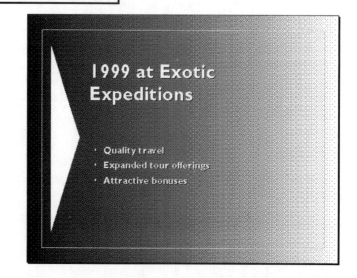

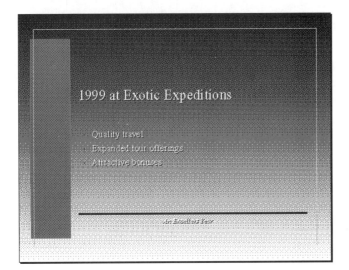

Design 27

1999 at Exotic Expeditions

Quality travel
Expanded tour offerings
Attractive bonuses

- Quality travel
- Expanded tour offerings
- Attractive bonuses

Design 28

1999 at Exotic Expeditions

- Quality travel
- Expanded tour offerings
- Attractive bonuses

Design 29

Design 30

1999 at Exotic Expeditions

· Quality travel
· Expanded tour offerings
· Attractive bonuses

1999 at Exotic Expeditions

· Quality travel
· Expanded tour offerings
· Attractive bonuses

Design 31

Design 32

1999 at Exotic Expeditions

· Quality travel
· Expanded tour offerings
· Attractive bonuses

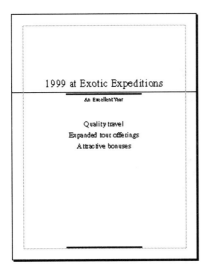

Design 33

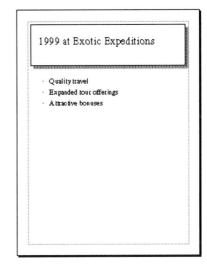

Design 34

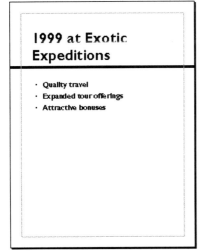

Design 35

345

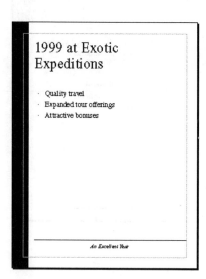

Design 36

1999 at Exotic Expeditions

· Quality travel
· Expanded tour offerings
· Attractive bonuses

Design 37

Transferring Slides Among Presentations

There will be many times when you want to transfer the slides from one presentation to another, so that you don't have to recreate them. For example, you may find that some of the slides from one presentation would fit well with the content of another expanded presentation that you are doing for a wider audience. Perhaps it would be easier to copy a slide containing a specially enhanced chart into another presentation, rather than taking the time to recreate the chart.

This appendix gives you two procedures that can save you time and effort:

- **Copying slides from one presentation to another**
- **Copying slides, along with their masters, from one presentation to another**

To copy slides from one presentation to another:

1. Open the source presentation. (Choose "Open…" from the File menu and double-click the name of the presentation you want to copy slides from.)

2. Make sure that the masters for the slides you are going to copy have the same name as those in the target presentation. This is important! Persuasion decides whether or not to copy the masters based on whether the master names are identical or different. If they are identical, only the slides are copied. If you need to rename one or more masters so that they have identical names, go to Master view in the source presentation and use "Define masters…" from the Master menu. Information about this command can be found in Chapter 12.

3. From Outline or Slide Sorter view, select the slides you want to copy, and then choose "Copy" from the Edit menu.

4. Close the source presentation, and then open the target presentation.

5. In Outline view, click a horizontal insertion point where you want to paste the new slides, or in Slide Sorter view, select the slide to the left of where you want to paste the new slides. Then choose "Paste" from the Edit menu. The slides from the source presentation are pasted into the target presentation, taking on the formatting of the default master slide.

To copy slides and their masters into another presentation:

Use the same procedure, but make sure that the masters assigned to the slides you want to copy have unique names—that is, master names that don't exist in the target presentation.

Glossary

Active layer Any drawing layer whose contents you can select and modify.

Alignment For graphics, how each one lines up. Using the "Aligning…" command, you can align graphics to the ruler increments or to each other. For text, how the text aligns within a text block. The alignment options are "Left" (even on the left side and ragged on the right), "Right" (even on the right side and ragged on the left), "Center" (starting from the center and flowing out to the edges), and "Justified" (even on both sides.

AutoTemplate A presentation file that contains only the elements that make up a presentation's design: slide masters, a background master, a color scheme, and/or formatting information. Persuasion comes with predesigned AutoTemplates that you can use to create your own presentations.

Background master The master defining background elements that can appear on every slide. Place elements that repeat from slide to slide, such as a graduated fill or a corporate logo, on the background master, and then assign the background master to the various slide masters.

Category The data on a chart that serve to categorize the values shown therein. For Example, if you are showing the department's profits for each month, the months are the category and profits are the values.

Color palette   Displayed by choosing "Colors" from the Windows menu. The Colors palette lets you select , define, and edit the colors in your presentation.

Color scheme   A working set of colors designed to complement each other and to be applied consistently throughout the presentation.

Current layer   The layer on which you are currently drawing and modifying objects. The current layer is displayed in the bottom center of the screen.

Data series   All values on a chart within a category. For example, if you are showing the profits for several company departments for each month of the year, each department represents a data series.

Data sheet   The spreadsheet-like window for a chart in which you enter the values you want to plot. Each chart in Persuasion has its own data sheet.

Default slide master   The slide master that Persuasion automatically assigns to all newly created slides. You can change the default slide master in the "Preferences" dialog box.

Diagonal-line tool   The tool used to draw lines.

Ellipse tool   The tool used to draw circles or ovals.

Export   The method by which an outline or slides in a file are saved on disk. The outline is exported as a text-only file; slides are exported as Windows metafiles.

Fill background   The white or colored area of a patterned fill.

Fill foreground   The black or colored area of a patterned fill.

Film recorder   An output device you "print" your slides to, which captures them on 35 mm film.

Font   A complete set of characters of a particular design, such as Times New Roman PS.

Freeform tool   The tool used to draw freeform shapes.

Group   A selection of objects that has only one set of handles around the entire perimeter and is treated as one object by Persuasion.

Handouts   Pages containing miniature representations of each slide in your presentation that you can distribute to your audience. Persuasion's AutoTemplates contain handouts designed so that your audience can take notes during your presentation.

Import   The method used to bring external text files or graphics into your presentation; it is performed by choosing the "Place..." command.

Independent   Text or a chart that is not formatted by a place-holder on a slide master.

Layer   An invisible plane on your slide that contains elements. Unless you specify otherwise, all elements you create or import are placed on Layer 1. For more complex slides, you can place objects on different layers, thereby controlling which objects can be edited (by setting layers to be active or inactive). You can also present information layer by layer. For example, each text level can be on a different layer, so that bulleted items are presented to the audience one at a time.

Line style   The thickness of a line or the style of line end it has. Line thickness and line end styles are set in the Lines palette.

Lower menu bar   The row of pop-up menus that appears at the bottom of Persuasion's working area. What pop-up menus are available in the lower menu bar varies based on the view you are in.

Notes   Pages containing a miniature of a slide and your own notes that you will follow when giving your presentation. There is one speaker note page for each slide in your presentation.

Orientation   How an item is printed on a sheet of paper. When the icon in the "Printer setup" dialog box is upright, the items will print so that the page is taller than it is wide. When the icon is rotated 90 degrees, the items will print so that the page is wider than it is tall.

Placeholder   A holding area on a slide master containing formatting information for text, charts, or organization charts.

Plot frame   The border surrounding the plotted area of the chart.

Pointer tool   The tool used to select and manipulate text and graphics.

Polygon tool   The tool used to draw polygons.

Rounded-corner tool   The tool used to draw squares or rectangles that have rounded (rather than square) corners. You can also use the "Round corners…" command to round the corners of squares and rectangles drawn with the square corner tool.

Rule tool   The tool used to draw vertical or horizontal rules. Rules, as opposed to lines, have square ends. Lines have round ends that attach easily to other objects. Use rules to underline or emphasize objects; use lines as part of a drawing that contains other objects.

Rulers   The objects on the top and left sides of your screen that are used to precisely place text and graphics on slides. Rulers reflect the currently selected unit of measure, which you can specify in the "Preferences" dialog box.

Selection   One or more objects that have handles displayed around them.

Shadow offset   The distance a shadow is cast from text or a graphic. Shadows can be cast down, up, left, or right.

Slide master   A slide model that contains design and formatting elements. For example, Persuasion's AutoTemplates contain seven slide masters, designed for specific purposes such as containing preformatted charts, text, or organization charts.

Square corner tool   The tool used to draw squares or rectangles with square (rather than rounded) corners.

Subordinate heading   A line of text in the outline that is below and to the right of the text above.

Subselection   A selection of a subcategory of objects. For example, you can select an entire organization chart, or you can subselect one of its levels.

Text block   A rectangular area containing text on a slide master. Text is entered in a text block with the text tool.

Text tool   The tool used to enter and edit text.

Value   The data within a category on a chart. For example, if you are showing the profits for each month of a year, the profits are the values and the months are the category.

Visible layer   The layers that are set to be visible in the "Set layer" dialog box. You can set a layer to be invisible, so that you don't inadvertently modify the objects on it.

Index

D

E

N

Power-duplicating, 200
.PR2 filename extension, 70, 285
"Preferences…" command, 51, 85-86, 89, 93, 185, 188, 299
Presentations
    based on AutoTemplates, 65-67
    compared to AutoTemplates, 70, 73-74, 285
    defaults, setting, 186, 299-301
    filename extension, 70
    formatting for your medium, 58, 69
    giving, guidelines for, 58-64
    medium, 9, 58-62
    merging, 347
    naming, 69, 136
    objective, determining, 62, 63
    opening, 65-68
    planning, 58-64
    previewing, 322
    producing, 327-331
        See also Printing
    saving, 69, 136
    setting up, 68
    starting, 68-70
    steps for creating, 7-11
    transferring slides among, 347
    writing tips for, 62-64
Previewing
    AutoTemplates, 79, 81, 252
"Print…" command, 158, 327, 329
Printers
    See also Film recorders; Slide service bureaus
    color printers, 17-19
    drivers, described, 19-20
    installing, 19, 27-28
    PCL printers, 16-17

PostScript printers, 16-17
    QMS ColorScript 100 printer, 19
    recommendations, 15-17, 25-26
    slide printer, 328
Printing
    handouts, 158, 275
    landscape orientation, 327
    notes, 327
    on transparencies, 329
    options in dialog box, 328
    outlines, 327
    overheads, 327
    portrait orientation, 327
    presentation, 161
    proofs, 331
Projection techniques, 24-25
Promoting outline units, 107
Pull-down menus, 50

Q

QMS ColorScript 100 printer, 19
Quotation marks
    codes for inserting, 40
    converting when importing files, 100

R

"Random" transition effect, 326
Range
    of slides, selecting in Slide Sorter view, 111
    of text, selecting, 103
Rearranging
    slides in outline, 107
    slides in Slide Sorter view, 110-113, 145

special characters, 139
text on slides, 167-168

U

Underline text style, 170
"Ungroup" command, 185, 209, 217, 256
Ungrouping
    charts, 209
    imported graphics, risks of, 209
    objects, 209, 256
    organization charts, 215
Units of measurement, 185, 189
Units, outline *See* Outline
User dictionary, 320

V

Value axis, 221, 243, 243-244
Value labels *See* Label
Vertex, 201
Vertical
    bar in Slide Sorter view, 112
    insertion point, 95, 107
    lines, drawing, 195
View menu, 42, 50
Views
    described, 42-49
    icons for, 52
    setting opening view, 93

switching, 43-49
Visible layers, 212

W

Weight, line, 191
Width
    of data sheet columns, 151, 236
    of table columns, 247
Window, Persuasion
    See also Microsoft Windows
    components of, 31
    defined, 31
    manipulating, 32
    panning within, 187
"Wipe down" transition effect, 326
"Wipe left" transition effect, 326
"Wipe right" transition effect, 326
"Wipe up" transition effect, 326
Words, selecting, 104
Working set
    defined, 309
    importing, 81, 83, 315-315
    replacing colors, 81, 83, 312

Z

"Zero lock" command, 185, 188, 217
Zero point, changing, 188
Zooming, 187